The Mackerel Years

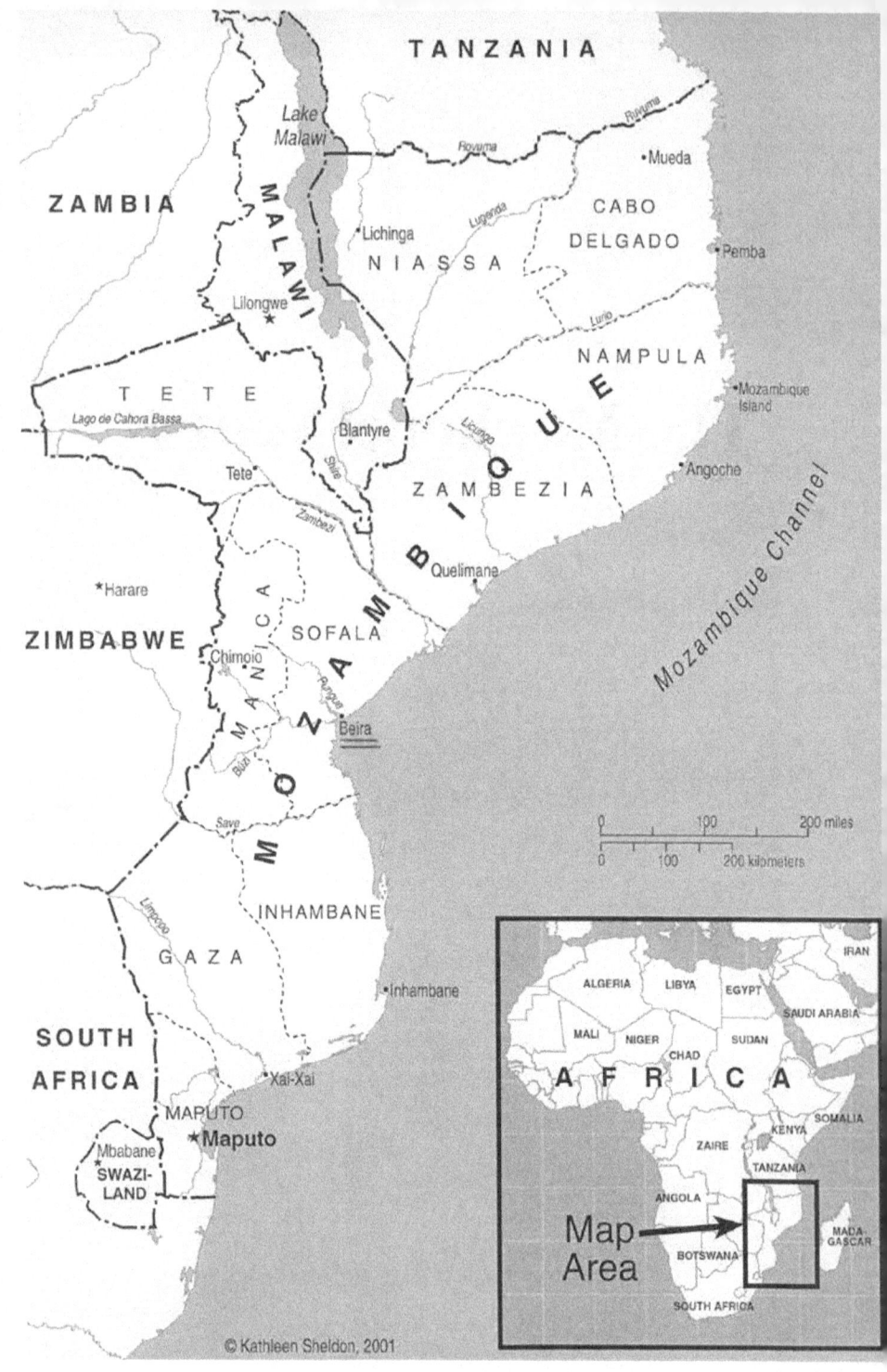

Map 1: Mozambique and its neighbors.

The Mackerel Years
A Memoir of War, Hunger, and
Women's History in 1980s
Mozambique

by
Kathleen Sheldon

AFRICA WORLD PRESS
TRENTON | LONDON | CAPE TOWN | NAIROBI | ADDIS ABABA | ASMARA | IBADAN | NEW DELHI

AFRICA WORLD PRESS
541 West Ingham Avenue | Suite B
Trenton, New Jersey 08638

Copyright@2024, Kathleen Sheldon

All rights reserved. No part of this publication may be reproduced, stored in a retrieval system or transmitted in any form or by any means electronic, mechanical, photocopying, recording or otherwise without the prior written permission of the publisher.

Book design: Dawid Kahts
Cover design: Ashraful Haq

Cataloging-in-Publication Data may be obtained from the Library of Congress.

ISBN: 978-1-56902-863-6
        978-1-56902-864-3

Table of Contents

1	Family, Travel, and History	1
2	Getting to Portugal and Mozambique	17
3	Gourmet Airplane Food and Arriving in Maputo	31
4	Beira at Last	45
5	Mercie Goes to Creche and Prawns for Lunch	57
6	Chickens in the Kitchen	71
7	Freshly Slaughtered Beef and Ration Cards	81
8	Pediatrics and Politics	93
9	Streets Scenes and Sabotage	101
10	Manioc and All the Trimmings	111
11	Organizing Research on Women and Health	119
12	Advances and Setbacks	127
13	May Day in Maputo	141
14	Hamburgers in Mbabane	151
15	Health Care for the People	157
16	Mexicana Life	169
17	Talking with Nurses	179
18	Day-to-day in Wartime Beira	185
19	Talking with Cashew Workers	197

20	Tea and Bread at the Provincial Women's Meeting	215
21	Guinea Fowl for Dinner in Zimbabwe	229
22	Talking with Garment Workers	239
23	Bureaucracy and Shortages	255
24	Talking with Market Women	267
25	Tragedy and Kabanga	279
26	Cake and Despedidas	293
27	Home and Back Again	309
Acknowledgements		321
Glossary		323
Index		

Chapter 1
Family, Travel, and History

Two loud explosions got us out of bed, our hearts beating hard. We were sweating from the humidity and at first we thought the noise was thunder. As the sounds reverberated through the night, we wondered if something in our building had blown up, but as my husband and I stumbled sleepily out to the porch of our fifth-floor apartment we could see flames and a plume of smoke rising about a mile away. Everything looked gray and grim and threatening. It appeared that downtown Beira was on fire. After the initial two explosions, a series of smaller blasts disturbed the night. Fortunately, rain began to fall about an hour later, stemming the spread of the fire. It was December 1982 and we had been living in Beira, Mozambique, for four months. We were still adjusting to the difficulties of daily life in a city that was virtually under siege from antigovernment guerrillas based in the adjacent rural areas. The attack we witnessed that night was the closest we had felt the conflict approaching.

We learned that the explosions were the result of South African saboteurs who came in through the bay and blew up the storage tanks that held gasoline for Zimbabwe, Mozambique's land-locked western neighbor. It was part of a deliberate strategy by the apartheid government, which then ruled South Africa, to destabilize the neighboring countries that were governed by independent black-majority socialist governments. South Africa bordered Mozambique to the south and west. We were aware of that larger situation before we arrived in Mozambique in July that year. But we had not anticipated the reality of war reaching within a few blocks of our home and our daughter's childcare center, nor had we realized that we would spend the next two years worrying about where each meal would come from as market supplies dwindled and food was rationed.

My memoir tells how we came to live in Mozambique among a small group of internationalists working for the revolutionary government. We were called *cooperantes*, which could be translated as "cooperators" or aid workers. We had traveled there so that I could pursue my doctoral research in African history. My husband, Steve Tarzynski, had a two-year contract as a medical cooperante with the Ministry of Health and he was a pediatrician in the local hospital. Our daughter, Mercie, who was with us as well, was not yet two years old. She was a good-natured and usually tolerant toddler who took life as it came. This narrative is mainly drawn from a hand-written journal I kept while we lived there and tells of our experiences during the Cold War period in southern Africa.

Many cooperantes came from Canada and from European nations such as Sweden, the Netherlands, Italy, England, and Ireland in response to a call from the Mozambican government for help in developing the newly independent nation. We also met cooperantes from Brazil, Uganda, Mali, and Zambia.[1] The European and Canadian cooperantes were sympathetic to socialism and supported what were viewed as positive revolutions in Third World countries. Those internationalists had organizations in their home countries that helped arrange their journeys and paid a portion of their salaries. They were there under individual and low-level arrangements, rather than part of governmental or international agencies. The cooperantes we knew from Cuba and the former Soviet Union were maintained by their governments. Their presence reflected

Chapter 1

Cold War policies regarding international connections between socialist nations. Although there was a solidarity movement for Mozambique in the U.S., there was no American organization to support our travel and work. We were there on our own and, for most of our stay, we were the only Americans in Beira.

I resisted writing about those years because I did not want to make it a story about myself, a reticence common among historians.[2] I was reluctant to report the many problems and obstacles I encountered, fearing it would reflect poorly on Mozambique and on my own capabilities. At that time (late 1970s and early 1980s), there was little preparation for accomplishing field research or for the practicalities of living abroad or the larger political and ethical demands of working in impoverished circumstances. In recent years, it has become more common for scholars to admit their own foibles and errors and there is less of a tendency to present one's research as a straightforward success.[3]

My initial goal was to describe life in Mozambique in the 1980s. That story is inevitably intertwined with various aspects of our experience, as there is no single story, primarily because we were there as a family with three different kinds of involvement. I begin with some background, in response to the many times I have been asked, "How did you end up going to Mozambique?" Then various aspects of our two years there emerge: I was discovering how to do research on the ground while learning the history of local working women; I was a mother accompanied by my child while doing international fieldwork; my husband was embedded in an African health care system; my daughter attended local day-care centers; we were constantly thinking about where each meal would come from; we visited two contrasting neighboring countries; we were socialists hoping to participate in the international socialist movement; and we were there during the early days of a devastating conflict. These stories are braided from the multiple strands of our experience into one story related here.

We went to Mozambique with the hope of contributing to one country's socialist transformation. We were eager to experience life under a new government whose leaders had fought a war that helped to bring down the Portuguese empire and who were trying to eliminate all forms of inequality. We shared with Mozambicans we met both a great hope for the future and many deep challenges that posed immense difficulties.

A New England Childhood

My desire to travel to faraway places is indicated by the "Life ambition" entry in my high school yearbook: I had written *To go to Baghdad*, a goal that seemed particularly ironic after the 2003 occupation of Iraq by American forces that resulted in that city becoming a center of violence and danger. I grew up in Glastonbury, Connecticut, the child of two descendants of old New England WASP (white, Anglo-Saxon, Protestant) families. Our house had many books and magazine subscriptions and I read everything, including encyclopedias and dictionaries. I particularly enjoyed historical fiction and biographies of prominent women. *National Geographic* came regularly, and there is a high likelihood that, when I was twelve, I read the 1964 article, "Mozambique: Land of the Good People." I still own that issue, rescued from the stacks of old magazines in my parents' attic.

Politics was not a focal point of our family life. My parents were registered as independent voters so that they could receive literature about candidates from both parties, though they generally voted for liberal Democratic candidates. I do not remember any specific discussions about Communism or anti-Communism, though at school we were subjected to the familiar worthless drills, going down to the basement at Academy School and curling up against the hallway walls to protect our heads in the event of a nuclear attack. Maps in the newspaper showed concentric circles of radiation reaching Connecticut from a nuclear attack on New York City, and I found that possibility frightening.

My town was perched along the Connecticut River, outside of Hartford. In the 1950s and 1960s there were no synagogues but there were three Congregational churches, one of which my family attended. I grew up in an overwhelmingly white Protestant community, as there were almost no residents of color among the twenty thousand or so residents. My graduating class of over three hundred included only a single black student and no Asians, Latinos, or other students of color. My understanding of race and racial politics was mainly informed by news coverage of the Civil Rights movement in the 1960s.

When I was twelve, my family moved to a larger house in a different part of town and we sold our postwar split-level home to an administrator for the Glastonbury schools, who was black. Most of our former neighbors welcomed him and his family, but when we visited our old neighborhood, members of one family pointedly turned their backs to us and walked away without a word, and another family that had been close friends didn't speak to us for years. Though a mild response in the context of what was happening nationally in 1964, it made an impression on me as I realized that they were angry about a black family moving in down the block. Looking back, I can see that my parents' decision to sell to that family was a minor but brave action, one of many taken by people across the U.S. who stood against racism in their own communities.[4]

In junior high school, the teachers introduced a social experiment. One morning the announcer read a list of student names, saying all of those mentioned should leave their class for a meeting. Everyone quickly realized they were calling all the redheaded students; I was included as someone with obvious redheaded ancestry. Some of my classmates remembered this exercise with anger and resented the manipulation, but I recalled that most of the students refused to comply with rules that insisted the redheads sit separately at lunch and be generally ostracized by the rest of the student body. I still have a badge made by the dissidents that says, "Stamp Out SARGE," calling for an end to Segregation Against Redheads in Glastonbury.

I was involved with my church youth group in activities with a partner church in Hartford's "inner city." In the late 1960s I saw a *Life* or *Look* magazine that ran a two-page spread of photos of the Black Panthers who had been killed by police, and I recognized that our government was purposely attacking black political activists and community leaders. I read James Baldwin's *The Fire Next Time* and Eldridge Cleaver's *Soul on Ice*. All these events and activities contributed to my knowledge of racial prejudice, but it was still an abstract idea and barely related to any direct personal experience with black people. Nonetheless, I developed a sincere desire to end racial discrimination. I became interested in understanding racism and inequality in the world and began to learn about history and politics in some of my high school classes.

In a more muted way, I started paying attention to sexual politics as well, reading Robin Morgan's important anthology, *Sisterhood Is Powerful*, from cover to cover. Though I understood how sexism stunted women's lives, I did not experience the worst kinds of oppression in my own life, where I found consistent support from family, friends, and teachers for following my own choices in my relationships and my career.

I was also getting caught up in the anti-Viet Nam war activities of the time. I began attending meetings and candlelight demonstrations in front of the post office led by local Quaker families. A small group of us protested American involvement in the war with regular silent vigils in front of the high school, enduring eggs and epithets thrown at us. My parents, though not always happy with my activities, supported me when the school tried to punish students who skipped class to picket. The day after four students were shot at Kent State University in May 1970, we again stood outside in a rag-tag row along the chain link

Chapter 1

fence and, in response to those deaths in Ohio, our principal, Mr. Bartolotta, came out to join us.

My awareness of Africa was also growing, and I spent many hours at the Hartford Public Library researching South African politics for my high school Current Events class. My paper addressed the recent history of racism in South Africa, discussing the post-World War II development of the stringent system of racial categorization and discrimination known as apartheid. I was learning about the links between racial attitudes in my local neighborhood, the war in Vietnam, and the extreme violence of the apartheid regime.

Dreams of Travel and Northwestern

When I was twelve, my career goal was to be a stewardess (as flight attendants were called in the 1960s) because that was a job that appeared to combine glamour with the opportunity to visit far-flung locales. That interest in being a flight attendant had long faded by the time I went away to college in 1970, traveling to Northwestern University in Evanston, outside of Chicago, farther than I ever had ventured before. I felt I was going to the Wild West, a great distance from my family and from everything that had defined me until then. In keeping with my desire to learn about faraway places and remote cultures, I expected to major in anthropology, and even took an introductory course during my first quarter there. The professor, a well-known scholar, was a poor lecturer, and he was unable to answer the deliberately pointed questions of one of the class members. Every time he fumbled a response, I grew more disappointed, and determined not to continue in that department. I did not know what to focus on after that and spent most of my first year taking language and science requirements and introductory classes in English and sociology.

During the summer between my first and second years, I thought about what I should do. My parents, with four daughters, had promised to pay for either our first year of college or a big wedding. I opted for the college year, as did all three of my sisters. I had some of my own money from regular work during high school as a waitress at the local Post Rider diner. When I first arrived in Evanston, I found a job near my dorm waiting tables at the Village Snack Shop, a small casual restaurant that was owned by Greek immigrants and had booths and a long counter. But that income was not nearly enough to cover the high cost of Northwestern, and I was not sure that I could afford to return to Evanston.

A major factor by that time was the man I had met in February of my first year, Steve Tarzynski, a pre-med student who lived in the dorm adjacent to mine on north campus. A thin man with thick brown hair, a broad Polish face, and wide-spaced eyes, he liked to wear his blue jeans with black motorcycle boots and an old green army jacket with the sleeves cut off. I was attracted in part to his intense commitment to anti-war activities at Northwestern, and we shared interests in music and cultural events. Steve and I were deeply in love and after spending most of that summer apart I was desperate to be with him. I decided to return to Northwestern and arrange for loans to pay for school.

Steve's father had been born in Warsaw and was forced to leave at age eighteen when the Nazis invaded. Most of his family perished in the Holocaust. He fought in the war against the Nazis and when the war ended he went to Bologna, Italy, to finish medical school. There he met Steve's mother and after they married, they emigrated to the U.S. in 1951. Steve was born the following year. His family spoke Italian in their home, and he did not learn English well until he began kindergarten. His parents were very suspicious of me. Steve and I could often be found volunteering at the Amazingrace Coffee House on the Northwestern campus, which was developing into a counter-cultural center of political activism, cheap healthy food, and cutting-edge folk music. Although Steve had been raised to oppose tyranny, his family believed that Steve's leftist politics had been learned from me and did not see how his anti-war activities were a continuation of their own beliefs. I was blamed for everything that bothered Steve's parents as he became an American hippie with long hair and radical politics rather than a devoted Italian Catholic son.

Steve had planned to live with his family at their home in Melrose Park during the summer after our sophomore year. Following an argument with them about his hanging a poster in his room that showed student protestors, he left. As happened in many families, the larger political conflict had very personal consequences. Steve arrived without advance warning at the large apartment in Evanston that I was sharing with half a dozen other friends, and from that point on we lived together. His parents then disowned him for living with me without benefit of marriage and we did not speak with them for over a year. They were willing to reconcile after he was accepted at Rush Medical College following only three years of undergraduate study. The painful relationship with his parents was difficult for both of us. Our warm relationship with my family provided a calmer, friendlier contrast; despite our geographical distance, we had remained close, and Steve was welcomed by them.

Studying African History

Even though history courses were among my favorite high school classes, I had not initially thought about majoring in history in college. I enrolled in a large lecture course on Western Civilization during my first year, but only focused on studying history seriously when I returned for my sophomore year. I then signed up for a seminar on South Africa with John Rowe, a historian who specialized on Uganda in his own research. I loved it. I enjoyed the reading and I appreciated the small class size, a welcome difference from the large lecture classes of my first year. I realized almost immediately that I wanted to study African history, attracted in part by the chance to learn something completely new, unlike the American history I had already learned in high school. I also appreciated the opportunity to study material that had political content and a connection to current events.

Though I had not been aware of it during my first year, Northwestern had a prominent African studies center, and I was able to focus on Africa in history, political science, and literature courses over the next three years. I benefited from studying with such internationally known scholars as Dennis Brutus, a South African poet living in exile; Gwendolen Carter, a pioneering political scientist who wrote scathing indictments of South Africa's apartheid system; John Paden, another political scientist who was known for his work on Nigeria; and Ivor Wilks, a charming Welsh historian who was a noted expert on the Asante kingdom in Ghana. Visitors who offered seminars for interested undergraduates included the Ghanaian historian Francis Agbodeka, so Northwestern offered ideal conditions for becoming immersed in the study of African history and politics.

There was also a lot of extra-curricular political activity related to African affairs. In October 1971 I looked forward to hearing Catherine Taylor, a United Party member of parliament in South Africa, speak on current events there. She opposed implementing trade sanctions against South Africa, which was one of the main tactics being espoused by American anti-apartheid activists to force a change in policy there. When I arrived at Harris Hall to attend her lecture, I found that black students had organized to prevent her from speaking. They occupied all the seats, chanted political slogans, and clapped and made noise so that she was unable to make her presentation. I was new to African studies and had little knowledge about Taylor's politics, and I was conflicted about the successful effort to silence her. I understood the motivation, but I still felt she should have been allowed to speak and have her views contested in a discussion. Years later I finally read her account of

Chapter 1

the Northwestern incident and similar events at other U.S. colleges in her memoir, *If Courage Goes*. I learned that she held quite reactionary views, referring to the Mozambique Liberation Front, known as FRELIMO (the acronym for Frente de Libertação de Moçambique), as a "so-called liberation movement" and saying that she felt like an anthropologist "in the midst of the wild, Black American scene" in Harris Hall. Perhaps if she had been allowed to speak, she would have condemned herself with her own words.[5]

History majors were required by the department to take at least two courses with an international focus, as most students concentrated on U.S. or European history. I had the opposite experience. After the first-year lecture course in Western Civilization, I only took two seminars in western history, one on the French Revolution and the other on countercultures in Europe, where we read about witches and millenarian movements. I did not take a single American history course in college, nor did I have very strong training in western history more generally. In contrast, I took everything offered on Africa, Asia, India, and Latin America. My concentration on world history became a drawback when I took the standard history GRE (Graduate Record Examination) for admission to graduate school, as I knew very little about American political history, which was the focus of much of the exam. I was learning about the assumptions of history education in general, which at that time centered on Europe and the U.S. while scarcely admitting that other areas of the world even had a history worth learning.

By my third year, I had developed a special interest in Mozambique, which was fighting a liberation war against its Portuguese colonizers. Portugal had been a presence in Mozambique for four hundred years, though its colonial control had never extended much beyond small enclaves along the coast, often under the control of chartered companies, and a series of large but isolated estates along the Zambezi River in the center of the country. Portugal was an extremely brutal and exploitative colonial power, with much of the colonized population subject to forced labor. In response to the harsh conditions, many Mozambicans fled to find work in neighboring colonies, working in South African gold and diamond mines, or choosing the comparatively benign experience of British colonialism. Those who remained toiled on roads, grew cotton, and labored at other tasks as virtual slaves, being forced to do the work in order to pay onerous taxes.

After World War II, much of Africa began to emerge from colonialism, beginning with Ghana in 1957 and followed by most of the French and British colonies throughout the early 1960s. But Portugal, ruled by a fascist regime first under António Salazar and then Marcelo Caetano, insisted that its colonies—Mozambique, Angola, Cabo Verde, Guinea-Bissau, and São-Tomé e Príncipe in Africa; Goa in India; and Macau in China—were not separate countries but were part of "metropolitan Portugal." Rather than begin the process of granting independence to its colonies, Portugal redefined them as "overseas provinces," emphasizing their incorporation into the ruling nation. There had been localized resistance to colonialism from the 1950s and earlier, though the armed liberation struggle only began in the early 1960s.

By the time I learned about FRELIMO, ten years after they began fighting, leaders of that organization had developed a socialist approach to politics. From their perspective, it was not enough to end colonialism while retaining other forms of inequality. Through debate and struggle they determined that the system that offered the best possibility for transforming their society for the better was socialism. Their decision positioned Mozambique within the complex international conflict of the Cold War. As I discovered through an independent study project on U.S.-Portuguese relations, the United States valued having landing and refueling rights at an air force base on the Portuguese Azores Islands in the middle of the Atlantic.

Chapter 1

The U.S. government thus resolved to continue their alliance with fascist Portugal rather than alienate that ally by supporting the independence of its African colonies. The U.S. administration also allied with the racist South African government, which was staunchly anti-communist as well. The 1970s were a time of heightened repression by the apartheid government. Nelson Mandela remained imprisoned on Robben Island and the leaders of the African National Congress operated from exile in neighboring southern African countries that made up the Frontline States (i.e., the black majority–ruled countries that bordered South Africa). Meanwhile, in the absence of support from many western democracies, FRELIMO turned to China, the Soviet Union, and the Warsaw Pact countries, for assistance in their struggle for independence, thereby falling on one side of the great international political divide of those Cold War decades. Although the U.S. saw Mozambique as a Soviet ally, Mozambican leaders considered themselves firmly in the non-aligned camp, as they also drew support from such western democratic nations as Canada, Italy, Sweden, and the Netherlands.

I admired the socialist politics of FRELIMO and I was particularly interested in the policies it advocated with respect to women. When choosing topics for required class projects, I wrote papers on Mozambican nationalism; the politics of the Cahora Bassa dam, a big project on the Zambezi that would supply electricity to South Africa; and the ethnic politics of the Makonde, a people who lived on both sides of the northern border Mozambique shared with Tanzania and who were known for their ebony carvings. I began to study Portuguese so that I could read documents for myself. I graduated in 1974 with a certificate in African Studies, and, in addition to earning a bachelor's degree in history, I completed the requirements for a degree in political science.

I spent the next year working in Northwestern's Transportation Library while Steve attended Rush Medical College in Chicago. We also continued to be active politically. Steve volunteered in the Uptown neighborhood in Chicago at a free medical clinic that was organized by the Young Patriots Organization, a group of white activists who worked with the Black Panther Party and the Puerto Rican Young Lords. The clinic served a neighborhood of poor white families, many from Appalachia. I accompanied Steve several times and was always impressed with the Rainbow Coalition's political work, which brought together a range of groups fighting poverty.

Unsure as to whether history or political science was my preference, I applied to the interdisciplinary Master of Arts in African Area Studies program at the University of California in Los Angeles (UCLA). I was accepted and awarded a small grant for my first year. Steve and I planned to move to Los Angeles, and he began organizing rotations, one-month clinical courses taken in the final two years of medical school, in various pediatric subspecialties at L.A. area hospitals. But his parents felt he was interrupting his medical education to follow me across the country. They did not understand my decision to pursue African history, which his father referred to derisively as "Afro studies." They disowned Steve a second time and again we were not on speaking terms with his family for over a year. During that time, we decided to marry, and though we invited his family to join our modest ceremony at my parents' home in Connecticut, to our deep disappointment, they did not respond.

Endnotes

1   Other nations, particularly eastern European countries, also sent technicians and other professionals, though we did not meet them ourselves. For information on European women cooperantes in Maputo, see, Elisa Fuchs, *Moçambique Marcou-Nos para a Vida: Grupo de Mulheres Internacionalistas 1980-1984, Retratos e Depoimentos* (Maputo: JV Editores, 2014), and for Latin American cooperantes, see, Mario Ayala and Ricardo Pérez Haristoy, "South America's Transnational Solidarity with Southern Africa: Chilean and Argentine Exiles as Cooperators in Mozambique, 1976-1986," *Journal of Global South Studies* 40, 2 (2023): 418-440.

Chapter 1

2   For more on historian's memoirs, see Kathleen Sheldon, "Telling a Historian's Story," *CSW Blog* (8 February 2019), available at www.kathleensheldon.net. While it is common, and even expected, that anthropologists will write about their fieldwork experiences, historians rarely do so. One exception is Elizabeth Jacoway, ed., *No Straight Path: Becoming Women Historians* (Baton Rouge: Louisiana State University Press, 2019), a collection of biographical articles by women who often took circuitous career paths before emerging as pioneering historians, most of them studying the history of women in the southern U.S. I concurred with a common refrain in this collection about their reluctance to write their own stories after a career focused on the history of others.

3   Ezgi Irgil, Anne-Kathrin Kreft, Myunghee Lee, Charmaine N Willis, and Kelebogile Zvobgo, "Field Research: A Graduate Student's Guide," *International Studies Review*, published online, June 2021, https://doi.org/10.1093/isr/viab023. Anne-Kathrin Kreft stated in a comment on Twitter that she considers it her "mission to de-mystify fieldwork and go beyond the sanitized accounts we find in published work and emphasize: no, we don't always know what we're doing, things often don't go as planned, we all make adjustments on the ground," https://twitter.com/Anne_Kreft/status/1439901657052196869?s=20, accessed September 20, 2021.

4   In the annual diary my mother kept, she noted that in 1964 our home was sold to the Sam Turners, with no mention of their race or of any related issues. Mr. Turner was a renowned educator and was a principal at one of our town's elementary schools before moving on to other positions (his obituary in the *Boston Globe*, November 13, 2015).

5   *The Daily Northwestern* published accounts of the Catherine Taylor event and the extended debate that followed about free speech; photocopies are in my possession, with thanks to Jason Nargis of the Northwestern Archives and David Easterbrook, then at Northwestern's Herskovits Africana Library, for their assistance.

Chapter 2

Getting to Portugal and Mozambique

1975 to 1982

The year I began graduate school was also the year that Mozambique became independent. In April 1974, members of the Portuguese military staged a coup in Lisbon that brought down the decades-old fascist regime. The Portuguese soldiers were motivated in part by their experiences in fighting the long and increasingly pointless anti-colonial wars in the African territories. Portugal was a poor country itself, and one-third of its annual budget was being poured into those military struggles. Many Portuguese saw that as a losing proposition and supported the soldiers' coup and their new socialist leadership. The following year, in June 1975, power in the former colonies was officially handed over to African leaders. In Mozambique, FRELIMO emerged as the single ruling party and the nation was officially called the People's Republic of Mozambique (República Popular de Moçambique). FRELIMO became the Frelimo Party, no longer an acronym but a word on its own. There is an immense literature about the history of the liberation struggle, the fierce internal disagreements, and intense political conflicts, which I cannot discuss here. As outsiders, we believed we could support the socialist efforts of Frelimo in the years after the end of the anti-colonial war.

I could start to think about traveling to Mozambique, a prospect that had been nearly impossible during the war. I began my graduate studies and prepared to develop a dissertation topic that would require me to go to Mozambique and do research on the ground. Without fully realizing it, I had stumbled into a program at UCLA, which then had a special emphasis on Portuguese Africa. As an undergraduate, I had not known the recognized scholars in the field, but I soon learned that UCLA's history department included Ned Alpers, who had already done research on Mozambique and had lived in Portugal and Tanzania, and he became my primary dissertation advisor. During my first week at UCLA, I saw an ad in the campus paper, the *Daily Bruin,* for a new course on African women and social change. I immediately sought out the professor and thus met Peg Strobel, who had just completed her own research on women's history in Mombasa, Kenya. Her class became an entry point for studying women's history more broadly at a time when it was an entirely new field of study. The friendship and mentorship of both Ned and Peg have been a vital support for me ever since. I was very fortunate to meet them both during my first week at UCLA.

I got involved in the campaign to convince the university to divest itself of stock holdings in companies that did business in apartheid South Africa. One day on campus, as I was collecting signatures on a petition to urge the University of California regents to divest, a black student challenged me, "Why are you doing this?" My response was to throw the challenge back, asking "Why aren't you?"—to which he had no reply. There was tension, as the presence of white student activists working to promote racial equality was sometimes resented by some black students. But I also had close friends of all races for the first time in my life, our camaraderie forged in long meetings, public demonstrations, and a shared passion to end apartheid.

The African Activist Association was a multi-racial UCLA student group that spearheaded the divestment campaign. One of our projects was leafletting workers at the Fluor Corporation at Irvine in Orange County. Fluor had developed a way to manufacture oil out of coal, a process that provided support for the South African government which had no oil holdings and was legally blocked by international sanctions from importing oil. But South Africa did have a lot of coal, and Fluor's invention allowed them to avoid the worst impact of sanctions. I was never at ease with political organizing because I did not like approaching strangers and trying to explain complex issues. But when a group of us drove down to Orange County one cold dawn, standing around the Fluor gates in a then-empty Irvine landscape and trying to describe to Fluor workers how their company supported the racist South African regime, I knew I was contributing in a small way to ending apartheid.

I also began participating in other political activities, including involvement with the local Socialist Community School, which was affiliated with the New American Movement, a nationwide democratic socialist feminist organization. As a member of the school committee, I helped plan the curriculum and recruit teachers for weekday evening classes at the First Unitarian Church on Eighth Street in Los Angeles. I also co-taught a course on socialist feminism. It was exciting to be part of a grassroots form of alternative education, and for several years we enjoyed success with hundreds of students passing through our classes.[1]

It seemed self-evident that injustices of various forms in the world were interconnected and that the common thread was capitalism. The best way that I could see to end racial, sexual, and class oppression was to change the system altogether, developing a democratic socialist society that would bring equal opportunity to everyone.[2] Sometime during those years, I purchased a beautiful poster illustrating my own ideas about international women's solidarity. Including nearly twenty different cultures with the slogan, "Women: Many Waves, One Ocean" in all the various languages, it has hung in my study for over forty years. I was especially pleased that African women were included with the phrase in Kiswahili.[3] Though the political optimism of American leftists was beginning to fade by the end of the 1970s, I had never believed (as did some) that the revolution was imminent, and I was able to maintain my hope for a socialist future. Living in Mozambique, a self-proclaimed socialist country, was my dream.

I was particularly inspired by the attention to women's oppression in Mozambique. Frelimo had strong policies on women's rights and in support of women's emancipation. They encouraged women to become active in combat and in society more generally. They also targeted customary practices such as polygamy (more specifically, polygyny, where a man could marry more than one wife) and bridewealth (an exchange of goods and money from the groom's family to the bride's kin) that were perceived as being oppressive to women. I later learned about the greater complexity of these practices, but at that time there was very little information available about women's issues in Africa. I relied on the official Frelimo magazine, *Mozambique Revolution,* and articles in the bulletin, *Southern Africa,* published in New York, to learn about the changes that were being introduced. Occasional pamphlets about Mozambican events or personalities appeared at independent bookshops like the New World Resource Center in Chicago, but there were few books on the topic. As a western feminist, I saw the new policies as exemplary, but I was frustrated by the limited information I could find. I wanted to go there and learn for myself from the women who were directly involved in these momentous changes.

But getting there was not an easy process in the late 1970s and early 1980s. I finished my master's degree in African studies in 1977 and entered the doctoral program in history where I wrote a dissertation proposal on Swahili settlements in northern Mozambique, with an emphasis on women and gender issues. I had studied Kiswahili, the Swahili language, for three years and hoped to contribute to Swahili studies. That field of study typically stopped

Chapter 2

somewhat arbitrarily at the southern Tanzanian border, excluding the northern Mozambican coastal communities that shared many cultural and linguistic features with their Tanzanian neighbors. Like most graduate students, I was looking for a topic that interested me while being relatively un-researched, so that I could make a real contribution to the field.

In 1979 I passed my doctoral qualifying exams and began applying for funding to do research in Mozambique. Steve had finished medical school in 1977 and was completing his pediatric internship and residency program at the Los Angeles County-University of Southern California Medical Center. Hoping to travel when he finished his residency, we originally planned to go in 1980 or 1981.

We responded with some optimism to the announcement in 1979 of a position with the American Friends Service Committee (AFSC), which hoped to continue their program sponsoring a physician to work in Mozambique. Paul and Andy Epstein, a physician and nurse with two children, were based in Beira, and the new announcement was designed to find their replacements once their contract ended.[4] The AFSC project appeared to be a wonderful opportunity, because we would have the support of a well-known organization while we were there. We worked hard on the lengthy application and felt that we met their criteria. Steve was fluent in Italian, conversant in Spanish, and had begun studying Portuguese. His training as a pediatrician was sorely needed. We had demonstrated the political commitment that was part of the AFSC requirements.

We each had to fill out applications that included short essays on our opinions on military service, an account of our community and political activities, and "the most important values and commitments in your life." Our idealism was evident in our earnest compositions. Steve wrote that the main three things he valued were "family, life work, and activism," going on to comment that "my commitment to building a democratic socialist society free of all forms of oppression is of central importance." In an oblique reference to the estrangement with his family, he wrote, "I feel confident that I can persevere and maintain these values and commitments because in order to do so up until now has required considerable personal sacrifice." My own essay also listed my primary allegiance to "marriage/family, my work as a historian, and my work as a socialist feminist." While we were trying to frame our beliefs to meet the interests of the AFSC, our application essays reflected the values that shaped our lives separately and as a couple.

However, we were extremely disappointed when we received a letter before the end of that year telling us that they had selected another American physician. The man they chose had already advanced farther through their recruitment process and, as they had finished interviewing him before they had followed up with our references, they decided to select him. Ironically, the physician they chose never made it to Mozambique. Though we did not discover that outcome of the AFSC project until much later, in response to my query an AFSC staff member replied that that physician did not go "due to a long delay in processing through the Ministry of Health" in Mozambique.

As part of my preparation for pursuing field research, I spent three months in Portugal, where I worked in the historical archives collecting documents and information on Cabo Delgado, the northernmost province in Mozambique. It was my first time traveling outside the U.S. and I loved living in Lisbon, grabbing a morning *bica* or espresso at the coffee bars, eating the typical lunch of *bacalhau* (cod), salad, and flan at one of the many small restaurants. I was happy just to walk around the streets, soaking up European urban life and admiring the blue-and-white tiled buildings and decorative sidewalk designs. I had a usable level of reading literacy in Portuguese that I had acquired in the classroom, but the limitations of my verbal fluency were suddenly very evident. I was often hesitant to use a language I spoke imperfectly, but living in Lisbon was its own immersion course. I was

Chapter 2

forced to speak in Portuguese to get my research done and to survive, and I was much more comfortable with the language by the time I returned to California.

Most of my research time was spent in the chilly rooms of the repository of colonial documents at the Lisbon Geographical Society or sitting in the modern reading room at the National Library, waiting for material I had requested to be brought down from the closed stacks. I savored the detective work of poring over old papers and files to find odd statistics and arcane but relevant pieces of information. I felt like a real historian, pursuing my own independent research while sharing the archive tables with other scholars who accepted me as a legitimate researcher.

I was helped by Greg Pirio, a fellow UCLA graduate student in history who had already been in Lisbon for most of the year before I arrived, and I met some other researchers as well. Steve joined me in Lisbon for a couple of weeks and we enjoyed Portuguese culture and participated in leftist Portuguese political activities. People in Portugal were still reveling in the end of fascism, and they brought a refreshing exuberance to events including a huge rally on May Day 1980 that ended with a gathering in the old bullfight ring. We went with our friend Martin Shapiro, who was also briefly in Lisbon that spring. Martin was another UCLA graduate student who already had his M.D. but was also researching a history dissertation on Portuguese colonial health care. Hearing thousands of people singing "The International," the familiar tune echoing in the huge arena, was thrilling, and we felt we were having a real revolutionary experience.

Martin also went with us to a downtown square for a large and lively demonstration protesting the rising cost of living. When the main gathering broke up, we followed a crowd down some side streets and inadvertently got caught in a police assault on protesters. We managed a narrow escape, as the police batons came uncomfortably close while Steve yelled, "Somos Americanos" (We are Americans), to little avail. That episode was a reminder that not everyone supported the changes that were taking place in Portuguese political life.

Figure 1: Cost of living demonstration in Lisbon, May 1980. Photo by Steve Tarzynski.

When I returned from that trip, it was evident that getting clearance and permission to go to Mozambique was going to be difficult. We simply had to accept the delays. We had been planning to eventually have children, and the question was not if we would ever have children, but when we would find the time. Realizing that it could be over a year before we would get to travel to Mozambique, we decided to start our family before that trip. Our daughter, Mercie, was born in March 1981. Her first name was an old New England family name, and her middle name, Josina, was for Josina Machel, a Mozambican hero who had died of disease during the armed struggle. The date of Josina Machel's death, April 7th, was celebrated as Mozambican Women's Day; in addition to the political cachet, I simply liked the sound of the name.

Because Steve was a pediatrician, we were not unduly concerned about taking a small child to Mozambique. But we had not anticipated difficulties with her birth. Mercie was born with a diaphragmatic hernia, a hole in her diaphragm that had allowed her stomach and intestines to migrate into her chest cavity in utero, pushing her heart and lungs to one side. She was operated on at three hours of age. Her entire chest cavity was opened so that the surgeon could push her organs into their proper places and insert a small mesh to close the hole in the diaphragm. She was born just after midnight, and I called my parents early that morning to tell them that their first grandchild had arrived. But when I started to explain about her surgery, I could not find the words and simply started weeping. Steve took the phone and coolly described what had happened, but he did not tell them or me until a year later that the mortality rate at that time for that kind of anomaly was as high as 80 percent. Since I did not know that the odds were against her, I blithely went along expecting a good result and a healthy baby, eventually. We were lucky. The surgery was completely successful and she had no lingering problems related to that initial malformation. We had planned to go to Mozambique once she reached nine months of age and was able to have her shots, especially the crucial measles vaccine, but we decided to delay until she was fifteen months and fully recovered from her ordeal.

While we were dealing with my pregnancy and Mercie's difficult arrival, we were simultaneously seeking further contacts and opportunities for travel to Mozambique. A formidable complication at that time was a serious breech in relations between the United States and Mozambique. The U.S. had supported the Portuguese government throughout the anti-colonial struggle and continued to distrust the independent socialist government that ruled Mozambique after 1975. The American administration persisted in the broader Cold War strategy that viewed southern African countries solely through the lens of anti-communism. Despite South Africa's abhorrent racial policies, the American government supported that regime rather than its socialist neighbors. South Africa in the late 1970s and throughout the

1980s viewed itself as the last bastion of anti-communism, surrounded by black-majority leftist governments in Mozambique, Angola, and, after 1980, Zimbabwe. In 1978 the U.S. Congress passed a foreign aid bill that specifically denied funds to Mozambique, as some members of Congress feared that Mozambique was becoming too closely aligned with the Soviet Union. Although that prohibition was waived in 1980, relations remained cool. In March 1981, the Mozambican government expelled four American embassy staff members and their families from Maputo on charges of "espionage, subversion, and interference."[5]

Affairs between the two countries improved over the next few years, but the time of greatest official difficulty coincided with Steve's attempts to find a job in Mozambique and my applications for funding. The rupture in relations between Mozambique and the U.S. meant that I was unable to obtain any financial support for my dissertation research because I was going to be in a country without an official American presence. We hoped that we would be able to find work for Steve with the Mozambican Ministry of Health, as his job would be our only source of funding or income.

The Portuguese colonial system was notorious for its lack of training and education for Mozambicans. At independence, in 1975, there were only twelve physicians for a country estimated to have twelve million people. The new government was determined to bring health care to ordinary people in rural and urban areas. Many health workers from around the world were already contributing as cooperantes in Mozambique, providing health care and training. But Steve faced numerous obstacles in the process of finding a position.

Steve wrote to anyone whose name came to us as having a connection to the Ministry of Health and, eventually, he applied directly to the ministry as an individual. Despite initial positive responses from Mozambique, the process was lengthy and subject to unexplained delays. Our friends Bud Day and Carol Thompson, both longtime activists on southern African issues, made an important connection for

Chapter 2

us with a Canadian obstetrician, George Povey, who had already been working in Mozambique for several years, supported by Canadian University Service Overseas (CUSO). We were able to arrange to meet with him when he visited his sister in southern California. He was an older physician and initially seemed skeptical of our commitment to undertaking such a post. He questioned us closely about our interest in Mozambique and our expectations of what our life there would be like. We were able to convince him of our determination and he became our friend and an important resource in Mozambique. When George returned to Maputo, he discovered that Steve's application had been misplaced and was languishing somewhere in the Ministry of Health offices. He was able to get it to the person who could approve Steve's contract, an intervention that was crucial to our obtaining clearance to go to Mozambique.

We were hesitant to tell the ministry that we really wanted to be posted in Cabo Delgado, where I expected to pursue my research in Swahili history, until we were sure that a contract would be granted. When we did request that posting, we learned that a team of Chinese physicians had just begun a contract in that province and the ministry did not want to send us there. There was a greater need for an American pediatrician in Beira, then the second largest city and a port on the central coast.

Beira was considered an undesirable placement by many cooperantes, in part because it was a center of anti-socialist activities. Jorge Jardim, a prominent Portuguese businessman, had been based there and his role in opposing Frelimo had an enduring impact on the political life of the city. It was also not a particularly attractive location, despite being located on a string of Indian Ocean beaches. We were somewhat disheartened by the news that we would be living in Beira, but we were committed to going to Mozambique and decided we would make the best of the unexpected placement. One month before we planned to leave for Mozambique, we were asked to send a telegram specifically agreeing to be posted to Beira, so that the government could feel secure in hiring Steve.

While I knew a bit more about Beira's history than most Americans, I had not done the kind of in-depth archival and library investigations on Beira that I had done on Cabo Delgado and Swahili history. I had even filed a dissertation topic titled "A Social History of Northern Coastal Mozambique, 1850 to World War I." But Beira was well south of the Swahili areas, so I could not transfer part of my subject or make use of my years of language study. I was busy packing up and getting ready to leave and did not have time to do any further research preparation in the month before we left. Even though our reason for going to Mozambique was so that I could do my research, we agreed to go to Beira, and I recognized that I would have to begin an entirely new project while in the field. I was apprehensive about my research, but I was still eager to go to Mozambique under the new circumstances. I was reassured by the experience of Bob Nelson, an astronomer friend, who pointed out, "I shifted my dissertation topic from one planet to another!"—switching from Venus to the moons of Jupiter and Saturn. Surely, I could manage to find a good topic in Beira that would result in a dissertation, as I was at least studying the same *country* as I had originally planned to do.

Though we were concerned about these events, we were not dissuaded from our plans to travel there. The international political situation under newly elected President Ronald Reagan only bolstered our resolve to go to Mozambique and promote the development of a poor country that was condemned by a right-wing American government as well as beleaguered by its much stronger white minority–ruled neighbor. We believed that our activities in Mozambique would be part of an international struggle to improve the lives of ordinary people and that we would be making a concrete contribution to the global socialist movement.

All these factors came together finally in 1982, when Steve's contract with the Mozambican Ministry of Health was finalized. Mercie had fully recovered from her surgery and was old enough to have all the immunizations needed for overseas travel. We were ready to begin our new adventure, voyaging literally to the other side of the world. Though it was not one of the usual destinations for Americans, for us the route to Mozambique was determined by a series of ordinary decisions coupled with optimism. The intersection of global politics and personal desires led me there, taking my husband and toddler daughter with me.

Endnotes

1. For more on the school, see Victor Cohen, "The New American Movement and the Los Angeles Socialist Community School," *The Minnesota Review* 69 (Fall 2007): 139-151.
2. My politics were part of the anti-imperialist feminist movement, as discussed in Say Burgin, "White Women, Anti-Imperialist Feminism and the Story of Race within the US Women's Liberation Movement," *Women's History Review* 25, 5 (2016): 756-770.
3. The poster was designed and printed by the Chicago Women's Graphic Collective, which was affiliated with the socialist feminist Chicago Women's Liberation Union. This poster was made in the 1970s and can be viewed online at https://www.cwluherstory.org/store/many-waves-but-one-ocean, accessed May 6, 2021.
4. We had seen the Epsteins' "Letter from Mozambique," distributed by the American Friends Service Committee; eventually there was a series of twelve letters from 1978 to 1980.
5. Bernard Gwertzman, "U.S. Blames Cuba for Expulsion of 6 Americans from Mozambique," *New York Times* (March 5, 1981).

Chapter 3
Gourmet Airplane Food and Arriving in Maputo

July 1982

In Santa Monica, we lived in a sunny, rent-controlled two-bedroom apartment, equipped mainly with used furniture and books. We arranged to sublet it to a friend for two years while we were away and proceeded to sell or store our belongings. The couch, an odd shade of green that we had found for a very cheap price and liked because it was a sofa-bed, was sold to a friend of a co-worker of Steve's. The sofa buyer arrived with a pickup truck, loaded the couch, and left for East Los Angeles. We went out to dinner that night with our close friends Paul Koegel and Ilene Bell and celebrated at Trader Vic's, where Steve had his favorite drink at that time, a Suffering Bastard. When we returned home near midnight, we called for Thika, our little beige cat, but she did not come running as she usually did. (I had been reading Elspeth Huxley's memoir of growing up in colonial Kenya, *The Flame Trees of Thika*, when our Thika came to live with us as a kitten.) Though we walked around the neighborhood, there was no sign of her.

The next morning it occurred to us that we had not seen her since the couch had been picked up. Steve called the new owner of the sofa, who said, "I haven't seen any cat, but a friend of mine slept on the couch last night and he said he heard weird noises, they kept him up half the night." Sure enough, Thika had climbed up inside the back of the couch to escape from the commotion of packing and had ridden across Los Angeles in her hiding place. Steve drove to the other side of town to retrieve her, but only for a day or so, as she would be living with our friends Bob Nelson and Peggy Renner while we were away. They had a cat named Max and were possibly more enamored with cats than anyone else we knew. When we brought Thika to their house in Pasadena, Max had "written" a welcome note to her.

We were packing a small footlocker and two small suitcases, and we had bought a larger trunk to ship the rest of our belongings. We also planned to have our bicycles shipped. When I tried to visualize how the rest of our clothing and supplies would fit into the suitcases we owned, it seemed like everything might fit, though Steve was skeptical, and kept telling me, "We have a lot to pack, we will need at least one or two more big suitcases." Finally, the day before we were to leave, we piled everything around the living room in an approximation of packing our luggage. It was suddenly obvious that we were desperately short of suitcase space. Steve went to Sears and returned with three very large, brown, not very attractive, faux leather suitcases. We proceeded to cram everything in, but even with more space, we were sitting on the lids and holding the edges while we struggled to zip the cases shut.

Our plan was to make our way to Mozambique by increments. Our first stop was Chicago, to see Steve's family, who had reconciled with us a second time when Mercie, their first grandchild, was born. While re-packing various items in Chicago, we found the key to our neighbor's pick-up truck in Mercie's diaper bag. He had kindly lent us the truck so we could transport some of our boxes to a rented storage space, but the key had disappeared. After we found it, we guessed that Mercie, who was just over one year old, had decided to help us pack and had carefully stowed the key away in her bag. Fortunately, he had had a spare key to use until we mailed the found key back from Chicago.

Chapter 3

We then spent a few days in Connecticut with my family. When my sister Carol gave me a rather large box containing a going-away gift, I said in despair, "I don't have room for anything else!" She replied, "Just open it," and it turned out to be a particularly useful tote bag. My parents drove us to New York to catch our TWA flight to Paris. From there we would fly on UTA, the French airline Union de Transports Aériens (later, part of Air France), to Mozambique. The Ministry of Health was paying our plane fare and had given us $710 for overweight luggage. We had decided to use that allowance to ship the trunk, footlocker, and bicycles, but our luggage was nonetheless vastly overweight, with three giant, jam-packed suitcases, a baby stroller, Steve's guitar, and other smaller but still weighty boxes and cases. The desk agent at TWA knew we were headed to work in Mozambique and she asked who was paying for the excess baggage; when we told her we would be, she charged us nothing, much to our relief.

In Paris, we showered and slept in one of Charles de Gaulle Airport's tiny very-short-stay rooms and then continued our journey at midnight on UTA. We enjoyed a gourmet French meal on the flight, which concluded with individual bottles of raspberry liqueur. Following the example of a few of our fellow passengers, we stashed salt and pepper packets from the trays, though we had not yet internalized a food hoarding mentality.

Finally, as we flew over the expanse of Africa, I could look out the window and, in the dawn light, see the continent stretching into the distance. Years of reading and study had not prepared me for the vast landscape, the towering thunderheads on the horizon, or my joyous feeling when I finally saw the place that had filled my head and caught my heart. We could not stop in South Africa, as it was at that time subject to international sanctions, so we re-fueled in Brazzaville, Congo. We de-planed briefly, sitting on rickety wooden benches with unsavory puddles at our feet. I was exhausted from all the traveling, steaming in the heat and humidity, and overwhelmed to be on the ground in Africa. After that quick stop we flew the final leg of the journey across the continent to Mozambique.

We landed in Maputo at 2 P.M. on July 7, 1982, Steve's thirtieth birthday. We were greeted by the slogan painted in large letters on the main terminal, "Bem vindo à Moçambique, zona libertada da humanidade" (Welcome to Mozambique, liberated zone of humanity). Colin (Coke) McCord, an American surgeon who had been working there for a while, was at the airport to meet us. We showed the officials our health cards, documenting all the shots we had accumulated over the previous weeks, and changed some dollars into *meticais* (the singular form is *metical*, the currency that replaced the Portuguese currency, *escudo*). But then we discovered that only Steve's visa was in order. Despite our many letters and communications, the Ministry of Health had not prepared for the arrival of the whole family. Coke and João Alfredo, a ministry employee, made two or three trips back and forth from the airport to the ministry arranging the paperwork. I cut up a photo I happened to have in my wallet to supply the required picture of me, and eventually my visa and Mercie's were assembled and approved.

It was then 6 P.M. We had been traveling for days and now were sitting in the dimly lit and sparsely furnished Maputo airport for over four hours, unable to move around without official approval, and the customs officers had gone home. We promised to return the next day to go through customs and declare restricted items in our possession, such as tape players and radios. Because it was winter in the southern hemisphere, it was already dark, and I had only fleeting views of the city as we drove away from the airport, glimpsing people walking along the streets and observing shanty neighborhoods gradually giving way to modern high-rise buildings before we reached the apartment building where Coke and his wife Susan lived, just a block from the Ministry of Health.

Chapter 3

Although we were posted to Beira, we spent three weeks in Maputo, sleeping on the McCords' floor, waiting to make sure that housing was arranged in Beira, and sorting out paperwork with the Ministry of Health. An extremely useful booklet was *Time Out in Maputo: A Cooperantes Guide*, published by M.A.G.I.C. (Mozambique, Angola & Guine Information Centre), the British Mozambique-support organization. The booklet commented that, "You will spend quite a lot of time, especially at the beginning, filling in forms you don't understand for purposes you don't comprehend," and that was certainly our experience.[1] The tangled bureaucratic web was usually blamed at least in part on the legacy of the Napoleonic-era Portuguese colonial bureaucracy, which involved special blue paper called *papel azul*, multiple rubber stamps (*carimbos*) from different officials, and the special purchase of tax stamps (*selos*), which were something like postage stamps but could only be found at designated shops. That cumbersome set of rules converged with the new Soviet-style socialist bureaucracy, which was interested in keeping track of everyone. The result was a mind-boggling and time-wasting experience whenever anything even vaguely official needed to be accomplished.

The McCords already had guests when we arrived, another American physician, Dan Murphy, his wife Janet, and their two boys, Liam and Conor, who were on their way home to Iowa after three years in Gurué in the northern province of Zambézia. We had previously been put in touch with them by David Train, a friend of ours who had worked with the Murphys in the United Farm Workers' organizing campaign in the 1970s. We had exchanged letters in which they reassured us about life in Mozambique and gave us copious and valuable advice about what supplies to bring along. It was fortuitous that we were able to spend a few days with them in Maputo. At the end of the 1990s, Dan began working in East Timor along with George Povey, both making good use of their Portuguese as well as their experience providing health care in conditions of war and extreme poverty. Dan received a United Nations Development Award in 2002 for his contributions to the Bairo Pite Clinic in Dili, East Timor.

The letters from the Murphys, who had lived in a rural area, had included encouraging stories about raising children without television and with access to plentiful fresh food. Not only had the Murphys had a memorable time with their sons, but Jon Cohn and Jeanne Raisler, a physician and a nurse-midwife, were living in Quelimane in northern Mozambique with their toddler son and their new baby daughter who had just been born at the end of June. They remained in Quelimane for the birth, where George Povey joined them as the birth attendant. We had learned some details about their experiences through letters from Jeanne that were published in *Africa News* in 1981.[2] And we were familiar with the "Letter from Mozambique," written by Andy and Paul Epstein, who were with their children in Beira at the end of the 1970s. The fact that Steve was a pediatrician, bolstered by those reports of American children who had thrived in Mozambique, allayed any doubts we might have had about living there with Mercie.

Mercie was even-tempered and adaptable, and she agreeably met new people and readily ate unfamiliar foods. One meal she enjoyed soon after our arrival was grilled local fish and onions with diluted condensed milk to drink, not a dinner most toddlers would find acceptable. She was rarely cranky, even on the long plane rides or while sleeping in strange beds and unknown rooms, and she learned Portuguese more quickly than I did. But making the trip to Mozambique with a fifteen-month-old seemed the height of folly to some people, including Steve's family, who were mystified by our plans. Years later, when Mercie was in college and told stories about her toddler years in a war zone in Africa, people responded by saying, "Were your parents insane?"

One of our first tasks was to arrange for a permanent visa for Mercie, which meant we needed to get an official photograph of her. I took her to the recommended studio, where she happily sat and smiled for the camera. The photographer became increasingly impatient, as it was supposed to be an Official Photograph and smiling was not permitted. That was impossible to explain to a tiny child who had been exhorted to smile for the camera all her life. The more he insisted, "Don't smile!" the more she twinkled and preened, but eventually she toned her expression down to a Mona Lisa level and an acceptable portrait was achieved.

Figure 2: Mercie's official photo on arrival in Mozambique, July 1982.

We began to get acclimated to life in urban Mozambique. I enjoyed the early morning smell of wood smoke that drifted over the city, and we went for lengthy walks just to see what was there. Many of the shops and cafes were closed due to shortages of food and supplies, though chairs and tables were still visible, and the permanence of the closures was not clear to passersby. In my journal I noted that there seemed to be plenty of food in the markets, though I already found it monotonous after the first few days. Every meal was rice with a vegetable sauce, sometimes fish or meat if it was available, accompanied by a salad of lettuce and tomatoes and a lot of bread. One day the *salão de chá* (tea shop) near us had a supply of small sweet rolls, with a line of customers stretching out the door and children eating them in fast bites on the street. I did not have a chance to buy any that day and by the next day they were finished, never to return during our entire stay. Local Polanaville chocolate bars also appeared one day at the salão de chá, and we did manage to purchase a couple of bars of the creamy dark bittersweet treat, but they also were never seen again.

People generally had access to basic food supplies through a ration system, distributed through neighborhood cooperative shops. The McCords' ration card listed thirty items, from cashews and coffee to beer, wine, milk, matches, butter, fish, meat, and onions. Cashews, a luxury snack in the U.S., were a major export crop in Mozambique and were often available in the stores and markets. Fruit was for sale in the markets and we ate apples, pears, and grapefruit, and once we enjoyed a tropical salad of pineapple, mango, and orange sections for lunch.

Other food was available at the diplomats' shop, then called the Interfranca and later the *Loja Franca* or Exchange Store. Only dollars or other strong currencies such as the South African rand were accepted there, but customers could buy Hero jam and Toblerone chocolate imported from Switzerland, liquor, and fancy cookies. Rationed items such as eggs and butter were not counted against the quota if they were bought at the Loja Franca, so those who had dollars could supplement otherwise restricted purchases. The system of having a separate "dollar store" was controversial as it allowed well-to-do foreigners and a few privileged Mozambicans to purchase food that was not available in the ordinary markets and grocery stores. Many of us who were able to shop there and who did so regularly were uncomfortable with the convenience and critical of the two-tier system. Most cooperantes had come to Mozambique to help develop a socialist society and were annoyed at having special access to such luxury. At the same time, the Mozambican government benefited from the modest quantities of foreign exchange that were acquired from those stores. Additionally, some believed it was important to allow small indulgences for cooperantes, who were generally living in much-reduced circumstances compared to their lives in their home countries.

Chapter 3

It was also possible to eat in local restaurants, though there were only a few that were open. The Piri Piri restaurant, which continues to serve customers from its site on the Avenida 24 de Julho, was one place where Mozambicans and foreigners ate often. *Piri piri* refers to the flavorful, uniquely Mozambican, hot pepper sauce that is used on all sorts of dishes, but especially chicken and prawns. We sat in the plainly furnished room one Sunday for lunch, paying the relatively high price of $5.00 each for very tough, nearly meatless bony fried chicken, greasy French fries, a strange bitter salad, and a glass of local beer. Piri piri sauce was not available.

Before we left the United States, we had heard that there were small counter-revolutionary anti-government groups operating in northern rural areas. Nothing we read had suggested that their actions were having an impact on daily life in the cities, and at first it was not easy to distinguish whether shortages were a result of poverty, isolation, government policies, or the rebels whom we all called *bandidos armados* (armed bandits)—BAs, or bandidos for short—or sometimes *kizumbas*, meaning hyenas. These rebels later were known as the Mozambican National Resistance (MNR) or Renamo (the acronym for Resistência Nacional Moçambicana) and we learned that they had substantial support from apartheid South Africa. But for the two years that we lived there, they were still somewhat mysterious in origin and motivation.

While still in Maputo, we learned that the bandidos had attacked the power lines that supplied Beira, cutting all electricity to the city for sixteen days. That was one of the first indications we had that our lives would be affected by Renamo, which we had assumed would be quickly brought under control by the Mozambican army. After all, the Mozambican soldiers of FRELIMO had won a revolutionary struggle against a modern western army less than a decade earlier. Adding to our concerns, George Povey shared a letter that he had received from Steve Gloyd, an American physician working outside of Beira in Dondo. Steve Gloyd wrote that, "Food is a real problem for everybody here. ... Folks in Beira haven't seen rice or *farinha* [flour] for quite a while, and fresh vegies [sic] and fruit are out of the question." Other cooperantes in Maputo were the source of rumors and unreliable information. My Steve was told by an Italian physician that "You should only go to Beira if you have a return ticket in hand," as conditions were so unstable. We were already committed to living in Beira, but we were beginning to worry about how we were going to manage once we got there.

I attempted to contact other scholars at the Universidade Eduardo Mondlane and I spent an afternoon on the campus visiting offices and trying to find people to speak with. The campus is slightly outside of the downtown area, so Susan McCord gave me a lift by car on my first visit. I found my way to the African Studies Center, a modern two-story building with a lot of glass and an interior courtyard. The first floor was mainly a public reception area and a small canteen, while the offices were found on the second floor. I walked around the corridor and knocked on various doors, but July was a vacation month and everyone was away on break. Ruth First, a prominent South African exile who was director of the African Studies Center, was with her family in England, and center co-director Aquino de Bragança was out of town as well. Most of the academics at the university were expatriates themselves and were not inclined to be supportive. In part they were responding to my own uncertainty about what my situation would be in Beira, as I had not yet defined a proper research project. The national historical archives were also closed. It seemed better to wait until I got to Beira and could arrange connections with local institutions. A few expatriates, including Judith Marshall, a Canadian employed in the Education Ministry; Julie Cliff, a British physician with the Health Ministry; and Signe Arnfred, a Danish researcher working with the women's organization, gave me much-appreciated encouragement.

Chapter 3

One day I was included in a group of Americans who were making a formal presentation of 18,000 meticais (just over $500, as, at that time, one dollar equaled around 30 meticais) raised to support Frelimo's Fourth Party Congress, which was scheduled for the following April. We were invited to meet with Eduardo Arão, a member of Frelimo's Central Committee. Four or five of us went in a minivan to his office. There had been no running water for several days, and I had watched women line up at the pumps outside the hospital opposite the McCords' apartment and walk away with immense tins of water on their heads. I had not been able to shower for three days, so I tied a silk scarf over my stringy hair. Nearly every woman in Mozambique wore a scarf on her head as a matter of daily fashion, and on special occasions scarves were chosen to coordinate with the rest of the clothing. But on the way to Senhor Arão's office, Susan McCord told me, "You can't wear that scarf, this is an official visit."

Head scarves were problematic. Mozambican women were supposed to be proud of their hair and not cover it up. While there was never an actual law concerning the wearing of scarves, President Samora Machel had made comments in several speeches about taking pride in being African and denouncing women's headscarves. On that day I removed my scarf and in my unwashed condition I took part in the small ceremonial presentation of funds. There were a couple of brief formal speeches and we all chatted while we were served coffee in cups with the Frelimo emblem. I did not encounter enforcement of the scarf rule again, though it was an issue in some schools.[3] Sadly, Eduardo Arão, after many years of service in the upper levels of government, committed suicide in the 1990s.

We were expecting our trunks to arrive any day and hoped they would come soon so that we could convey them with us to Beira. We feared we would never see them if we went on to Beira without them. We learned in a phone conversation with my mother that it had cost nearly $1,500.00 to ship them. My parents paid the $755.00 difference, the beginning of thousands of dollars that we would owe them before we returned to the U.S. We were also waiting for housing to be arranged in Beira and for our installation fee of $800 to come from the Ministry of Health. But because we would not be permanently based in Maputo, there was little for us to do each day and the inactivity was wearing us down.

The night before we left Maputo, Coke came home late because there had been a shooting at the Chinese embassy. One of the Chinese employees had shot nine of his colleagues, killing each of them with a bullet in the head. There was not actually anything that the doctors could do, but they were kept at the hospital as a precaution. We never saw a report that explained what had happened, but it seemed ominous and suggested that even individuals from other parts of the Third World found it impossible to cope with life in Mozambique.[4]

Most expatriates found their own non-violent solutions to help them deal with the difficulties. Steve and I noted that Coke and Susan began each evening with a glass of whiskey and accompanied their dinner with beer when it was available. We were social drinkers at that time, drinking beer or wine occasionally at parties but not otherwise. From our perspective as new arrivals, we were concerned about what seemed like a high level of alcohol consumption by the McCords. Our time in Beira, however, would lead to a shift in our own drinking habits and we came to have a far less self-righteous interpretation of the practice of having a pre-dinner cocktail followed by beer with every meal.

Endnotes

1   M.A.G.I.C. (Mozambique, Angola & Guine Information Centre), *Time Out in Maputo: A Cooperantes Guide*, 2d ed. (London: ca. 1982). M.A.G.I.C. replaced the Committee for Freedom in Mozambique, Angola and Guine after those countries became independent. Both organizations' archives are held in the Bishopsgate Institute: https://www.bishopsgate.org.uk/collections/committee-for-freedom-in-mozambique-angola-and-guine-cfmag.

Chapter 3

2   Jean[ne] Raisler, "Notes from a 'Cooperante'," *Africa News* 16, 20 (May 18, 1981); 17, 1 (July 6, 1981); 17 (November 16, 1981); 18 (March 1, 1982).

3   Chris Searle reports on this in *We're Building the New School: Diary of a Teacher in Mozambique* (London: Zed Press, 1981), 119-122.

4   A report on these murders is on Reddit, https://www.reddit.com/r/TrueCrime/comments/qfuwb1/the_1982_the_chinese_embassy_maputo_shooting_that/?rdt=45119, accessed March 28, 2024.

"Third World" is a term that has been the subject of much discussion and has fallen out of favor in the twenty-first century. I use it in this memoir because our mindset in the 1980s concurred with this analysis: it was "a beacon of hope. Leftist groups, student protesters, and social movements in Europe and the US, anticolonial activists in Asia and Africa, as well as reformers and revolutionaries in Latin America collaboratively created the idea of the Third World as a promising alternative to the destructive antagonism of the Cold War;" quote from Cristoph Kalter, "When 'Third World' Still Meant Hope," blog post at Cambridge University Press (4 November 2016), http://www.cambridgeblog.org/2016/11/when-third-world-still-meant-hope/.

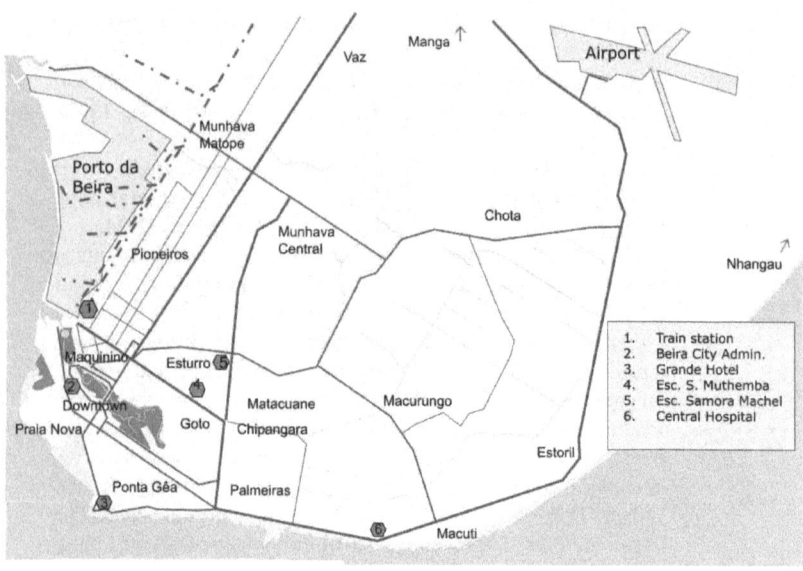

Map 2: Central Beira, modified by Kathleen Sheldon and used with permission from a map by Jon Schubert, which he adapted from Open Streets Maps.

Chapter 4
Beira at Last

July to August 1982

Finally, on July 31st, we arrived in Beira. The city sat along the Indian Ocean coastline and was marked by large swampy areas, a lot of sand, tropical heat and humidity, seasonal rains, and not much else. Since then, I have read other travelers' accounts, and they have rarely been complimentary in their descriptions of the city. A 1957 geographers' report on port activity commented that "It is notable that Beira has achieved such prominence as a seaport despite a mediocre physical site. Located at the confluence of Pungue [Púnguè] and Buzi rivers . . . the oldest part of the city spread . . . over a low, unstable flatland of marsh and silt fringed with mangrove swamps."[1] It was never a center of Portuguese colonialism despite the presence of the chartered Mozambique Company after 1894. It was an essential port for land-locked Southern Rhodesia (which became Zimbabwe after 1980) and the local paper was published in both Portuguese and English during much of the twentieth century in recognition of the importance of its English-speaking residents and British colonial influence. There had also been a thriving camping and resort area just north of the city along the shore where hotels and restaurants had catered to white Rhodesian tourists, but that was largely abandoned in 1982. Central to Beira's economy, however, was the port, which was a notoriously high-maintenance site. The harbor silted up easily and required regular dredging and repair to accommodate large tankers and other ships. The port facilities had fallen into serious disrepair by the time we arrived.

We were met at the Beira airport by a representative of the provincial Ministry of Health and were loaded into a beat-up tan Land Rover with another foreign health worker, a woman from Guinea (Conakry), who was also in Mozambique with her two-year-old daughter. She was dressed in a stylish outfit of printed cotton cloth, including a long skirt, overblouse, and elaborately tied headscarf typical of West African women. We drove into the city along a lengthy straight road lined with eucalyptus trees, with extensive flat rice fields stretching off in all directions. That Land Rover ride became an odyssey that lasted nearly two hours. First, we needed to find the local pediatrician, Dr. António Gama, who was at the hospital and was expecting Steve's arrival. He was to become a constant colleague of Steve's during our two years there, a tall man of South Asian descent, in his late twenties, who worked hard to provide decent health care in a difficult situation. Steve was stationed in Beira with the expectation that he would help train Gama (as everyone called him) in pediatrics so he could become one of Mozambique's first two pediatricians.

Then we went to the Ministry of Health offices, where the never-ending requirement for further paperwork was satisfied. We were taken to the Embaixador (Ambassador), a large downtown hotel. The people at the reception desk claimed at first that they had no rooms, as we sat around with our luggage and baby looking disheveled and distraught. After further negotiation with Ministry of Health agents as our mediators, a room was found.

The Embaixador retained an aura of faded elegance from its days serving well-to-do white Rhodesians on holiday. We were assigned to a suite furnished with a bed, dressers, a desk, and a make-up table, all painted white with green trim, surrounded by a curving balcony affording a view of the Chiveve River, a tidal stream that ran through the center of Beira.² We even had hot water, though the pressure was erratic and the shower stall was equipped with a window that opened directly to the public hallway.

The hotel had two dining rooms, a smaller room designated for families with children, and the larger main dining room for adults. We had dinner that night in the family restaurant and we were served Portuguese style, with new dishes and cutlery provided for each course. After potato soup we had fish and boiled potatoes, followed by meat (possibly pork) and fried potatoes, and flan for dessert. Being served two main courses was almost too much food and was an unusual experience in Mozambique during those years. There was not a lot of choice, however. We were not offered any fruit or vegetables other than the various potato preparations and there was only bottled water or hot tea to drink. There was no bread, which boded ill, as I assumed that if bread were available in Beira our relatively upscale hotel would be serving it. Breakfast the next morning consisted of tea and nothing else, so we relied on cheese and pears that we had brought with us from Maputo.

We remained at the Embaixador for five days while Steve tried to arrange permanent housing and to sort out his situation with the Ministry of Health. Then we learned that our rooms were promised to a government official who was just arriving in town. As our apartment was not yet ready, we were moved to another hotel, the infinitely more horrible Hotel Mozambique. We were offered a choice of rooms. One was larger but was located on the twelfth floor, which by our American reckoning was really the fourteenth as the floors were numbered from the bottom up, "ground floor" and "restaurant," followed by the first floor. We were concerned about being on the higher floor because the elevator was out of order, and we were warned that during the electrical cuts of the previous month the stairwells had been pitch dark and the hotel had lost its water supply (a common problem in high-rise buildings that depended on electric pumps to deliver water to rooftop cisterns).

The Mackerel Years

We chose the smaller room on the fifth (seventh) floor. It was infested with cockroaches. Even worse, while we were waiting in a dank hallway for dinner to be served at the hotel restaurant, we saw a rat running along the baseboard. We spent the night with the lights on and in intermittent wakefulness to ensure that no rats bit Mercie, and that no cockroaches went into her ears while she slept. Steve had had experience with rat bites at Los Angeles County Hospital, as well as with extracting cockroaches from children's ears. He did not want to perform that minor operation in Beira on his own daughter. The next morning, our breakfast of weak tea accompanied by bread and flavorless, yellow-colored jam was much delayed and I felt the first strong pangs of homesickness. All I wanted was to be in a diner back home with a waitress pouring endless cups of hot fresh coffee before taking food orders.

Beira made an initial impression of being left behind, a literal dusty backwater. We had been cautioned that the open-air produce markets would be empty from December to April, but there was little on display even though August and September should have been the season of greater supplies of vegetables and fruit. Steve began work on the pediatric ward at the hospital and I did errands at the bank and post office and walked around with Mercie trying to learn a little about the city. After a month in Mozambique, I had met people who had each given me the names of other individuals that I should try to meet. But none of these contacts had offered concrete advice for how I should proceed in my research. I still had to figure out the first steps for myself.

One of the first people we met in Beira was Murray Dickson, a genial bearded Canadian dentist, accompanied by his wife Gerri, a nurse, and their two sons, Michael and Brennan. Murray was writing *Where There is No Dentist*, a companion text to the widely distributed basic health-care book, *Where There is No Doctor* by David Werner. Murray knew that the apartment next to theirs in the Mexicana building was vacant. It was assigned to Yacine, a French nurse, but she had moved in with a Brazilian pharmacist named Juarez and had no immediate plans to move back to her original quarters. Murray made the arrangements with the ministry and after two horrid nights at the Hotel Mozambique we moved into that two-bedroom apartment. Initially we thought we would be there temporarily until permanent housing was arranged, and that we might camp out at other cooperante homes in the interim. But Yacine's place was ours for a year.

The Mexicana (pronounced in Portuguese, "Meshi cáh na") was a seven-story apartment building about two blocks from the ocean, and if we leaned out from our balcony, we could see a sliver of water and sand. It was located in the Ponta Gêa neighborhood, an area that had been reserved for white residents during colonialism. An observer in the 1950s sketched its ambiance in glowing terms: "The aristocratic neighborhood of Ponta Gêa is enchanting, with beautiful homes enjoying a lovely panorama of the beach, which is just two steps away."[3] It was less aristocratic by the 1980s, though still adjacent to the shoreline. Many cooperantes were housed in the Mexicana building, but, in a significant change since independence, about half of the apartments were home to Mozambicans.

The first floor of the Mexicana was a tea shop that was closed and dark, though the tables and chairs were still there. As we stopped to peer through the large dirty windows, Murray mentioned, "This shop used to serve nice little rolls and tea, up until a few months ago," to which I responded optimistically, "Oh good, maybe we'll be able to buy some bread here." During the two years we lived in the building it was never open as a salão de chá, though they did on rare occasions sell sacks of bread rolls.

*Figure 3: Mexicana building at dawn, Beira.
Photo by Steve Tarzynski.*

When we arrived at our assigned apartment, a sturdy young man was on his hands and knees scrubbing the wooden floor. It transpired that he had been cooking and cleaning for Yacine and expected to continue working in the same apartment for us. We were not used to having someone clean for us and were hesitant about the prospect of a full-time person taking care of our housework. After observing the McCords' household, where Feliciano, an African man, did all their cooking and cleaning, we had been discussing whether we would hire someone or not, but we had not reached a conclusion. Francisco Agostinho, the floor scrubber, seemed to be already working for us and we never made an actual decision about retaining him. We did not ask him to leave, however, in part because we did not want to be responsible for making him unemployed, and in part because housework was arduous and time-consuming. He stayed with us the two years we were there and became an important part of our household.

I had harbored vague ideas about equality in a socialist society, ideals that seemingly precluded hiring a local person to do the dirty work. But as skilled international workers, we were expected to devote our time to the jobs

Chapter 4

we had been hired to do, whether it was teaching, providing medical care, or helping with other technical tasks. The absence of labor-saving devices, the difficulty of finding and buying food, the need for all laundry to be hand-washed, hung to dry, and ironed, meant that housework was truly a full-time job. Steve was also told bluntly by another doctor that cooperantes were not there to waste the struggling government's money waiting in long lines for food and cleaning their apartments.

An additional issue was that Europeans tended to require fewer hours of toil from their employees, yet they paid a higher monthly salary than African families, making a position in a cooperante household extremely desirable for many Mozambicans. While the cooperantes were trying to be fair in their unaccustomed role as bosses, their presence as employers skewed the economics of the whole system of domestic service. The reality of trying to introduce socialism into one of the poorest nations in the world (at the time Mozambique was at the bottom in the United Nations ranking) was rife with contradictions. The presence of fulltime domestic workers in every middle-class household, both foreign and Mozambican, was simply one example of the struggle between ideals and reality.

We were curious about Francisco's family and where he was from, so about a month after he began working for us, he wrote an autobiographical sketch for us. Composed in ball-point pen on lined paper, with careful penmanship and impeccable official-style Portuguese, he outlined his background.

The Biography.

I, Francisco Saize Agostinho, Native of Mopeia, Student of the Secondary School of Luabo

I certify on my honor that my father is deceased and I am obligated to support my mother and my four (4) sisters as for example by buying clothes for them and sending money for their expenses and I also need clothes and other important things.

That is all. I wrote this biography to explain to you my situation.

Beira, 13/9/82

Revolutionary Greetings.

The apartment was already furnished with a modern-style blue vinyl couch and chair, some bookcases, a dining table and chairs, and a bed. The floors were parquet, which had been neglected and abused for years, and the walls were painted institutional green. There was an imposing front door that led to the common open hallway that ran along the back of the building, but everyone used the kitchen door, which was immediately adjacent to the front door and also opened onto the shared hallway. A double door with a space for a glass window in the top half led from the living room to a small balcony that protruded from the front of the building itself. Many of those windows in the building had broken over the years and ours was covered with cardboard when we moved in. We used to relax on the balcony and watch the city residents walk past. The government Marriage Palace was around the corner and every weekend wedding parties would drive past, honking their car horns, accompanied by children racing alongside, chanting, "*Casamento, casamento!*" (Wedding, wedding!).[4]

The kitchen was narrow and dark, presumably built on the assumption that the white apartment dwellers would not be working there, though the conditions were considered adequate for the African cook. Our kitchen was in especially poor shape, with one countertop missing entirely and moldy and decayed cupboards underneath. One cabinet above the sink seemed especially placed for bumping one's head. The tiny refrigerator needed to be defrosted nearly every week when the electricity was working. The stove ran on a canister of propane gas, but only one of the three burners worked, making it tricky to organize meal preparation. Francisco

Chapter 4

found that a charcoal brazier on the back porch was more reliable. A poky laundry room, with a cement washboard and sink, was outside the apartment in the common hallway.

By late October, we were dealing with a serious and continuous leak that apparently originated in the bathroom of the apartment above us. At first it was confined to our bathroom, but as weeks went by with no repair despite repeated requests, we faced water seeping into our bedroom floor and inside the closet, causing extensive damage to the parquet floors. These problems caused Steve to note in his journal that the obstacles to finishing the most basic tasks were perhaps to be expected when living in the Third World, and that he was trying to find the patience needed to avoid getting an "ulcer/hypertension/coronary/nervous breakdown."

The entire kitchen was heavily infested with cockroaches, and we had no means of eliminating them. If one of us went into the kitchen at night and turned on the light (when we had electricity), dozens, or even hundreds, of big ugly roaches would scoot back into hiding. One night we noticed a three-inch long cockroach on the wall of our bedroom, and we watched in horror as it spread its clumsy wings and lumberingly flew across the room to the opposite wall. In the U.S., flying cockroaches were a kind of mythical insect, but we were living with the reality, and it was disgusting. Mercie learned to call a roach a *bicho* (pronounced BEE-shoo) for bug and copied her friends from childcare who went into attack mode when spying the bugs in their classroom, crying out "Bicho! Bicho! Bicho!" while running to stamp wildly on the nasty creatures.

Mercie was sleeping in a hospital crib on loan from the Ministry of Health. To protect her from malaria-bearing mosquitos, we shrouded that bed with unsightly green mosquito netting from a camping store in Los Angeles, at the time the only netting that we had found among the limited supplies for a tropical journey. She became accustomed to sleeping in her green cocoon and, long after we returned

The Mackerel Years

to the U.S., she preferred to have her head covered when she slept. We kept her crib in our bedroom for the first few months. We also burned mosquito-repellant incense coils every night and managed to scrounge bits of wire mesh to mend the holes in the window screens. Finding the screen for patching was an adventure, as there was none readily available in Beira. After many inquiries to friends and co-workers we located a supplier, but when new holes appeared later in our stay, he no longer had mesh for sale.

The threat of malaria was a serious one and a newspaper report in December 1983 stated that 43.7 percent of Mozambicans were infected. Residents of Beira were especially prone to contract it due to the swampy nature of the land surrounding the city. Mosquitoes were everywhere. Even the patch of land behind the Mexicana was an acre of swamp most of the year. In the dry season it filled with dry reeds that swayed and rattled in the breeze and, once, a fire blackened the yard, causing a mortar shell hidden in the grass to explode, causing some neighborhood excitement. In addition to the nets, screens, and coils, we faithfully took our chloroquine tablets every Sunday (malaria was not yet fully resistant to that common treatment), crushing the pill and mixing it with jam to disguise the harsh taste for Mercie. She quickly learned that intense bitterness was hidden in the sweet treat and convincing her to swallow it quickly and then drink a cup of water was a recurring struggle.

Another health concern was tuberculosis and, as we planned to enroll Mercie in local day care, Steve wanted her to get the TB vaccine, BCG (Bacille Calmette-Guérin), which was not normally given in the U.S. Mercie and I went to the neighborhood health center, a pleasant, two-story colonial building surrounded by dirt yards and shade trees. Located in the middle of our Ponta Gêa neighborhood, it had been the hospital "for whites" under colonialism. The old hospital "for blacks," transformed into the main hospital for Beira after independence, was on the outskirts of the city. When I arrived at the health post with Mercie, there were already dozens of women sitting along the porch wall waiting in line with their sick children. The nurses insisted that I move to the head of the line and despite my discomfort with the special treatment I could not resist them. Being singled out for such privileges was a persistent issue while we lived there. It was partly a relic from colonial days when white Portuguese insisted on preferential treatment. That courtesy was also a way that Mozambicans could acknowledge that we were making sacrifices to assist Mozambique during a difficult period and should not waste our time waiting in line. The longer we were in Beira, the more people knew us, particularly because Steve provided care to thousands of Mozambican children. Wherever we went, parents who had met him in the health centers and hospital wanted to make sure he and his family were given advantages. Nonetheless, we knew how exhausting everyday life was for ordinary Mozambicans and always felt a bit guilty when we were invited to the front of a food queue or given other privileges.

Endnotes

1 William A. Hance and Irene S. Van Dongen, "Beira, Mozambique Gateway to Central Africa." *Annals of the Association of American Geographers* 47, 4 (1957): 307–335, quote on 311.
2 The Chiveve finally got an upgrade in 2020, when a new green space with a park and shops as well as improved flood control was inaugurated: "Nyusi Inaugurates Beira Green Park," *Club of Mozambique* (December 21, 2020) https://clubofmozambique.com/news/mozambique-nyusi-inaugurates-beira-green-park-watch-180545/
3 Octávio Rodrigues de Campos, 1953 (Full citation lost, possibly "Notas sobre a cidade da Beira," 1954); "Encantador é o bairro aristocrático da Ponta Gea, com residências lindas de onde se disfruta em belo panorama para a praia, situado ali a dois passos."
4 After we returned home to Santa Monica, where a train occasionally went past on tracks a block from our apartment, a train whistle blew one morning, and 3-year-old Mercie piped up, "Casamento!" It was one of the only times that she uttered a word in Portuguese after leaving Mozambique. The iconic Wedding Palace was in severe disrepair and a likely candidate to be demolished by 2020: "Study Advises against Rehabilitation of Beira Architectural Landmark

Palácio dos Casamentos," *Club of Mozambique* (February 8, 2021) https://clubofmozambique.com/news/mozambique-study-advises-against-rehabilitation-of-beira-architectural-landmark-palacio-dos-casamentos-noticias-report-183802/ (accessed May 28, 2021; includes links to further information about the building).

Chapter 5
Mercie Goes to Creche and Prawns for Lunch

July to August 1982

We arranged for Mercie to attend a local childcare center, called a creche. I visited the Primeiro de Junho creche (named June 1st for International Children's Day) with Mercie. The center was for children under two years of age and Mercie attended it on a regular basis for nearly a year. It was on the third floor of a high-rise residential building and, after Mercie began going regularly, I would take her there in her stroller, a walk of about thirty minutes. The bottom two floors were parking garages, which were completely unused and dark while we were there. The elevators did not work, so we climbed the unlit concrete stairs, toting the stroller with us. After our bicycles arrived, I would lock my bike inside the garage so I would not have to carry it up the stairs. I never felt at ease climbing those stairs, shining my flashlight up the steps as we went along, but I never found another way in, so Mercie and I would take a deep breath and climb up to the creche. Once, when I returned after dropping Mercie off, I discovered that someone had stolen the little blue nylon pack I had strapped on the back of the bike seat. The pack was empty, so I did not lose much, but my anxiety about who might be skulking around the garage area increased.

The creche director was Dona Caterina (*Dona* is a title of respect), a woman with a close-cropped natural hairstyle who had fought in the armed struggle to end Portuguese colonialism. On our first visit, she was warm and informative as we toured the facilities. Most of the childcare workers were Mozambican women, though there were two white Portuguese nuns who had been working in Mozambique for decades and had remained after independence. The center appeared very well organized, with fifty-eight children in attendance, divided into groups according to their ages—newborn to six months, six to nine months, nine to twelve months, and one to two years old—and there seemed to be many adults around to provide care. They served two meals a day to the children, who were mainly the offspring of Mozambican professional and civil service workers. They had cribs for naps and the clean bright rooms were surrounded by a large veranda where the children could get some outdoor playtime.

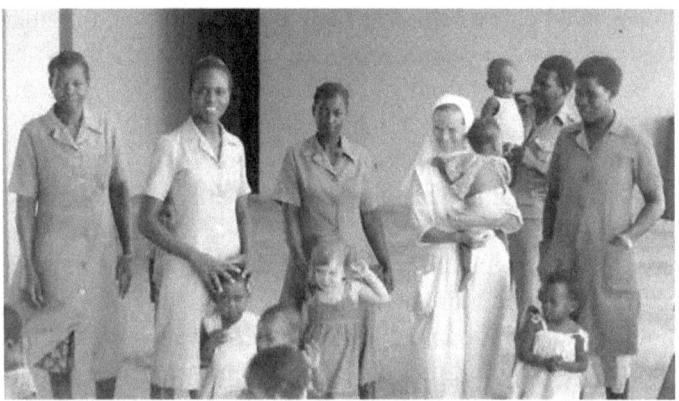

Figure 4: Primeiro de Junho creche, 1983. Photo by Steve Tarzynski.

The creche was open from 6:30 A.M. until 6:30 P.M., Monday through Friday, and a half-day Saturday as well, so that care was available during normal work hours. For the first few months Mercie attended three days a week—Monday, Wednesday, and Friday—which seemed to suit her energy

Chapter 5

level but limited the time I could devote to my own research. The program for the one-year-olds was well planned, with attention to learning words and songs, a lot of free play time, and regular group potty training. The "socialist potty-training project," as we called it, was very effective. After every meal and snack, they sat the children on little gray plastic potties imported from Bulgaria and in a surprisingly short time they no longer needed diapers. I had to laugh the first time I caught sight of a dozen toddlers chatting casually as they sat on little pots together, but I was very glad to end the nightly practice of soaking dirty diapers in buckets of harsh Napi-San detergent.

When Mercie first began, I spent several hours over two days observing the creche, and though it went well there were fewer trained staff on site than I had thought initially. When we arrived on the first day, the children were playing on the veranda with no adult in sight. We did see Kadi, the daughter of the Guinean woman who arrived in Beira with us. The older children, who were at the most only twenty-three months old, were helping keep the younger ones close by, retrieving those who began to wander off and helping others who fell as they tried to walk. At 8:30 Mercie's group of seventeen children sat in a circle for their morning snack, which, on that first day, was a piece of bread with a sweet tomato spread. There were two adults to care for the group.

After snack and potty time, the children went inside and sang a song about a train, "*Comboio* . . ." while walking around as if they were a train of children. They had time for drawing pictures, and then they went outside again. Play equipment and toys of any kind were scarce, so free play meant a lot of aimless wandering around in the sun. Lunch was macaroni, which Mercie loved, and vegetables served with cornmeal porridge called *massa*, which she did not care for at first. She never liked foods with a pudding-like consistency, and that first day she simply refused to eat more after taking one taste, but she grew to enjoy it over the next few weeks. After more potty time, they all napped from 11:45 to 2:15. The afternoon was more of the same: snack time, free play, songs, and potty training. They also had lessons in concepts such as *grande* and *pequeno* (big and little).

The veranda could also be dangerous. People living in the upper-level apartments often tossed their trash over their balconies and it landed on the play area. A large proportion of urban residents were recently arrived from rural villages, and they had little understanding of the constraints of apartment living.[1] The trash at times included burning embers, dead cockroaches, and even human waste. One day the children ate pieces of Styrofoam packing peanuts that had fallen. I spoke about the problem to Sister Alzira, a tiny energetic Portuguese nun who wore a traditional grey habit and white cowl. She agreed that it was a difficult issue, commenting that recently, "Another child ate *chloroquine* pills," the potentially poisonous malaria medicine. I wondered if that story of a more dangerous incident was supposed to allay my concerns about the Styrofoam! One day a teacher had a narrow escape from a coconut grater, a heavy wooden bar with a sharp metal rasp on one end, which, to my knowledge, was the most treacherous item that plummeted from above. One night a board fell and broke a window in the creche. Fortunately, those items did not actually fall onto a child, but clearly the conditions were less than optimal.

Steve and I were uneasy about these deficiencies, which would have immediately closed down any childcare center in the U.S. I had not previously enrolled Mercie in day care and, since her birth, I had not been away from her for more than a couple of hours at a time. I was concerned about leaving her in a strange place with new people, and the substandard conditions certainly increased our apprehension. But as we had come to Mozambique to do our work, we had to find some form of childcare, and the alternative of hiring a Mozambican woman to care for her at our home was a much less satisfactory solution. A nanny would have watched over Mercie in our apartment

Chapter 5

during the day when I often was doing work related to my research. I had observed other expatriate families where the Mozambican caregiver simply sat around listlessly watching the children play with sticks by the front stoop of their building. Avoiding that situation would have meant that I would likely be more involved in Mercie's day-to-day recreation. I loved spending time with her and watching her learn and grow, but I also knew that I did not have the skills or interest to spend hours on preschool instruction. The teachers at the center had training in early childhood education and knew how to provide organized learning activities. We continued to be vigilant and kept Mercie at home from time to time but felt that the creche was the best choice we could find in Beira. I later wrote an article—one of the first that I published based on my research in Beira—that analyzed the importance of providing childcare for working mothers, which was a priority of the Mozambican government.[2]

The creche organized a parents' group and the first gathering of that group in October was also the first official meeting I attended in Mozambique. There were about thirty-five parents, apparently professionals, as most of them were well dressed and wearing shoes, an uncommon sight on the streets of Beira. One of the mothers was the personal secretary for Armando Guebuza, then the governor of our province, Sofala. A representative from the Social Action section of the Ministry of Health, the government entity that oversaw day-care programs, opened the meeting by explaining that it was important to organize as parents in order to foster regular links with the creche workers. At first, people were reluctant to take on the responsibility and wanted the man from Social Action to run the organization. One father was worried about the role of foreigners. Since the only non-Mozambicans were me and Ibrahim, Kadi's father, it did not seem to be a potential problem. In the end, four parents agreed to serve as president, vice-president, secretary, and treasurer, and Ibrahim was secretary. Although mostly men had spoken up during the discussion, the officers who were elected were two men and two women, without any reference to achieving a gender balance.

It was common for parents who did not have childcare to simply leave their children home alone. I noted that small children often had the responsibility of watching even tinier tots and girls as young as four or five could be seen on city sidewalks with their infant siblings wrapped on their backs with a length of cloth in imitation of their mothers. I saw children playing unsupervised with charcoal braziers and climbing trees that clearly could not hold their weight. Steve treated wounds, especially burns and kerosene ingestion, suffered by children who had been left on their own. The weekly newspaper, *Domingo,* printed an article in late 1982 describing twenty-four hours in the emergency ward at the Central Hospital in Maputo, with a special sidebar on the injuries incurred by children playing in the streets. The children often organized team games, such as dodge ball (a girls' game) and soccer (played solely by boys). Boys also constructed elaborate cars from wires and discarded cans and wheeled them around the city at the end of long sticks. But they planned these entertainments with little or no adult oversight.

On a typical day, roosters crowing would awaken us just before our alarm rang at 6 A.M. and we would hear dogs barking throughout the neighborhood. The sun was already bright. We ate our breakfast of home-baked bread spread with imported peanut butter and drank instant coffee (also imported) while sitting at the dark wood table circled by six heavy chairs. We rinsed off the dishes in cold running water since all hot water had to be heated on the stove. We listened to the BBC World Report or the U.S. Armed Forces Radio on our shortwave radio. Francisco would arrive around seven to begin his work, which he always initiated by sweeping out the apartment. We bought him a push broom to replace the bundle of straw tied to a stick that was the usual, not highly effective, broom used throughout the city.

Chapter 5

My hair was long, so most days I would braid it and pin it up, a concession to both the limited shampooing opportunities and the extreme heat. Though I had brought blue jeans with me, I usually wore skirts and blouses in recognition that a skirt or a length of colorfully printed cotton cloth called a *capulana* was the typical clothing of Mozambican women.

By 7:30 each morning, we were out in front of the building, where Steve waited for transportation with other doctors, nurses, and health technicians, several of whom also lived in the Mexicana. The Ministry of Health provided transport for workers to the hospital and the more distant health posts, usually in a minibus or Land Rover. Once a decrepit truck arrived with chairs loosely placed in the back, not bolted in, and the cooperantes refused to ride in it. If there was room, I would occasionally ask for a lift to Mercie's creche. Mercie loved riding in the health department Land Rover. Despite the dilapidated condition of the vehicle, she thought it was luxurious, saying "Nice *carro*" as we climbed out at her creche.

If there was no room for us, I would walk through Beira pushing Mercie in her stroller to her day care. A wheel once fell off the stroller, a result of constant bumping over torn-up roads that were paved but in disrepair in our neighborhood and downtown. I had the wheel soldered at the Ministry of Health machine shop and continued the twice-daily walk. The streets were broad and empty of cars, large trees provided shade, and I could investigate city life as we went along. One day a group of small boys playing in the street waved at Mercie and she waved back. They came closer, saying, "*Ta ta amiga*," meaning "Hello friend," though "ta ta" usually means goodbye in British usage. Each in turn carefully shook her hand with great formality. Mercie beamed at me, pleased with the attention, we all smiled at each other, and I enjoyed the feeling of acceptance that came with such small encounters.

The Mackerel Years

There was a primary school on the corner near our building, and as we walked by the children would be lining up, all wearing bright blue shorts or skirts. A few blocks further on we turned onto a wide road lined with private homes and apartment buildings, Eduardo Mondlane Avenue, named for the leader of the anti-colonial struggle who was assassinated in Tanzania in 1969. The lovely shade trees had destroyed the cement sidewalk as their roots spread, so I walked in the road itself. For several days I watched as a menacing six-inch black spider built an impressive web nearly six feet across between two trees along our route. I spied a Red Bishop, a small bright red-orange and black bird, as it glowed and flashed in the sun in the trees in front of our apartment. Later I learned that they were considered pests because they ate peoples' rice seed. Flame trees and flowering plants brought beauty and color to the neighborhood. Chickens squawked, goats were often tethered in vacant lots, and everywhere women were working in their small plots of corn or rice or were sharing the work of grinding grain in the large wooden mortar and pestle called a *pilão*. Every morning men were out using bundles of leaves to sweep the streets clean of debris.

As we neared downtown Beira, I would venture down narrow streets lined with small shops, most of them owned by Indian families. Throughout East Africa, the colonial rulers had restricted Africans from owning businesses, and that essential position in the economy was filled with immigrants from the Indian sub-continent, referred to as "Asians." Their presence added to the multi-cultural mix of African communities, as women in saris walked along the streets and men in turbans could be seen in the shops. When we first arrived, most of the shops posted signs in their windows warning that "Não há sal, carne, pão" (There is no salt, meat, bread), sometimes listing up to a dozen such items that were not available. We had marveled at the rows of empty shelves seen in nearly every shop, as even stores that called themselves supermarkets might have half a shelf of rough gray toilet paper and nothing else for sale. But on my route, one store sold fresh milk every morning and by 8 A.M. there was a line of people carrying a variety of bottles, pots, and other containers to collect their purchase. A sign at a bus stop along the way warned "An organized people are a disciplined people. Please, comrade, form a line!" Finally, I would cross the bridge over the Chiveve, which rose and fell with the tides, and we would arrive at Mercie's creche.

At noon Steve and I enjoyed a two-hour lunch break at home, following the Mediterranean custom. After a meal of fried fish and rice that Francisco prepared, we would relax and read. For a while, we tried to teach ourselves chess by following games published in books, but that did not really capture our interest. We read all kinds of books, some we had brought with us and others sent by family or borrowed from other English-speakers living in Beira.

I often bought a copy of the local newspaper, *Diário de Moçambique* (*Mozambique Daily*), from young men hawking papers on street corners, though eventually we arranged to have it delivered. I was struck by the markedly different focus of the news which emphasized local information followed by news about Africa and the Third World.[3] Many topics that were ignored in American newspapers were on the front page of Beira's paper. One typical day in November 1982, the headline story concerned who should represent Chad at the Organization of African Unity, concluding that Chad, then involved in a brutal civil war and partly occupied by its northern neighbor, Libya, was a pawn being used by enemies of African unity. Two other front-page stories were about a Red Cross meeting in Maputo and a sports agreement between Mozambique and the Soviet Union. The next three pages covered Mozambican events: the lack of coal and energy sources that undermined the production goals of a cement factory in the northern city of Nacala, the delivery to Beira's maritime administration of a French gift of motors and replacement parts for a passenger ferry boat, and various meetings by

Frelimo party cells in Beira in preparation for the upcoming Fourth Party Congress. The following three pages reported on mainly African international events, such as stories on new technology to control the tsetse fly (whose bites spread sleeping sickness), a Senegalese purchase of railroad cars, the Namibian struggle for independence (which was finally won in 1990), Saudi oil supplies of concern to *Ianques* (Yankees, presumably referring to the U.S.), and news from Venezuela, Ethiopia, Turkey, and East Germany. The two-page centerfold story was about President Mubarak of Egypt taking a more pro-Arab position. After a few pages of advertisements, a crossword puzzle, sports, and letters to the editor (which often featured complaints about poor service from some government entity), the back page carried more immediate news. On that particular day, the stories were about three bank branches opening, the export of Mozambican wood to Algeria under a new agreement, a meeting between the women's organization and a Hungarian visiting delegation, and other similar stories.

The news thus seemed more parochial that what we were used to from the *Los Angeles Times*, but it also emphasized the connections between Third World nations, relationships that took place outside of U.S. influence and which were never even alluded to in the American media. The perspective of the news gave us a new sense of how the nations of the world interacted, with their own agendas and interests, utterly independent of the United States. In fact, reporting about events in the U.S. was almost absent, or was flawed when it appeared, such as the report about the celebration of Martin Luther King, Jr.'s birthday, which stated that January 21st commemorated his death rather than his birth. On that occasion, Steve and I stopped by the newspaper office to see if we could provide more accurate information to the reporters, an effort which had absolutely no impact. The converse situation was true after we returned to the U.S., when I wanted news about Mozambique, which

Chapter 5

was generally ignored by the U.S. media unless there was a dramatic event such as horrific floods.

On one of our first Sundays in Beira we ate at the Oceana. As most restaurants had limited food and other supplies, they were seldom open, and Oceana was one of the few restaurants that served customers from time to time. It was located on the beach, with a lovely veranda offering a resort-quality view of the Indian Ocean. The food options did not match the setting, and on that day were confined to omelets, potatoes, and rice, all served cold.

We were expanding our social life as we met some of the other cooperantes in Beira. Niall Crowley was an engineer from Ireland who later in the year was joined by his companion, Melanie Reidy. Mike Muller, a water engineer, was in exile from South Africa. He had been in Mozambique for several years already and was an endless source of advice, support, humor, and encouragement.[4] One weekend in August, we all went downtown to eat at Johnny's Place, also called the Arcadia Restaurant. The restaurant was famous for its prawns, a well-known Mozambican delicacy, and we had dozens of delicious fresh prawns, grilled and piled high on metal trays. We ate them with our hands, tearing off the heads and peeling back the shells, to relish the succulent meat. Niall had a bar of Mozambican chocolate that we all shared for dessert. Steve wrote optimistically in his journal that, "We may make Saturday lunch at Johnny's a tradition—certainly has potential."

It was not to be. In January 1983, Mozambique signed a trade agreement with the Soviet Union that included the export of prawns as well as sisal and cashew nuts. For the next two years, Johnny's remained closed and we were not able to get prawns there again. We frequently grumbled that all the good prawns were being shipped out, and rumors abounded that the Soviet fishing trawlers were over-harvesting the shrimp beds in the Mozambique Channel. A study done in early 1984 claimed that the fishing licensing

The Mackerel Years

program was well-managed, though it also reported that nearly every prawn caught was being exported.[5]

I was trying to sort out my possibilities for doing research. All I knew at that early stage was that women obviously lived in the city and had lived there for many years, so those women had to have a history that had not yet been written. I began to visit the Municipal Library, a modern building near downtown Beira that had been funded by the Portuguese philanthropic organization, the Calouste Gulbenkian Foundation. Following the practice of many European libraries, readers and researchers needed permission to use the materials. I had to leave my identification at the front desk each day when I arrived. As there was no card catalog and no obvious organization to the books, I just started at one end of the shelves and book by book began perusing material as I searched for information on Beira's history. The collection was so limited that over the course of a few weeks I was able to at least glance at every book owned by the library.

That week in August, when Mercie was just beginning day care and I was starting to find material in the library, we turned on our shortwave radio to catch the BBC report one morning and learned that South African security forces had sent a package bomb to the African Studies Center at the Universidade Eduardo Mondlane in Maputo. Ruth First was killed as she opened it, and Aquino de Bragança, Bridget O'Laughlin, and others were injured. Bridget was an American economist whom I had met briefly in the U.S. before either of us moved to Mozambique. The news of Ruth First's murder deeply shocked us. I had not been able to meet her, but I had been in that exact office only weeks before the attack.

I had difficulty comprehending that the South African government was willing to kill scholars in their university offices and I felt acutely frightened about the future. I was fearful on two divergent levels. One was the evident escalation of hostilities between South Africa and

Chapter 5

Mozambique, with the possibility that South Africa would stage increasing attacks on Mozambique. In addition to that uncertainty, I wondered what the new situation at the African Studies Center would mean to my own work, and whether I would be able to do any research at all while we lived in Mozambique. Those two concerns weighed equally on my mind, though I knew quite well that my research meant little to anyone but me, while the vicious assassination of Ruth First was a major loss to the world. Her husband, Joe Slovo, continued his political work in the African National Congress and later became Minister of Housing in post-apartheid South Africa. Their daughters told the family story in the film *A World Apart* and in the memoir *Every Secret Thing*.[6]

Beira was extremely isolated from Maputo. Phone service was non-existent, mail was excruciatingly slow and unreliable, and computer-based communications and cell phones were in the distant future. We had just arrived and had no thoughts at that point of leaving, but the situation was much more serious than we had expected. Regarding my research, I was on my own and it appeared that things would be getting worse.

Endnotes

1   This issue and others related to urban living in Mozambique are discussed in David Morton, *Age of Concrete: Housing and the Shape of Aspiration in the Capital of Mozambique* (Athens: Ohio University Press, 2019); see p. 153 and throughout.

2   Kathleen Sheldon, "*Creches, Titias*, and Mothers: Working Women and Child Care in Mozambique," in *African Encounters with Domesticity*, ed. Karen Tranberg Hansen, 290-309 (New Brunswick, N.J.: Rutgers University Press, 1992).

3   Kalter, "When 'Third World' Still Meant Hope," see chapter 3, footnote 14 about the meaning of "Third World" in the 1980s.

4   Mike Muller's story of exile is briefly described in Nadja Manghezi, *The Maputo Connection: ANC Life in the World of Frelimo* (Auckland Park, South Africa: Jacana, 2009), 60; cooperantes in general are discussed on 124-126.

5   The 1984 report is now lost, but the story of shrimp and the Soviet Union's activities in Mozambique, including a license in 1982 to fish 500 tons of prawns from Mozambican waters, is discussed by Elizabeth Banks, "Socialist Internationalism Between the Soviet Union and Mozambique, 1962-91," Ph.D. diss., New York University, 2019, chapter 4, 216-262, "The Economies of Internationalism, or, Tales of Friendship, Shrimp and Debt," see p. 248 and following.

6   *A World Apart*, dir. Chris Menges, screenplay, Shawn Slovo (1988); and Gillian Slovo, *Every Secret Thing: My Family, My Country* (Virago, 2010).

Chapter 6
Chickens in the Kitchen

August to September 1982

We mainly socialized with other English-speaking cooperantes, either eating at each other's homes or sitting on the beach on the weekends. There were several Swedish families, including a plastic surgeon and a social worker, a Dutch nurse named Hanny who worked with Steve, and Len Limpus, a Canadian who worked for FAO (the UN Food and Agriculture Organization) and lived in a magnificent modern house in the beachside neighborhood of Macuti with his wife, Judy, and two children, Adrian and Inalla. Most of the other cooperantes were in a much more secure financial position than we were. We had a single local income, only from Steve's work since I was not employed, and with no funding from any U.S. organization. In many other cooperante families, both spouses had jobs, and the European solidarity organizations usually paid a supplement to match their local salaries. They therefore had four times our income, since they earned two salaries and also received support from their sponsoring group.

We also got to know Soviet and Cuban cooperantes, most of whom were physicians and other health workers who worked with Steve at the hospital.[1] Many of the Soviet physicians had to leave their own children back in the Soviet Union for the duration of their stay in Mozambique, and they enjoyed seeing Mercie and helped us when they could. Their government provided them with food, and they were happy to share surplus milk and apples, often trading with Steve for the American postage stamps they collected. I refer to them as "Soviet" because I do not want to assume that they were all Russian. Some were from the Ukraine and others might have been from other regions that later became independent nations when the Soviet Union broke up in 1991. Though it sounds archaic, at that time they were all "Soviets" from the Soviet Union.

More cooperantes arrived during our first month in Beira. Mike Muller's wife Ruth and their five-year-old daughter Marika returned from a visit to England, and Marika became Mercie's good friend despite the three-year difference in their ages. They shared books and dolls and generally played happily together on weekends when we were visiting. Another dentist arrived also, Steve Boyle, and his wife Jacky, who was to teach English at the high school. They were from Liverpool and spoke Scouse, an accented version of English that I frequently misunderstood, much to their amusement. Steve was tall, thin, and blond, while Jacky was shorter and rounder, her brown hair usually styled in a kind of bowl cut. They had a motorcycle, and that form of transport combined with no child to tote around made them quite a bit more mobile than we were. Our bicycles had yet to arrive, and for the first few months we walked everywhere or tried to arrange rides, a difficult undertaking in a city with few cars and almost no gasoline. Steve B.'s wicked sarcasm about the difficulties of life in Beira was a welcome form of gallows humor and Jacky proved to be a wizard at concocting meals from an odd assortment of ingredients. Their friendship was an essential part of our ability to live—and even live well—during the years we shared in Beira.

We were still waiting for our trunk and bicycles to arrive, and one day a Ministry of Health driver took us out to the airport to see if there was any information. We were driven through Munhava, a vast *bairro do caniço*, a shanty

Chapter 6

neighborhood of reed houses, which contrasted sharply with the *cidade do cimento*, the cement city where we lived. Hundreds of people walked along Munhava's unpaved roads on their daily business, going to market, trying to find goods, visiting friends, and looking for work. Once we arrived at the airport, we learned that there were no trunks and no news about where in the world they might be.

The trunk finally arrived near the end of August with everything intact. We had shipped dishes and kitchen supplies, books and toys, and extra clothing. Steve was thrilled to get his medical texts as well as all the medications he had packed to meet any contingency, and even supplies of deodorant. Before we left Los Angeles, we had bought appliances at a 220-volt shop, and the trunk held our toaster oven, hot plate, and food processor, which had been recommended by Dan and Janet Murphy to grind up tough meat we might encounter. Not a single glass was broken, and we finally could set up housekeeping.

Francisco lived quite a distance away in Manga, a suburb of Beira. Without informing us, he began to sleep on a mat in the laundry room in what were legally uninhabitable conditions, rather than travel the distance to his house each night. Some families expected their workers to be on call until nearly midnight and on the weekends, but we had explained to Francisco that he was only to work regular hours from around eight in the morning until five at night. Besides not wanting to exploit his labor, we liked having the apartment to ourselves in the evening. He would cook a substantial lunch for us and for himself and leave food for dinner before he stopped work. Usually, he preferred to eat massa himself and made other food for us. One day when he lucked into corn on the cob, he roasted a few ears and brought one to share with me. It had a wonderful nutty taste, but my enjoyment was short-lived as I chipped a big corner off a tooth when I bit into it. It did not hurt, but I could feel the jagged edge, and I was embarrassed to tell Francisco, as I did not want him to think I did not appreciate his gift of a special treat. The corn was not particularly tough, but I must have had a weak section on the tooth. I went to see Steve Boyle, who filed down the uneven area and a week later put in a filling that lasted until we returned home.

Food was very scarce in the markets, and Francisco spent long hours shopping and waiting in line at the cooperative store around the corner from our apartment that honored foreign cooperantes' ration cards. One day he bought a few live chickens, and though they were small and not very meaty, we enjoyed eating two of them over a couple of days. I had never had to contend with butchering my food and, like most urban Americans, preferred not to make the connection between the animal and the food we ate. I considered myself a vegetarian of somewhat slack standards, occasionally eating tuna fish or other seafood, but I had not had chicken, pork, or beef for about ten years. There had been times when my eating preferences had caused problems, such as Thanksgiving with my family, or once when friends of Steve's father had included us in a barbecue where the main course was a huge steak for each guest. I had politely refused to eat even one bite, and I am sure our hosts thought I was self-important and arrogant.

I was willing to be more flexible in Beira, recognizing that food in general was hard to come by and I should eat whatever was available. Nonetheless, I was glad to let Francisco handle all aspects of killing, cleaning, and cooking these "micro-chickens." Two or three days after we had eaten the chickens, I discovered that there were two more chickens living in the cupboard under the kitchen sink. Francisco wanted to make our meat supply last as long as possible and hoped to fatten them up a bit before their slaughter. The cupboards were half-rotted, and we did not store any dishes or food in them because their condition was so atrocious. The chickens sat there perfectly silent for days, eating when Francisco fed them something but not gaining any observable weight. When the acrid chicken-coop odor began to be noticeable, Francisco killed them, and we ate the remaining two micro-chickens.

Chapter 6

Steve occasionally bought chickens on our ration card when he saw that they were available, and he would carry them home through the streets, holding their legs and letting their heads hang down. They would try to escape by attempting to peck at his hands, and he learned that chicken beaks are sharp! He found that they could be stunned into passivity if he swung his arms around in a circle, forcing their blood to their heads. I always relished the image of him walking along swirling chickens through the air. Later during our stay, we again kept live chickens in the cupboard. Once, one of them died, which we only discovered when the nasty stench began to spread through the apartment. Another day as Jacky Boyle and I were visiting in our living room, one chicken escaped and came walking into the room cocking its head and eyeing us distrustfully.

One of our first visitors was Isac Chival, who knocked on our door and introduced himself. He was a Mozambican who lived down the hall and told us he was a lieutenant in the armed forces, though we realized eventually that he was also with SNASP (Serviço Nacional de Segurança Popular), the secret police. One day when Steve was visiting his apartment, he spotted an AK-47 stored in a closet. We should not have been surprised that we were under (somewhat lax) surveillance given the poor relations between the U.S. and Mozambique, but we had not really anticipated this situation. Isac became a real friend in any case, playing guitar and singing with Steve one evening, and telling us stories of how badly he was educated under Portuguese colonialism. The nuns assumed all black children were incapable of learning, and he remembered clearly that one holy sister condescendingly commented on what good Portuguese the *pretinho* or little black boy spoke. Isac also became part of our network of food sources. Most Mozambicans had connections to rural relatives or friends, or to land they could cultivate, which we did not have, so they sometimes had food that never appeared in the market.

Isac brought us potatoes and we shared our own surplus food in return. Another time when we had not been able to buy fish for a month, he stopped by with three or four kilograms of fish in his hands and said, "Here, take these, I'm going to Maputo and I don't want it to spoil."

Another day two *responsáveis* (a term for people with specific official responsibilities; singular, *responsável*) from the Ministry of Health came by to collect our immigration papers. Senhor Agostinho admired the game of solitaire I had spread out on the table and Senhor Carlos scanned the few books on our shelves. He was very interested in history, and like many Mozambicans, he was pleased to know that I was fascinated with Mozambique's history, and he encouraged me in my research. He also made it a point to call Mercie by her middle name, Josina. Samora and Graça Machel, Mozambique's president and first lady, named their daughter Josina, but I never personally met a Mozambican named Josina, though our Quelimane-based colleagues, Jon and Jeanne, had named their new baby Josina (and called her Jo Jo). Mozambicans were often pleased and touched that we had named our daughter after their heroine.

Weekends came and we welcomed more relaxation. Sometimes we would take walks with Mercie and look around our neighborhood. We discovered a park a few blocks from our apartment that was mostly empty space and was clean but barren. The frame of a rusty swing set remained, but the swings themselves were nowhere in sight. The grass was worn to a few gray patches, while city workers swept the rock-lined paths and watered the skimpy plants that struggled to survive in the hard-packed ground.

Other times we would go to the beach and paddle around in the water, and then eat at the Oceana. Our second meal there consisted of greasy fried fish, bland spaghetti without any sauce, and boiled cabbage. Dessert, for 60 meticais or about $1.50, was *fruta em calda* (fruit in syrup), and was exactly half of a canned peach. On another visit the Oceana served a decent crab curry over rice, and they even had

Chapter 6

shrimp once or twice, but when they had shrimp, they had no beer.

In early November, as the weather got hotter and more humid, we went with a group of cooperantes on an excursion to a beach near the airport. We drove several miles on unpaved roads lined by modest homes built of cinderblock, parked by a cluster of buildings marked "off limits," and walked across salt flats, over fields, and along a makeshift bridge of wooden planks that spanned water irrigation channels. At the end we came to a nearly empty beautiful beach with white sand stretching into the distance and shallow waves washing the shore. A few Mozambicans were fishing near the water's edge. We built a tent with poles and capulanas and stayed from 9 in the morning until 3 in the afternoon, eating bread and butter and a cake baked by Jacky, and drinking beer. While walking to the beach we saw an eight-inch-long iguana by the roadside. In the city we rarely saw any wildlife, in contrast to assumptions among westerners about life in Africa being filled with teeming hordes of animals. We did have a little gecko resident in our apartment, which we felt was a good omen; we hoped it was getting fat on its diet of cockroaches and mosquitoes.

There were occasionally *despedidas* (goodbye parties) for cooperantes whose contracts were up. One of the first was for a Dutch pediatrician, Bart Wolf. The Zambian cooperantes brought good dance music, and everyone contributed food and drink, including shrimp and special treats such as a papaya and mango pie baked by Annette, one of the Dutch cooperantes. At that party I met another historian, a Brazilian woman who was teaching in the high school in Beira. She lived on the floor above us with her husband Iris, a Brazilian ear-nose-and-throat specialist, and their three children. In October there was a party at the Zambian consulate to celebrate their national day and the food was remarkably abundant. In addition to shrimp, a dozen different hors d'oeuvres, platters of deviled eggs, imported cans of Heineken beer, and cakes and puddings for dessert, there was lobster and a whole roast suckling pig!

We had dinner with António Gama, the Mozambican pediatrician we had met when we first arrived. His wife, Ilde, and another guest, Jorge, were also physicians. Mercie was able to play with Gama and Ilde's son Pedro, who was a couple of years older. We enjoyed a meal of *caldo verde*, the classic Portuguese vegetable soup, tasty shrimp samosas, slices of grilled pork, fried potatoes, and coffee flan, along with our contribution of raw vegetables and cheese for appetizers. The conversation ranged over a variety of topics. We learned that their salaries were quite low. Gama was the director of pediatrics in the city, and earned eighteen *contos* a month, or approximately U.S. $450.00, based on the 1983 exchange rate of about $25.00 to one conto (1,000 meticais). The other two physicians earned a monthly salary of 13 contos ($325.00). Although Gama's apartment was large, it was sparsely furnished. It was a struggle for such highly trained people to remain in Mozambique, as they could potentially earn a lot more money as physicians in Portugal. One of their colleagues, formerly chair of the local Frelimo party cell, had left for Portugal after finishing his medical training in Mozambique. Ilde did eventually leave for Portugal with Pedro, and Gama reluctantly followed them later. That night they complained about the *bichas*, a term that literally means "worms" and colloquially referred to the long lines of people waiting for food, and about how people in Beira frequently and rudely cut in line.

Steve, in his position as Clinical Director of Pediatrics (appointed by Gama, who was his boss), was earning 27 contos ($675.00). Nearly half of that was paid in *divisas* (foreign exchange), but the remainder, around 15,000 meticais (approximately $375.00) was paid in local currency each month and had to be spent in Mozambique. He was paid in cash, and we would take part of his salary to the bank to convert it into dollars. Sometimes Steve would come home with his entire monthly salary in 100-meticais notes, a stack of 250 or 270 bills. We usually just stored the cash in our trunk, taking out what we needed for local expenses. Everything was paid in cash and during the two years we lived there I only saw one person writing a check.

We used some of the divisas at the Loja Franca but sent $300 a month back to my parents, who were making regular payments on Steve's medical school loans. We received the first divisas payment in November, for work he had done in July. Converting the meticais into dollars involved monthly visits to the bank. I would spend an entire morning waiting in a series of lines and filling out several different forms in duplicate and triplicate, converting a portion of Steve's salary into a check in dollars to mail to the U.S. The second check we got was made out to my father and, as I commented in a letter home, "It's too hard to explain the confusion that resulted in this check being made out to Dad." After we had been there for more than a year, I had trouble collecting one of Steve's checks at the bank. After six trips to the bank in two weeks, I convinced a bank worker to let me see the list of names he had for foreign exchange checks. It transpired that there was one for Steve, but the worker had confused the two English-speaking Dr. Stivs; Steve Boyle was also known as Dr. Stiv, and the worker thought our check was his. Despite such complications and delays, Steve received all the money that he earned, and we never lost a check that was mailed back to my parents.

In June, just before we arrived, Samora Machel had made a speech calling for "arms for the people," hoping to develop local militias to assist in the escalating conflict with the bandidos. Machel was the charismatic president of Mozambique who had been a leader of the liberation struggle. In August, there was a demonstration in Beira in support of that call to arms, despite a general lack of weapons to distribute. I went to a public meeting with Mike Muller and we were joined by Jon Cohn and Jeanne Raisler, who were visiting Beira from Quelimane with their two small children. Many of the people who were present carried sticks and hoes and other implements as weapons, which they brandished against the bandidos, a scene that might have been comical if it were not so tragic. Militias continued to be organized during our stay and it was a common sight to see companies of people running in formation through the streets, barefoot, chanting pro-Frelimo and anti-Renamo songs and waving their sticks around, often with women setting the pace at the front.

There was no evidence that these militias had any impact on stemming the progress of the war, which grew more violent each month. Shortly after we arrived, we learned that assaults on civilians were increasing and occurring closer to the city. A train was attacked at Dondo, a town outside of Beira, and we heard that fourteen people had been killed. Teachers and others associated with the Frelimo government were being targeted and suffered atrocities such as having their ears, noses, or other parts of their bodies sliced off. I never read a report in the local paper about these events, but news traveled quickly. Steve treated some of these victims when he was on duty in the hospital emergency room, including a badly mutilated schoolteacher. Stories of brutality, even in the form of hearsay and rumor, were frightening, but we still felt safe in the city. We avoided traveling out of Beira, as the roads in the surrounding area were unpredictably perilous, prone to the danger of landmines and sudden attacks on trucks and buses. It appeared that Renamo was not recognized as a serious enemy and, at least in the city, the attitude seemed to be that if everyone ignored them, they would go away.

Endnote

[1] Sarah LeFanu has a truthful though partly tongue-in-cheek entry on cooperantes in *S is for Samora* (New York: Columbia University Press, 2012), 41-43, including an informal ranking of cooperante physicians with Americans the best, then British, Cubans, Italians, and Russians.

Chapter 7
Freshly Slaughtered Beef and Ration Cards

September 1982

Though the war was encroaching, everyday life continued, as Steve worked long hours at the hospital, and I tried to find sources of information for my research. Eduardo Mondlane, the founding leader of Frelimo (and a graduate of Northwestern) had mentioned in his book, *The Struggle for Mozambique*, that Sebastião Soares de Resende, the Catholic bishop of Beira from 1943 to 1967, had written critiques of Portuguese colonialism. I began visiting the cathedral to see if they had any of those writings and met a young African priest, Padre Guilherme. He was interested in any project related to Beira's history and lent me several booklets that Bishop Resende had written. Those booklets were primarily religious tracts, but there were other random bits of information. During the colonial period, the Catholic Church was the official church with responsibility for educating all African children, but the pro-African sentiments expressed by Bishop Resende were notable and unusual.[1]

Mike Muller was also finding material for me at the municipal water department where he worked. After independence in 1975, thousands of Portuguese settlers fled Mozambique. Many of them moved to South Africa and others returned to Portugal. A large percentage had immigrated into Mozambique only after World War II and did not have the deep roots that settlers in South Africa had in their country. But many of the Portuguese settlers resented their loss of status after Frelimo took power, and they committed widespread sabotage as they left, including driving twenty-five thousand cars and trucks across the borders into South Africa and what was then still white-ruled Rhodesia. Mike told us that one of the acts of vandalism was the theft of all the plans and maps of Beira's sewers and water supply, leaving nothing for people to work with when they needed to make repairs.[2] Whenever there was a problem, workers had to guess where the pipes were and how they were connected. It was often a grim predicament as water was potentially contaminated and cholera was a constant threat.[3] We regularly boiled water and stored it in old gin bottles lined up in our refrigerator door, giving any visitors an impression of serious alcohol abuse on our part.

We finally began to get mail from family and friends in the U.S. There was no home delivery, so we had a box in the downtown post office, which Steve had arranged after meeting with a postal official whose children were his patients. I went daily to see if anything was there. At times, mail, even large envelopes, would arrive quickly, taking less than two weeks from the U.S. At other times, mail would appear months after it was sent. Even items that said "airmail" sometimes went by sea and presumably spent weeks sitting on a ship or dock before reaching us. Occasionally there would be nothing for days, followed by an accumulation of a dozen envelopes and small packages or even two deliveries to our box in one day.

Mail was a regular treat for the two years we lived in Beira, as my mother sent a weekly set of clippings of entertaining articles, Doonesbury cartoons, and whatever else she thought might divert us. One box of food from friends was broken into and the M&M candies they had promised were gone, though our mail was rarely lost or stolen. Other cooperantes received almost none of the packages sent by their family and friends. In April 1983,

Chapter 7

a post office theft ring was uncovered, and those arrested apparently included the official that Steve had met. We speculated that our mail was left alone because he had taken a liking to Steve, his children's pediatrician.

The post office was centrally located in the main downtown square, which was marked by imposing colonial buildings, the city hall, several shops, and Cafe Capri, a salão de chá. The center of the square was always filled with people, mainly men, sitting around and talking near a socialist-realist sculpture of victorious workers. I discovered that the tea shop often had sweet or plain rolls for sale, so occasionally my sojourn to downtown Beira to check the post office box included a stop to buy a small bag of rolls as well. The shop was frequently crowded, and one day I sat at a table to discover what attracted the customers. I ordered the local version of Portuguese pastry and *galão*, which should have been a glass of sugary coffee and milk. But I found it was barely edible, consisting of hot sweet watery milk missing the key ingredient of coffee and plain rolls cut in half and spread with slightly rancid coconut margarine. With so much hunger all around I could not simply abandon the food I had ordered, so I sat and put bite after sour bite into my mouth, finally reaching the end of my dismal snack.

Figure 5: Praça dos Trabalhadores, Beira, with Kathie and Mercie. Photo by Steve Tarzynski.

We were thrilled when a new shipment arrived at the Loja Franca that October, which was less well supplied than its sister shop in Maputo and had declined further in recent weeks, when the shelves had been completely empty. Finally, I was able to buy canned ham, milk, tomatoes, cookies, and pasta. The downside for us was that we had to use our limited divisas rather than Mozambican meticais to buy goods there. Spaghetti and macaroni along with rice and bread were also available at our local cooperative that honored cooperantes' ration cards. Steve and Jacky, with two jobs and therefore two cards and only two people to feed, were generous with their support, and often purchased

Chapter 7

their full ration and shared the surplus with us as we tried to feed the three of us on only one card.

In the face of such scarcity, stratagems for "arranging" food were ubiquitous. Cooperantes working in health care sometimes formed a group to make large or complicated food arrangements. Early in our stay they organized the purchase of half a steer from the local slaughterhouse. I managed to avoid being part of the group that went to the slaughterhouse but was not spared the post-abattoir butchering. After the animal was killed and cut into smaller pieces, the meat was brought back to our building for further division and distribution. Gerri Dickson and some others set up a table and knives in the common hallway between our two apartments.

I was repelled by the sight of so much raw meat. We had bought a share of the meat so that we could celebrate September 25, which was Mozambican Armed Forces Day and marked the beginning of the armed struggle against the Portuguese in 1964. But the Renamo bandits also wanted to mark the date, and they cut the electricity to the entire city just as we were beginning to divide up the meat. Some of the beef was stored in the Dickson's large freezer, which they had to move during the weekend to the house of a friend who had a generator. With no electricity our own small freezer was useless, and we could not use the food processor. We tried to chop it with a hand-operated grinder, but it was tough meat and difficult to make into ground beef. It was still leathery after it was minced, when we tried to cook and eat as much as possible before it spoiled. The memory of facing hamburger and bowls of goulash, meal after repugnant meal, still informs my subsequent avoidance of red meat. The Zambian health cooperantes knew how to salt the meat and preserve it, but everyone else ended up throwing out unthinkable quantities. I looked forward to returning to the luxury of a vegetarian diet.

The electricity remained out for over a week while we relied on candles and flashlights, though batteries and

The Mackerel Years

candles were in short supply in local shops. Francisco lent us a kerosene lamp and we then faced the problem of finding a supply of kerosene. The water tank for our building was on the roof and relied on an electric pump to keep it filled, so water had to be carried up the stairs in buckets, a task that Francisco usually accomplished. He came back during that first weekend because he knew we would need his assistance. When he saw Steve carrying a pail of water he was mortified and scolded him, saying that a person who had an *empregado* or domestic worker should not have to carry water.

Steve had been ill for several days with what he initially believed to be hepatitis, and I joked that he did have a jaundiced view of life in Beira. Because we were worried about our exposure to hepatitis, we tried to get gamma globulin shots regularly, though the efficacy of our first dose was uncertain because it required refrigeration and the cold chain had been broken briefly when there was no electricity. We learned that he had malaria, fortunately a relatively mild case, but debilitating, nonetheless. He ran a fever, slept constantly, and had no appetite or energy. He was treated and recovered after a few days, though he was much thinner.

The electricity was frequently cut during the two years we lived there. I kept a log of the outages, all attributed to Renamo attacks on the pylons, and we averaged an outage every two weeks, usually lasting five days or more. It often was difficult for Mozambicans to repair the sabotage, as the pylons were in remote areas and Renamo was known to plant landmines around the electric lines. The city organized a rolling supply using limited electricity, so that certain neighborhoods would have power for a few hours, then they would go dark, and another neighborhood would have power. Most of the residents of Beira lived off the electric grid in the bairros do caniço and they never had power, but in the cement city we depended on the regular provision of electricity.

Chapter 7

During that first outage and often in subsequent electricity cuts, we would get power from time to time, usually from 11:00 at night until 8:00 the next morning. That allotment was not long enough to really get the refrigerator cold, was pointless for using lights as we were normally asleep, and was useless with the water supply since our building's water pump was turned off at 9 P.M. every night. By the time the pump was turned on in the morning, the power supply was turned off. One night during that first outage the power came on at 8 P.M., so Steve ran and took a cold shower and then the water ran out. I went nine days with no shower, relying only on sponge baths in the sink and attempting to wash my hair (which reached halfway down my back) in a bucket. We learned that when the power went out, we had to immediately dash and fill the bathtub before the rooftop tank ran out so that we would have a water supply in the apartment. More than once we discovered that the entire city had power including neighboring buildings, but the Mexicana remained dark. We never learned why our building was not properly connected and we sometimes visited nearby friends for showers when everyone else had water and power.

In early October, compounding the difficulties, the pipeline that supplied the entire city was sabotaged and we had no regular water for over a week. Again, there was no official warning, but we learned with enough advance notice to fill the bathtub and a few of our larger pans. Mike Muller, in his position at the water department, worked thirty hours straight to get the pipeline repaired. There were wells around the city, including one in front of our building, but that water was not considered potable. Mercie's creche was reopened after a few days, but they recommended keeping the children at home because their water supply was not pure. I had also kept her home from creche during the power outage, as I was concerned about how disorganized and difficult the situation must have been at the creche in the absence of electricity. At times when the creche lacked

87

electricity, the teachers carried huge buckets of water up the dark treacherous stairwells. Once water returned, though we only had cold water, it felt like a luxury to turn on the taps and have water pour out. The disruption to the local economy and to city life in general because of the constant power outages was beyond measure and the delays to my own work were unremitting.

Francisco devoted most of his time to waiting in line at shops. He often spent the morning hours in line at the neighborhood cooperative shop where we were members. Once he left our big woven-reed shopping basket to hold his place, and it was stolen along with the beer bottles he was returning. The loss of those bottles was a serious problem, as new beer could only be bought when old bottles were returned. People lent empty bottles to newly arrived cooperantes so they could make their first purchase and get started on the cycle. The beer was brewed locally at the Manica brewery and, though it tasted fine, it often was not well-filtered. We used to look at the small mysterious bits of flotsam in each bottle and decide that it was drinkable in any case, as the alcohol must have killed off anything that might cause illness.

I relied on Francisco to do most of the shopping, so it was troublesome to learn that he was buying food for himself on our ration card. At first it seemed that he simply was not keeping careful count of the food money. As I wanted to demonstrate trust in him, I was sometimes a bit lenient about keeping track of the expenses. But I finally had to talk to him about a shortage of 250 meticais; he simply repaid the money when I asked him about it, so I thought it was just a matter of poor bookkeeping. Then a month later I found a receipt in the cupboard for sugar and crackers that we had never seen. I went to the cooperative myself and discovered that those items had been bought on our card. They did not allow me to buy more crackers as our rationed amount had already been purchased, and the shop's sugar supply was *acabou* (finished).

Chapter 7

I asked Francisco directly, "Did you buy crackers and sugar at the cooperative?" He nervously replied, "No, I didn't; I don't know anything about sugar or crackers!" I then told him, "I have the receipt," and he admitted that he had bought them for himself. I was seething with anger; he ate most of his meals in our house on our ration card as it was, and we only had access to items on one card. He did bring the sugar back. While it was a serious issue in the situation of chronic food shortages, I also felt terrible that missing out on a couple of bags of crackers had made me so furious. I was reminded of *Les Miserables*, where the theft of a loaf of bread brought on years of persecution, and I certainly did not care to see myself as Inspector Javert. We gave Francisco another chance, as it was a minor infraction, and he was otherwise a decent and reliable young man.

Nonetheless, the lack of food was critical. The cooperative did not have any meat, fish, or eggs for all of October, and during a lengthy power cut at the end of the month they had no bread. We had been able to buy a small sack of rolls there on a regular basis, but with no power the bakery could not bake the bread. We had thought we were done with the meat from the steer we had butchered, but when the Dicksons opened their freezer during that outage we discovered another package. We gave that meat to Isac, our neighbor the army officer.

Steve told Rui Bastos, the physician who was head of the hospital and provincial director of health, about the difficulty cooperantes were having in obtaining enough food. We suspected that he spoke to someone at Comércio Interno (Internal Commerce, the government agency in charge of food distribution and rationing), as eventually chickens, eggs, and beer came into the cooperantes' cooperative.

This list of purchases from various times during the month of October 1982 indicates what was typically available and the limited choices, especially when compared to the huge supermarkets with aisles of food that we had been accustomed to:

The Mackerel Years

- bread – ten pieces for 10 mts ($.25), or sometimes for 30 mts (*mt* is the abbreviation for metical; plural is mts)
- crackers – 35 mts per bag (just under $1.00)
- beer – 234 mts for six 1-liter bottles (plus six old bottles returned)
- tomatoes, cabbage, peppers, onions, eggplant – all 30 mts per kilogram, and we usually bought at least 3 kilos (or 7 pounds) at a time, which was a lot of vegetables
- carrots – 30 mts per kilogram; we bought 6 kg (over 13 pounds) in one shopping trip
- flour – 11 mts per kg (sold in 5-kg bags, so it was 11 pounds for a bit over $1.00)
- corn flour (*milho*) – primarily cooked into massa and eaten by Francisco
- sugar – 90 mts for 3 kg, or 58 mts for 2 kg
- rice – 34 mts for a 2-kg bag
- eggs – 29 mts for 6 eggs
- mangoes – 15 mts for ½ kg
- papaya – 15 mts per kg
- fish, 25 mts per kg
- grapefruit and oranges – 150 mts for a large sack
- coconut oil for cooking – 69 mts for 2 liters
- soda – 36 mts, plus 6 returned empty bottles, for 6 bottles of Fanta, Coke, or Pepsi (about $.05 per soda)
- matches – 30 mts for 2 packages of 8 boxes each
- soap – 35 mts for 2 long bars of locally milled soap

Altogether we spent about 5,000 meticais ($125.00) a month on food, the low prices reflecting government pricing policies. The problem was availability. It was common practice to simply join a line whenever you saw one and then ask what was for sale. There were many small fruit and vegetable shops that were generally closed but at odd times one might suddenly have supplies, and we regularly would simply walk into any open shop and ask, "Do you have anything for sale?" That is how we found that there were Indian-owned shops that sold lentils and that other

Chapter 7

stores sold beans, so we had sources for protein other than micro-chickens and tough beef.

I once met Ruth Muller in line for eggs, though we gave up when they said it would be several hours before the eggs went on sale. But after months of shortages, events sometimes could escalate. One time I got caught in the middle of a shoving match while in line for tomatoes, though it ended quietly as everyone joked nervously about what was happening to good manners. The one time during the two years that the bakery on the ground floor of the Mexicana sold small hard rolls, unruly bichas circled the building and blocked the entrance. I watched a soldier trying to organize a crowd of women into a line at a downtown shop, but they refused, shouting *"Não, não"* (No, no) at him until he gave up. I noticed a broken window at the downtown boutique called "Craque" one day and was told that a bicha for shirts had gotten rowdy and one man had been seriously injured when he was pushed into the plate glass. Later in our stay, there were long lines at all the bookstores because ordinary ballpoint stick pens had arrived, and students were desperate for that rare item.

Finding decent coffee was tricky. We usually could buy South African Ricoffe, powdery instant coffee enhanced with chicory, which was at least drinkable. Even though we had boycotted South African goods in the U.S., we realized that the economies of southern African nations were tightly bound with South Africa's, which was (and remains) the regional power. So, we consumed coffee, peanut butter, and other supplies imported from South Africa that were sold in Mozambican shops. In one of the ironies of daily life in Mozambique, we set aside our many years of boycotting Nestlé products in protest of their promotion of baby formula over breast-feeding in Third World countries. Many local markets sold Nestlé's powdered milk and dried baby cereal and we depended on those foods for Mercie.

At one point in mid-November, we learned that the local coffee distributor, a Tanzanian man who imported Tanzanian coffee, had coffee for sale. We followed the hand-drawn map given to us by a friend and found a nearly hidden shop at the far end of a dusty row of deserted storefronts. The man who answered the door at first claimed there was no coffee, but we could smell it and see the burlap sacks piled behind him, and he eventually consented to sell us a few pounds of beans. When we returned a few months later to replenish our stash of coffee, he no longer had any to sell and the shop remained shuttered for the following two years.

Endnote

1. Eric Morier-Genoud, *Catholicism and the Making of Politics in Central Mozambique, 1940-1986* (University of Rochester Press, 2019).
2. Ian Frayling, also a water engineer in Beira in the 1980s, confirmed that plans for the sewer system were missing; he also noted that only one out of fifteen pumps was in operation (conversation, January 2021). A persistent but false rumor suggested that cement had been poured into toilets as the Portuguese left; any reflection on this act would reveal it was highly unlikely. For a discussion, see Sean Christie, "The Great Unblocking of Beira," *Mail & Guardian* (March 19, 2010).
3. For a report on flooding and cholera the year before we arrived, see Paul Fauvet, "Cholera: Killer Disease that is Haunting Beira's Shantytown," *New African* (August 1981), 89.

Chapter 8
Pediatrics and Politics

October 1982

One day I accompanied Steve when he made his rounds of the pediatric ward at Hospital Central da Beira. The hospital had been built as the "native" hospital during the colonial era. Black Africans were usually referred to as *indígenas* or natives in the colonial lexicon, a pejorative term that is now avoided. The hospital was composed of a series of five white-painted buildings in a gated compound across the road from the beach. There were nearly seven hundred beds in the entire hospital, with the pediatric ward accounting for sixty medical beds and sixty surgical beds. The conditions were extremely poor. The rooms were dimly lit, with a shockingly low level of cleanliness, made worse by ongoing problems with the plumbing, resulting in a dank and malodorous ambiance. Workers did their best to keep things clean, but their efforts in swabbing the floor with an old mop could not easily overcome the obstacles presented by a limited supply of usable water and little or no detergent.

There was virtually no equipment, and doctors and nurses faced chronic shortages of medicines. Antibiotics were hard to procure, and one day early in our stay the penicillin supply was used up. While we lived in Beira there was a time when not even aspirin was available in the pharmacies. There were no ventilators or specialized therapists to help children who were lapsing into respiratory failure. Medical personnel would simply resort to mouth-to-mouth resuscitation. Steve could usually obtain basic laboratory tests as well as necessary x-rays, though the quality was poor. It was impossible to get accurate urine and blood tests because of the contamination of materials and a lack of reagents.

Steve was responsible for a room with four beds that was considered the intensive care unit for pediatrics because they could administer intravenous lines there. But only one-liter bags of normal saline and Ringer's solution were on hand. Smaller bags were safer for use with children, but a greater variety of intravenous solutions was not available. Oxygen was given only at 100 percent levels from a World War II–vintage U.S. Navy oxygen tank and there were none of the machines or labs that could monitor blood gas levels and other more sophisticated aspects of patient care. Children with illnesses like pneumonia or asthma who required oxygen received humidified air through the efforts of a relative, usually the mother, who would keep a wet sheet tented over the bed. Mothers were required to stay with their children who were under five years old, as that personal attention had been demonstrated to reduce child mortality by 25 percent in low-income countries. There were too many sick children and not enough doctors and nurses to observe all of them.

A larger pediatric room was devoted solely to children with diarrhea, with a further four beds for those suffering severe dehydration. There was no way to measure serum sodium, potassium, bicarbonate, or other electrolytes, and Steve became adept at judging a patient's condition based on the history and physical examination, which was very basically how the patient looked and responded to treatment. The life-saving rehydration formula they used was called *mistura oral*, an oral mixture. It was usually impossible to obtain pre-mixed powdered formulas, so they administered their own blend of one liter of cooled boiled water with six teaspoons of sugar and two teaspoons of salt, given to the child from a small cup or by the spoonful. Even such a simple recipe could be difficult to prepare if there was a shortage of fuel needed to boil water or supplies of sugar or salt ran low.

The next room was just a couple of beds off to the side behind a curtain, and it was reserved for babies with neonatal tetanus, which was nearly 100 percent fatal. Polio was a problem as well, and Steve saw three cases in his first six months in Beira. The Frelimo government had introduced inoculation programs to combat polio as well as measles, tetanus, and other diseases, and they were notably successful in reaching practically all children. At independence (1975), infant mortality in Mozambique had reportedly reached nearly 200 out of 1,000, one of the highest rates in the world. Less than a decade later, in the early 1980s, it had dropped to around 150 per 1,000, primarily attributable to the expansion of services and outreach to the community introduced by the Ministry of Health. That rate was still a terrible toll and far worse than the 4 deaths per 1,000 births in the U.S. The life-saving extension of services under Frelimo's socialist health program was almost completely destroyed by Renamo attacks on hundreds of health posts and health workers in the 1980s and early 1990s. Over 450 rural posts were destroyed between 1982 and 1985, and the increasingly destructive war continued for seven years after that.[1]

The biggest room of the pediatric ward contained about twenty beds that were reserved for malnutrition, primarily kwashiorkor (protein deficiency) and marasmus (calorie deficiency). Steve also saw a few cases of pellagra, which is easily treated with niacin, normally provided through a diverse diet. Most malnourished children never made it to the hospital but were treated at outlying health posts. Many of those who did arrive at the hospital were already in a seriously deteriorated condition, with hemoglobin readings of 2 or 3 (normal should be 11 to 14), indicating that their red blood cells were severely depleted. Steve successfully treated one child who arrived with a hemoglobin reading of only 0.9. Many of the malnourished children were suffering from intestinal worms and other parasites, and advanced tuberculosis was also common. The treatment for malnutrition was a high-calorie drink called LOA for *leite-óleo-açucar* or milk-oil-sugar. Despite the incredible severity of the children's conditions, the nurses and doctors had a set of protocols and procedures that led to a high rate of recovery once the children did get into the hospital.

The cooperante doctors learned quickly how to sterilize and reuse so-called disposable items such as syringes and gloves. When Steve first arrived, he was appalled to see nurses routinely drawing children's blood from their jugular veins using vintage big glass syringes. He thought he would help by showing them the modern way it was done in the U.S. But he found to his chagrin that the butterfly needles that were available in Beira were used over and over after being sterilized in an ancient autoclave machine, and the repeated use made them too dull to use on a screaming, writhing child. Also, glass syringes would begin to leak if it took too long to draw the blood, which was a problem when dealing with the small veins of children. As he admitted after a couple of attempts, the large needles in the external jugular vein worked better because they got the blood faster and with less pain for the patient.

Steve was kept exceptionally busy seeing patients. On one day in his first month at the hospital, he saw forty children, with treatments that included setting the bone in a radial arm fracture and putting on the cast, administering a spinal tap and diagnosing a newborn with meningitis, admitting a child who had been injured in a car accident, and giving chemotherapy to a child with Burkitt's lymphoma. Burkitt's lymphoma was an aggressive and deadly cancer that was rarely seen in the U.S. (fewer than 300 cases a year), but was the primary form of cancer affecting children in central Africa, where it most often appeared as a tumor in the child's jaw.

Chapter 8

Steve was not accustomed to seeing children die under his care, and learning to tolerate the high death rate was a debilitating aspect of his work in Beira. Children suffered from malaria and infections, and many died from malnutrition, pneumonia, and diarrhea, conditions that were rarely fatal in the U.S. But in addition, he had to treat children injured by bullets in the war with Renamo, and one day during his first month of work a child arrived at the hospital with a shrapnel fragment lodged near his spine. The reality of war cast a pall over all his efforts to improve health care for the children of Mozambique. As he wrote in his journal, "South Africa can make you feel angry and vulnerable at the same time." It was a frightening and infuriating time for everyone.

At the end of October, I noticed flyers posted in our neighborhood calling women to come to a meeting of the women's organization, OMM (Organização da Mulher Moçambicana) to learn how to support the upcoming Fourth Party Congress of Frelimo. I was tremendously eager to have an opportunity to observe and even perhaps participate in a women's political meeting. My expectations were colored by the romantic vision of women revolutionaries that had commonly been put forward on the international stage during Mozambique's armed struggle. I was accustomed to socialist feminist meetings in the U.S. where we organized classes on Marxism and women and talked about abortion rights and other issues important to American women. The OMM gathering would be my opportunity to attend a similar political discussion among Mozambican women.

As Mercie was napping when the meeting was scheduled to begin, I waited for her to wake up and arrived a bit late. It was held in a basement room of the Grande Hotel, just down the street from us. That five-story, white-painted hotel had never been successful despite its fantastic location just half a block from Indian Ocean beaches. According to one report, it had suffered from a lack of wealthy tourists and its rates had been too high for ordinary visitors. The owners spent one million South African rands to build it in 1952, and they had expected to include a casino that would generate considerable gambling income to cover their expenses. But their application for a gaming permit had been denied by the local government, which was under the sway of the Catholic Church.[2] By 1963, it was a vacant, dilapidated building looming over the Ponta Gêa neighborhood. In the early 1980s, when I visited the site, it provided housing for military families.[3]

The OMM gathering was attended by about thirty women, for the most part, apparently, hotel residents. The long, narrow meeting room was in the abandoned branch facilities of the telegram and post office. Chairs were arranged in three rows that stretched from one end of the room to the other. Over half of the women present had small children and babies with them, as I did. When I entered, a woman standing at the front was describing the process for making macramé bags to sell as a fundraiser for the upcoming Party Congress as well as for income. I found an empty seat in the front and settled in with Mercie on my lap. When the first speaker finished, another woman rose to add her comments. She had her baby tied on her back with a ragged cotton capulana. She raised the problem of poor conditions in the Grande Hotel, discussing how it was dirty, no one took responsibility for cleaning it, and reporting that there was a big kitchen that they were not allowed to use. As far as I could tell, no action was agreed upon by those in attendance regarding making macramé bags or opening access to the hotel kitchen. We ended the meeting singing "*Kanimambo* (Thank you), Frelimo," and walked out to the strains of another political song.

I was disappointed that the meeting had not provided any political discussion but had been held solely to recruit women to perform a typical female task in service to the male-dominated ruling party. I left with no sense of ongoing feminist organizing and no connection to any kind of socialist feminist group. But I nurtured a shred of hope, as

Chapter 8

the meeting indicated that there were OMM women who met in Beira, and if my work went well, I thought I would have a chance to get to know them and learn more about their political achievements. Nonetheless, when Gerri Dickson went to a subsequent meeting, she reported that the macramé bags were again a major discussion item, and that they were to be made for an upcoming trade exposition planned for Beira.

It was not only the women's organization that contributed to our increasing disillusion. A few months later, Frelimo published a booklet called *A Situação Actual no Nosso Pais* (The Current Situation in Our Country), which discussed the economic crisis Mozambique was facing. The booklet was supposed to be used as a study guide, and notices were posted announcing neighborhood and workplace meetings where people could discuss Frelimo's analysis of the deteriorating conditions. At a similar event later in our stay, Steve observed a Frelimo representative, facing limited literacy and a shortage of printed copies, haltingly read a policy statement to a group of workers. That method of sharing information left no time to discuss the issues.

Another meeting that Steve found more inspirational followed a similar format. In November 1982, he attended a hospital assembly to discuss the upcoming Party Congress. Gathering outside the hospital building under shade trees within sight of the sparkling ocean, about two hundred workers sat in rows, with physicians at the front, then nurses, and finally *serventes* or orderlies wearing bright blue smocks. A table at the front was covered with a red cloth and decorated with a vase of tropical flowers. The party and national flags flanked the table and swayed in the ocean breeze. Gama and Rui Bastos were joined at the front by José Namburete, the Frelimo party secretary at the hospital. They outlined a series of initiatives, including building a day care center at the hospital for workers' children, writing a history of the hospital and health care in Beira, making long-neglected repairs to the hospital buildings with the assistance of local industry, and collecting money to help fund the Party Congress.

Given the interracial character of the song-filled gathering, Steve noted in his journal that the meeting was one of the few times that he felt the reality matched the image of Mozambique we had developed back in the U.S.: "I kept pinching myself and looking around at everyone else to make sure it was real. After all the years of preparing, dreaming, planning, and study, I was *really* here!" Concluding his description of the meeting, he wrote, "It was a real up, and I'm feeling energized by the experience." His optimism was not entirely misplaced, as both the history and the day care center were goals that were realized while we were there, and the other objectives were also met over time.

Endnotes

1 Hilary Andersson, *Mozambique: A War Against the People* (New York: Palgrave, 1992), 84.
2 Douglas Alexander, *Holiday in Mozambique: A Guide to the Territory* (Cape Town: Purnell, 1971), 126-127.
3 *Grande Hotel*, a 50-minute documentary made in 2007 by Anabela de Sainte-Maurice, discusses the history of the hotel and the broader story of Beira, particularly its architecture and the diverse populations who settled there; available online at https://www.cultureunplugged.com/documentary/watch-online/play/7430/Grande-Hotel, accessed 13 October 2020. And see João Sarmento and Denis Linehan, "The Colonial Hotel: Spacing Violence at the Grande Hotel, Beira, Mozambique," *Environment and Planning D: Society and Space* 37, 2 (2019): 276-293.

Chapter 9
Streets Scenes and Sabotage

October to December 1982

My Portuguese was improving with daily immersion in the language, but I was still caught off guard from time to time. One day, when I arrived to collect Mercie at her creche, the teacher greeted me by saying, "Mercie está mordida," which I heard as "Mercie está morte" or "Mercie is dead." My heart began to pound, and I felt lightheaded, but I was also thinking that while the teacher seemed concerned, she was not overly upset, so she must be saying something else. The confusion between *morte* for dead and *mordida* for bitten was only clarified when they showed me the tooth marks on Mercie's back. The aggressive biter was a boy named Rui who eventually had to leave the creche because he continued to attack the other children. That was a memorable vocabulary lesson.

Mercie was learning Portuguese at creche and just beginning to speak English with us, pointing to her nose and saying "no," poking herself in the eye and saying "eye." One of her first words was "cookie," and she had started saying "See you later!" to us in the morning. When I picked her up at creche after she had been there for a few months, she pointed to the flashlight in my hand (needed to negotiate the dark stairwells) and said, "light." Her teachers, in amazement, said, "She talks!" It transpired that she never said anything during the day, and they were astonished to learn that she was singing songs from creche when she was at home. Her language acquisition was clearly slowed by the effort of learning two at once, but she eventually became proficient in both at a toddler level and used them appropriately. Near the end of our stay when I arrived to collect her at creche and spoke to her in English, one of her teachers was surprised because she spoke Portuguese all day and they did not realize she could also handle English. She used to follow Francisco around the apartment and jabber at him in Portuguese, amusing him hugely with her funny pronunciations. She was not confused about which language went with which people.

The streets of Beira were always filled with beggars and children. On the walk to Mercie's creche, I normally would pass three or four groups of a dozen or more people dressed in rags. Children flocked around those they perceived as being well-off, saying, "Dinheiro, por favor" (Money, please). We sometimes observed people with malformed legs or twisted backs, but we rarely noted disabled people begging. One man we saw regularly was forced by a spinal deformity to walk completely doubled over and he wore shoes on his hands as he made his way about the city. Similar conditions were routinely corrected in the U.S., where people also had better access to wheelchairs and prosthetic devices. But health care had been strictly segregated under colonialism, allowing few black Mozambicans access to necessary medical attention. Wheelchairs and other aids were a luxury and most handicapped people persevered with makeshift crutches or canes.

People tried to dress well, but it was difficult as there were no clothes being sold in the shops, and older clothing had to be repeatedly repaired, providing work for the many tailors working in the doorways of darkened storefronts. Once or twice, I noticed men wearing just the tops of socks, so even though there was no material inside the shoe the

Chapter 9

ribbing around their ankles gave the pretense of socks. Similarly, people wore backless shirts, appearing fully dressed from the front, and only revealing the subterfuge when they turned around. Hand-me-down clothes were common and T-shirts claiming to be from the U.S. were popular. I had to laugh at one shirt that was emblazoned "USA" over the Confederate flag, long before renewed efforts to educate Americans about the racist history of that emblem. A counterfeit Levi's T-shirt pronounced that the company had been "Founded since 1850," clearly a direct translation from a romance language. We also took note of the many UCLA shirts, and one proclaiming "California Surf." Half of the people we saw on the streets had no shoes at all and, reflecting what she saw every day, Mercie removed the laces from her sneakers and announced that she had "Mozambiki shoes."

One morning as I crossed the Chiveve River with Mercie in her stroller, we were approached by a group of street children. Unlike the boys the previous month who simply wanted to say hello, this time a particularly grimy-looking boy reached out to touch Mercie, curious about her straight blond hair. I anxiously cried out, "Deixe-la!" (Leave her alone!) and made a motion with my hand as if to brush his hand away. To my horror the boy reacted by cringing away with a look of terror on his face. The incident distressed me because of the immediacy of his reaction, as he obviously expected me to hit him, and because it was a reminder of the overwhelming character of hierarchical racial and colonial relations. Though I thought I was responding only to his extremely dirty hand and instinctively protecting my own child, I could not escape the reality that I represented the privileged west with my white skin and decent clothing.[1]

In many ways it was possible for me to consider race in a completely different way while living in Mozambique. The community where we lived was overwhelmingly black, nearly all our work-related interactions were with black colleagues or interviewees, and on most days, we did not experience race as a decisive or divisive factor. We socialized more often with other cooperantes, who were mostly white, but who were also mostly English-speaking, and it was easier to relax in our own language. Occasionally, a child might call out a greeting to us, saying "*mzungu*," meaning a European or white person. Race was ever-present, though racism was mitigated when the majority was black and in power. It might have been idealistic or politically expedient to believe otherwise, but small events such as that street child's fear reminded me of the pervasive nature of racial politics.

The electricity was cut in mid-November, and it remained out into early December. We had been using Francisco's kerosene lamp, but we finally managed to buy our own for three hundred meticais ($9.50) from our cooperative. The Dicksons bought a small generator to run their freezer and, even though we connected a line to the generator so that we could have one light on at night, the noise of that machine on the back porch was infernal. Combined with the unpleasant gasoline odor of our kerosene lamp, it made our evenings at home anything but relaxing. We were running out of wearable clothing because Francisco could not iron anything, and the handwashed and line-dried clothes were far too wrinkled to wear.

One evening we went out with a group of cooperantes to the Aero Clube restaurant at the airport and had a decent meal right next to the runway, with small planes taking off and landing as we ate our omelet, sausage, and fried potatoes. Though the food was prepared in an unsophisticated way and not especially memorable, it was noteworthy because even a simple meal was so difficult to obtain. When we returned to the Aero Clube in December with Jacky and Steve, it was closed and we were told, "Acabou a comida" (The food is finished). So, we went to the railway station, a dramatic modern structure built in the 1950s. The restaurant there was very smart in appearance, but the food was limited to beef, rice, soup, bananas, and coffee, with water to drink, for which we paid about 300 meticais each. It was not a great meal, but we needed a respite from the noisy generator.

I began to try some new baking projects, motivated by Jacky's success in making marmalade, orange cakes, and other treats. Although my attempt at marmalade never jelled, it worked well as an orange sauce, and I used it to flavor pancakes and to make a cake myself. I also tried a quick-rising yeast bread recipe which became a staple for the three of us:[2]

Casserole Bread -- Batter Method

- 1 cup milk
- 3 tablespoons sugar
- 1 teaspoon salt
- 1½ tablespoons shortening
- 1 cup warm (not hot) water
- 2 packages or cakes yeast, active dry or compressed
- 4½ cups sifted flour.
- Scald milk; stir in sugar, salt and shortening. Cool to lukewarm. Measure the warm water into a bowl. (Use lukewarm water for compressed yeast). Sprinkle or crumble in the yeast. Stir until softened. Blend in the lukewarm milk mixture. Add flour and stir until well blended, about 2 minutes. Cover; let rise in warm place free from drafts about 40 minutes or until doubled in bulk. Stir batter down. Beat vigorously about ½ minute. Turn into greased 1½-quart casserole. An 8x8x2-inch square pan may be used. Bake uncovered at 375° F. about 1 hour. Makes 1 loaf.

Since it could be baked in an eight-inch square pan, I could use our toaster oven, which was more reliable than the propane gas oven installed in the kitchen. I developed a routine to fit the bread-baking into the on-and-off pattern of our electric power. When the power came on, I would immediately mix up a batch of dough, which then needed less than an hour to rise before baking. I could then beat it down, put it into the pan, and get it into the oven while we still had electricity. Even if we only had three or four hours of power every other day, I could make enough bread to last us for two or three days. The other constraint was the erratic supply of flour, and once or twice we arranged to buy fifty-kilogram sacks to split among our cooperante friends. We usually ate the bread for breakfast, sliced in small squares and spread with White Rhino peanut butter that friends brought back from shopping trips to Zimbabwe and Swaziland and sometimes South Africa.

Then, in early December, the gasoline storage tanks were sabotaged. In a prior explosion in 1979, the tanks storing gasoline for Malawi had been blown up and the South Africans sent in special fire fighters to extinguish the blaze that their own commandos had ignited. In 1982 that did not prove necessary, but the sight of those flames and oily black smoke rising into the sky over Beira was alarming and disturbing. Steve wrote to friends that "any lingering romantic notions about 'the struggle' both here and at home were vaporized as I watched the fires and the tens-of-thousands feet high smoke column." We later learned that Porfirio, a Brazilian friend who worked for the oil company as a computer specialist, had been out at the tanks that evening until 11 P.M. or so. He was subsequently questioned for ten hours, but he had no information about the sabotage. He told us that twenty-nine tanks had been destroyed, twenty-three belonging to Shell and the other six to Petromoc, the Mozambican petroleum company, with a total value of $100 million. Most of the gasoline had been destined for Zimbabwe, which had only a half-day reserve and faced serious transportation problems as a result of losing the stored gasoline.

Figure 6: Oil tanks burning, Beira, December 1983. Photo by Steve Tarzynski.

Even though the event was frightening, we did not seriously contemplate breaking our contract and leaving. No other cooperantes were leaving and, as we had arrived only a few months earlier, we had not even begun to accomplish what we hoped to during our stay. And if we left early, we would have to pay our own plane fare home, a serious consideration in our precarious financial situation. Our mounting anxiety and stress were balanced by our increasing anger at apartheid South Africa and our determination to remain and contribute to developing Mozambique.

December ushered in the rainy season as well, beginning with a downpour on the evening after the gasoline tank sabotage. But that year the rains did not continue and a serious drought developed, reputedly the worst in fifty years. Food supplies were critically affected. The markets seemed to be full of cabbage and nothing else. We had found watermelon for sale in November, a delicious sweet and juicy treat, with a richer flavor than the mass market watermelons we bought in California, but we never found them again during our two years in Beira. One day I managed to buy two cucumbers. Mozambicans preferred their cucumbers overripe, and piles of soft yellow cucumbers filled the market stalls. When I picked through the piles looking for greener crispier cucumbers, the women vendors would always tell me, "Those are no good, they are not ripe enough! We have plenty of ripe cucumbers." We could not find green peppers or onions or other vegetables, though one day I found carrots for sale. Another day when there were tomatoes, the bicha was so rowdy that I sent Francisco in my place, with the result that he was robbed of 600 meticais (about $15.00). I resorted to using imported canned tomatoes bought with foreign currency at the Loja Franca. Even the rice that was sold in the cooperative was imported from Taiwan because the Mozambican rice harvest was insufficient for the local demand.

One evening a group of Brazilian cooperantes hosted a number of international cooperantes for dinner, and they served a shrimp salad and grilled goat that was very tasty. I preferred the milder taste of goat to beef, though I was not comfortable eating meat of any kind. We knew that a few of our friends turned to the black market, known as *candonga*, to buy such treats and, though we were content to be included in their generosity, we resisted turning to that illegal system of purchasing difficult-to-find food. Candonga was also a way of circumventing the ration plan and it undermined the official attempts to develop a workable food distribution process. We completely understood why other cooperantes bought food off the legal market but decided not to do so ourselves.

Juarez, the pharmacist from Brazil, arranged for some nice fish for the medical cooperantes. That fish was a wonderful change from the horrid and much-hated *carapau*, which was becoming our regular source of protein. Carapau was horse mackerel, and it was so bony and oily that we found it nearly inedible. We would buy several pounds in a frozen block of ice and fish, marked by sharp edges that easily cut anyone trying to separate the fish. Francisco usually fried the carapau in coconut oil, making it even less appetizing. We had to be careful because it was so bone-filled that we could feed it to Mercie only by carefully picking through every bite before giving shreds of fish to her. Years later, when I mentioned to a young Mozambican of Portuguese descent that I had lived in Beira from 1982 to 1984, he exclaimed, "Ah, os anos do carapau!" (The mackerel years!). Other Mozambican friends remembered trying new recipes for risottos and fritters, curries and grills, in their attempts to make the carapau palatable.[3] What I called "nice fish" in my journal was a real treat.

Endnotes

1 Alma Gottlieb discusses the difficulty of overcoming these divisions in "Processing Privilege: Reflections on Fieldwork (Early, and otherwise) among Beng Villagers of Côte d'Ivoire," *Mande Studies* 20 (2018): 123-135, in a special issue on "First Fieldwork in West Africa."

2 From Culinary Arts Institute, *250 Breads Biscuits and Rolls* (Chicago: Consolidated Book Publishers, 1965).

3 I never heard a joke that supposedly made the rounds, that carapau was "a whale that has gone through the process of socialist transformation," cited in Jason Sumich, *The Middle Class in Mozambique*, 90. Colin Darch, in a review of the book, notes that Sumich "misses the point about carapau (p. 90), a nutritious species of mackerel that was widely believed at that time to have been overfished by Spanish vessels in the Mozambique Channel, leaving only the 'small bony' juveniles for local consumption," Colin Darch, "Review of Sumich, Jason, *The Middle Class in Mozambique: The State and the Politics of Transformation in*

The Mackerel Years

Southern Africa (Cambridge: Cambridge University Press, 2018), H-Luso-Africa, H-Net Reviews (November 2020).

Chapter 10
Manioc and All the Trimmings

November and December 1982

We arranged a weekend trip to Quelimane in November, to spend Thanksgiving with our fellow cooperantes, Jon Cohn, Jeanne Raisler, and their children. The name "Quelimane" evoked romantic images of nineteenth-century coastal Africa and I was really looking forward to the visit, though I realized that it might not live up to the town of my imagination. We had been told that, since it was a vacation, one of the benefits Steve was allowed in his position, the Health Ministry would purchase our plane tickets, and we only learned a few days before we planned to go that the tickets had not been bought. We scrounged for the 11 contos ($275.00) and literally at the last minute managed to get on the plane and fly half an hour up the coast. After landing in the sleepy, dusty town, we waited over an hour to collect our suitcase, slapping at mosquitoes in the infested airport. Quelimane, closer to the equator, was much hotter and more humid than Beira. Jeanne had promised "manioc and all the trimmings" for Thanksgiving—manioc, also called cassava, is a bland-tasting tuber that is a common ingredient in the Mozambican diet because it is drought-resistant and easy to grow. Another American couple, Trip Van Noppen and Rivka Gordon, were also visiting as part of a journey across southern Africa, and they had purchased a duck at the Loja Franca in Maputo. In the end, we managed a fine semblance of a festive dinner, complete with roasted duck, mashed potatoes, wine, a fruitcake that Jacky had made and sent along with us, and no manioc.

We walked around the city and admired the wharf where the Rio dos Bons Sinais, the River of Good Signs, went into the bay. It had been officially renamed the Qua Qua River, but many people continued to use the colonial name bestowed by Portuguese explorer Vasco da Gama in 1499. The city was exceptionally low and marshy. We saw a big ship coming up the river and it looked like it was plowing through the fields near Jon and Jeanne's apartment. We came upon a small youth festival with booths offering prizes for trying your luck at toss games and a stage filled with young girls and women singing Frelimo songs. They were undaunted by the unreliable generator that caused the stage lights and microphone to flicker off and on.

The next day we joined a Dutch cooperante couple and drove for thirty minutes through acres of coconut plantations with trees planted in lines running off to the horizon. We stopped at a stand to buy immature coconuts, called *lanho*, and drank the sweet water inside (called *ilaneer*, and not to be confused with coconut milk). We paused a second time to try some coconut candy that was sold along the roadside. We reached a magnificent beach with broad white sand ringed by more palm trees, spreading for miles in both directions. In that gorgeous tropical setting, we discussed the increasing bandit attacks, which were much more severe in the north, with many burned-out farms, factories, and health posts. There was still no official acknowledgment of the extent of the attacks, though Anneke, the Dutch woman, reported that assaults in the rural areas had made it difficult and even impossible for people to work in the fields. From her position working in agriculture, it was clear that they would have difficulty reaching even 20 percent of the projected cotton production that year.

Chapter 10

Mercie slept a lot that weekend, worn out by the heat and the new surroundings. When she was awake, she was often singing little songs, one of which sounded something like "I see, I see." We were able to ask Jon and Jeanne's four-year-old son, Josh, if he knew a song like that, and he immediately launched into a song with the line "Assim, assim":

> Tenho uma boneca
> Assim, assim
> Vem de Inhambane
> Para mim, para mim
> Ela diz 'papa'
> 'Mama' tambem
> Fecha-la os olhos
> E dorme bem.

In English, that means: "I have a little doll, like this, like this; she came from Inhambane, for me, for me; She says 'papa,' and 'mama' too; she closes her eyes and sleeps well." Mercie was learning a lot of Portuguese nursery songs in creche, and when I mentioned creche to her she began singing the "boneca" song and clapping her hands. A few months later, as we listened to the proceedings of Frelimo's Fourth Party Congress on the radio, we heard President Samora Machel merrily sing "Tenho uma boneca" with a group of children.

One evening, shortly before Christmas, we went to see a show put on by Grupo Polivalente 7 de Abril (the Multicultural Group 7th of April, the date of Mozambican Women's Day). Based in Manica province in central Mozambique, they were one of several similar groups formed to carry on traditional song and dance from a variety of ethnic groups. The tickets were only 100 meticais ($2.50) and we were excited about seeing a live musical performance. Most of the audience was local young men, but there were a dozen cooperantes in attendance as well.

The show began with performers planted in the audience saying, "Eu nunca vi" and "Eu também nunca vi," until they had a crowd on stage saying together "Nunca vimos" (I have never seen this, I also have never seen this, We have never seen this). They began with a traditional dance, followed by drumming and dancing routines, an older man with a *chizambe* (a traditional single-stringed instrument similar to a mouth-harp) who sang two or three songs, a choral group, a trio of guitar players, and a young man who sang a song praising the upcoming Party Congress, "Este congresso será um successo" (This congress will be a success). There were a couple of skits about the problems related to the Renamo bandidos and one discussing colonial times when the Mozambican people did not have improvements such as the metical, the People's Assembly, and so forth. The audience was particularly pleased by the scanty costumes worn by the women in one or two of the dance sequences.

Several months later at the same theater we saw a show from the Soviet Union. It was a different kind of traditional dance display, and it was very much appreciated by the African audience. Their favorite acts were a knife dance, in which the knives were flung into the stage like mumblety-pegs and two of them went skittering into the audience, and a sword-fight dance that sent sparks flying as the swords clashed. When the audience applauded, the performers simply did an immediate reprise of that segment of the show rather than waiting to do an encore at the very end.

Christmas 1982 was back to basics. December 25th was an official holiday, but to maintain the secular ideal of a socialist state, it was called "Family Day." I found a card to send to my family back home, with a vibrant drawing on the front of a man and woman hoeing their garden, the sun shining in the background, a fat baby on the woman's back, and lush vegetables growing. The inside phrase was not "Happy Holidays," but the familiar slogan, "Defender a Pátria, Vencer o Subdesenvolvimento, Construir o Socialismo" (Defend the nation, overcome underdevelopment, build socialism). A poem on the facing

Chapter 10

side lauded the efforts of the Mozambican people to plant and grow their own "tree of national independence . . . A tree that grows in each one of us, in the hands of the peasant, in the arms of the worker, in the courage of the soldier, in the voice of a teacher, in the eyes of a child." I still find the sentiment moving, if not particularly Christmas-y.

Figure 7: Frelimo holiday card, 1983. Artist unknown.

We bought Toblerone chocolate bars and alcoholic beverages from the Loja Franca as gifts for each other. I had saved the green paper used to wrap purchases in the shops and I cut it into the shape of a fir tree, which we decorated and taped to the wall. We had been getting packages from family and friends, enjoying such treats as a big can of Almond Roca from Rick and Marianne Brown or several bags of Pepperidge Farm Milano cookies from Steve's parents. My parents sent two big boxes for Christmas, so we had some brightly wrapped packages to look at with anticipation. Their gifts for Mercie included a rag doll and a stuffed toy cat. We were thrilled to receive items we had requested, things you could buy in any drugstore in the U.S.

but were not to be found in Mozambique, such as ball-point pens, plastic drinking glasses, and a new pack of playing cards. Packages from other family members included blank cassette tapes and candles, much needed and welcomed.

Our friends Dave McCloud and Bobbie Mahoney, who were working for the U.S. Agency for International Development (USAID) in the neighboring nation of Malawi while we were in Mozambique, sent us a book I considered a "nice surprise," *Karl Marx's Theory of History: A Defence*. Although we called ourselves socialists (or, more descriptively, democratic socialists or socialist feminists), I never regarded myself as a Marxist, mainly because I had not read more than a few small pieces of Karl Marx's voluminous writings. Frelimo had declared itself a Marxist-Leninist vanguard party at their Third Party Congress, in 1979, though that was destined to change at the Fourth Congress, in 1983. But in late 1982 I was grateful for the opportunity to expand my understanding of Marxist theory while living in the midst of one kind of "Marxist" reality, though in the end the book was not particularly explanatory.

We had Christmas dinner with Jacky and Steve, and she once again made a great meal of roast pork, potatoes, and fruitcake. A few days after Christmas there was a holiday party at Mercie's creche with plates full of shrimp, chicken, and rice, lots of soda and beer, and plain sugar cookies for a treat. It was a pleasant, low-key event. The children were all served first and they enjoyed themselves immensely, talking among themselves and smiling at their parents as they ate the unusual delicacies. For entertainment we listened to songs by two young men with guitars, one of whom turned out to be a locally prominent singer (he may have been Alexandre Langa, though I did not note his name in my journal).

The Dicksons got some bad news right after Christmas. Murray's parents had both perished in a house fire in Saskatoon. All our families in North America and Europe were so worried about us living in an apparently dangerous situation that it seemed completely wrong that tragic death

Chapter 10

would reach those in Canada. The circumstances were made more difficult by our isolation. Murray's sister had called the Maputo office of CUSO, the Canadian aid organization. They had then used ham radio to contact Jean Menard, a Canadian electrical engineer working in Beira, and he had come over to tell the Dicksons. The message was ambiguous, as it asked for "the whole family" to return, so Murray flew to Maputo to try and reach Canada by telephone and sort out his return voyage. We all shared the fear that something could happen to family members back home and it would be days before we got the news. Fortunately for Steve and me, our families remained well during the two years we were away, though I missed one sister's wedding and the births of three nephews.

Meat and fish had arrived in the shops for the holidays along with sugar, rice, and beer. Capulanas, imported from Tanzania, were for sale for the first time in months, prompting huge bichas as every woman needed a regular supply to replace those that had worn out. Many women had been wearing terribly faded and torn capulanas simply because no new ones had been on the market. We spent most of the week after Christmas eating our unusually abundant supplies of food so that it would not spoil, as we assumed Renamo would do something destructive to mark the holiday. As expected, the bandidos celebrated the New Year by cutting the electricity at 8 P.M. on December 31st. The power was out for several days, and we initially had no electricity at all for sixty hours straight.

Chapter 11
Organizing Research on Women and Health

December 1982 to February 1983

My initial research strategy was to tell everyone I met that I hoped to investigate the history of Beira, with a particular focus on women. Rui Bastos, the provincial director of health and Steve's chief at the hospital, wanted to help, and he conceived the idea of writing a history of the hospital. His support was the spark that I needed to get started, as well as giving me an official way to introduce myself and obtain a guia or permit from the provincial Ministry of Health.

One day in December, I went to the City Council archives with an older male nurse named Francisco Coimbra. We took our guia to Sr. Gomes, the head of the secretariat of the city council offices. He first told us that any information we were looking for would be found in the Public Works department rather than the City Council archives and he led us from one office to the next in the council building. Every person he spoke to referred us on to another office, but eventually Sr. Gomes telephoned the archives directly and we descended to the basement rooms which housed the repository of municipal history. The walls were lined with shelves bulging with manila file folders, arranged by neighborhood and apparently pertaining to land and property ownership. Sr. Coimbra and I were given

The Mackerel Years

permission to borrow a couple of small folders concerning the hospital, including one describing gardens at the hospital in the 1970s. Despite his initial resistance, Sr. Gomes spent his entire morning with us and, once he understood what our project was about, he went out of his way to be helpful. I used my permit from the Ministry of Health to go to C.I.S. (Construtora Integral de Sofala, E. E., the state construction company), to look at architectural plans of the hospital. Although I found the maps interesting, they were not dated, so it was hard to know how to use them as a historical source. The guia also gained me access to the *Diário de Moçambique*, where I began reading through back issues. It was monotonous, although I did find information about the hospital from the 1940s. I was frustrated because the newspaper covered only the white community. I found just one photograph of an African in that entire decade, a man arrested for theft. A few days later, a newspaper employee gave me a tour of their archives as well as the printing press and ancient typesetting machines. It soon became apparent that I would not be able to do any fruitful research in their very poorly organized and incomplete files, and my guide advised me that I would find what I needed in the main historical archive in Maputo.

I also visited the local bureau of *Notícias de Moçambique* (*Mozambique News*), which was published in Maputo. The resident editor, Rogério Sitoe, was interested in my project, but he could not do much in a concrete manner, as the Beira office was essentially a regional agency with little to offer for my research. The stories from the 1950s were limited to small-town news about neighborhood sporting events and white colonial social affairs, with Africans appearing in print only in the police blotter column, reported for thefts and assaults. Once again, it was suggested that I pursue research on Beira's history in Maputo, at the *Notícias* headquarters.

In a startling coincidence, I discovered one useful article among pieces of trash that were blown onto our apartment balcony. As I picked up the tattered newspaper to throw it away, I realized that it included a few pages from a month-

Chapter 11

old *Diário de Moçambique* containing a centerfold story about workers at the local sugar mill, including interviews with women workers. With no easy way to find back issues of the paper, I doubt that I would have found that article through another avenue. Conventional written sources and archives brought me limited information about the history of women in Beira, and I turned to other means to find their history.

Steve also helped me organize an approach to accomplishing my research. He spoke with Maria José, an older Portuguese nurse at the clinic near our apartment. She told Steve that she had worked in Beira for forty years and she agreed that I could come and interview her. But when I met her, she repeatedly insisted that she had nothing to say. She continued to see patients and give injections while I tried to conduct a serious interview, the first one I had ever done under any circumstances, never mind in Portuguese and with a recalcitrant interviewee with a syringe in her hand. I did learn that she had previously worked on the maternity ward. She asked if I wanted to know about her work and I said yes, her work and her family. "Oh, well," she responded, "My family is all dead, here and in Portugal." I said I wanted to talk to women about colonial times and she said (contrary to all historical evidence), "It was all the same, just the same." She thought I should talk to Mozambican women, which of course I planned to do, but I was also interested in hearing the stories of a variety of women who lived in Beira. She introduced me to Lília Fortes, another nurse, and I arranged to interview Lília later in the week. Despite the lack of information collected from that potential informant, I was encouraged by simply having begun the process of talking to working women in the city.

Lília lived in a house near us in Ponta Gêa, and we sat in her backyard drinking tea while I interviewed her about her work as a nurse. Her three children and a niece who lived with them came and went. In her garden she was growing vegetables and corn, and dogs, a cat, chickens, and a mother duck with eleven ducklings roamed the yard. She even had a monkey! She was a bit younger than most of the other nurses, not yet forty when I met her. She was a very friendly light-skinned woman with her thick hair in a bun on the back of her head.

Lília had been born in a village in the northern province of Zambézia and lived with her grandmother in Chimoio when she attended school. She had been a teacher for three years and during that time had met her husband when he was posted there with the military. Her uncle was a nurse and, when Lília became dissatisfied with teaching, he suggested she think about nursing. She realized that was what she wanted to do and moved to Beira in 1971 to study nursing. She and her husband married in 1974 when she finished her training. They settled into their lives while he found employment as a mechanic, and she began working on the pediatric ward at the hospital. Then, in 1980, he was hit by a car and killed. She had been walking out of the hospital gate with him when a car came along the road that paralleled the beach in front of the hospital and hit him. She was left with two small children and a third on the way. Her niece arrived to help with the household chores so that she could continue to work and support all of them. Despite the tragedy, they were doing well, living in a pleasant house called Vivenda Alegre (Living Happily).

I interviewed two male nurses, Francisco Coimbra, who was part of the hospital research project and had gone to the city archives with me, and Muange Bernardo, a tall man with a long face who was among the first Mozambicans to be trained as a nurse under Portuguese colonialism. Muange began work in 1937 for the Mozambique Company, the large, chartered firm headquartered in Beira that had held administrative responsibility for Sofala and Manica provinces. Unlike many other parts of the world, nursing was not a primarily female activity in Mozambique. Under colonialism, many more men than women had trained as nurses, though women were more likely to be nurse-midwives. Samora Machel had famously trained as a nurse before getting involved in anti-colonial politics. Even in the 1980s, at least half of all nurses were men and the students enrolled in the nursing classes that Steve taught were nearly all men.

Muange Bernardo's father had wanted him to be a driver, a job that was considered a good option for African men and one of only four jobs thought to be appropriate for them. In addition to nursing and chauffeuring, other jobs most often held by African men under colonialism were teaching in the mission schools and interpreting or other office work. But Muange decided he wanted to be a nurse, explaining, "I don't know why, I just decided for myself, it was my own courage" to defy his father. When he began nursing school in Beira there were no female nurses, and colonial health care was rigidly segregated by race. Eventually Portuguese nuns arrived and began working as nursing sisters in the hospitals. Muange said, "I was a native nurse, so I worked in the Native Hospital." The doctor on call for emergency service remained at the European hospital in Ponta Gêa and had to be reached by telephone if he was needed at the Native Hospital. African nurses could not make the phone call, they had to get the Portuguese nursing sister to contact the doctor. He recalled a great deal of suffering during his forty years working under colonialism. He remembered how one daring man commented on the abuse of African workers, saying, "There isn't a factory that manufactures blacks," though the Portuguese treated Africans as though they were not human and could be replaced by new recruits from some kind of warehouse if someone was injured on the job.

It took me several days to transcribe the tapes that I made because of the high humidity. As I sat with the tape player, pushing "pause" while I wrote down their comments, and "pause" again to restart the tape, the interior of the machine began to get steamy from the proximity of my hand. I was forced to work in brief spurts so that

I would not ruin my only tape recorder. Transcribing was extremely tedious, and I especially hated listening to my own voice speaking Portuguese, as I could only hear my errors and poor pronunciation and it made me cringe. Despite my misgivings, the people I spoke with understood my Portuguese and I had many informative interviews, though I never enjoyed transcribing them.

I began suffering from an itchy rash on my left wrist which appeared to be worsening in reaction to the heat and humidity. It looked like impetigo with a lot of little blisters on the surface of my skin. None of the salves or unguents we tried was effective, and the inflammation seemed to be expanding across my arm as I watched it. Finally, I went to see a Soviet dermatologist and he recommended their cure-all, gentian violet, as a drying agent. That did seem to ease the itching but exacerbated the ugliness with a much more noticeable patch of purple covering my left forearm. I considered the rash a generic kind of tropical rot, and it never healed completely until we returned home to a more temperate climate.

Steve and Jacky Boyle had to move out of the apartment they had been living in, within sight of the Mexicana, and they thought they had been promised a newly vacant apartment in one of the Swedish buildings. The Swedish cooperantes mostly lived in what we jokingly called the "Viking" neighborhood, an unpaved street near the hospital and just across from the beach, with large houses where several Swedish families resided. Meanwhile another Swedish family arrived, Anders Hellstrom and Marie Ekman, who expected to live in housing with Lars and Cecilia Salemark. They all had children and hoped to share in childcare arrangements. Anders and Marie said they had only agreed to come to Beira if they had access to a generator, and there was one already installed at Lars's house. We wished we had known to make such demands, but that information simply underscored the relative advantage of having a cooperante solidarity group in your home country. Out of frustration with the slow-moving bureaucracy, Steve Boyle had been impatient with people in the Ministry of Health over other issues and some of them were unwilling to go out of their way to help him sort out the confusion over the housing. After a bit of discussion, Steve and Jacky found alternate housing and the new Swedish family moved into the house they had been promised. The male Swedes were all physicians or surgeons, including Lars, a pediatric surgeon who Steve worked with daily. As a group they brought critically needed skills and positive energy to the hospital.

Two of the female Swedish cooperantes who worked in Acção Social (Social Action), then part of the Ministry of Health, offered to help me make contacts. Cecilia Salemark and her Mozambican colleague Saraiva Felix worked at an old people's home and suggested that they could help me arrange interviews with women living there. That never did work out, in part because of difficulties in getting transportation and in part because Cecilia, as a sociologist, was doing statistical research and it was not clear how the more open-ended interviews that I hoped to carry out could intersect with her work. I knew that I wanted to start talking to older women about their lives in Beira, but in the early months of my residence I did not have a clearly focused research agenda. I simply hoped that a broadly conceived investigation would clarify the issues and help me formulate a project. I did write up a research proposal, suggesting I might interview nurses, cashew factory workers, and women who brewed traditional alcoholic beverages, though in the end I had to drop the last group. Cecilia critiqued my proposal, and I benefitted a great deal from her comments and suggestions.

Christina Hernborg, also at Acção Social, introduced me to women she knew at OMM, the women's organization. She was involved in a project to set up neighborhood maternal health programs coordinated by OMM and the Health Ministry, but she had faced a lot of obstacles. She told me that OMM often did not even send representatives to meetings with the health officials, so nothing ever developed in Beira, though we heard that other regions in Mozambique had greater success with similar maternal health projects. Although I had known the Swedish women for several months, I had not learned what their responsibilities were or how they might be able to help me, so I had never pressed them to make introductions. I was pleased to have their assistance, but I was also frustrated, as one-third of our stay had already passed (eight months out of twenty-four) and I had barely begun my research.

Christina took me along to the OMM headquarters, located in a nearly empty building. Several rooms held one or two desks, a few chairs, and bags of baby clothing that members had made and hoped to sell. We met with Maria das Dores, a key member of the local OMM leadership, and I explained that I hoped to do research on the history of women in Beira. Some other women were also present, and they all expressed interest in my work and said they would try to help. But I left with minimal expectations, as the organization was clearly not very active. OMM was not alone in its lack of activity, though, as morale across the city was slipping lower due to the recurrent Renamo attacks, electrical outages, and lack of food and other essentials.

Chapter 12
Advances and Setbacks

January to April 1983

Early in the new year we finally got a phone, a heavy black 1950s model that was especially useful for Steve's work. Gama had gone to Maputo and Steve became the lead pediatrician in the city, supported by four pediatric cooperantes: a Cuban woman, a Tanzanian man, and a Soviet couple. He was regularly scheduled to be on call, though he could be at home on those nights and weekends. But when there was a problem that needed his intervention, the hospital would send a car; the driver would knock on our door without warning, and then take Steve to the hospital. Most of the issues could have been easily handled by phone, so, once we had one, he did not need to go to the hospital for every problem.

The telephone bureaucracy was an incredibly tangled web of many entities and offices, so we needed the Ministry of Health to acquire the phone for us. Even then, the first number they assigned to us belonged to another family. Sorting out that mix-up required two weeks of back-and-forth discussions with the ministry and the phone company. After the phone was installed, I spent an entire morning each month dealing with the intricacies of paying our phone bill, which had to be paid in cash and in person at the telecommunications office in downtown Beira.

There was no regular telephone connection to Maputo. Calls were supposedly possible between the two cities, but even the monthly newsletter from the Mozambique Information Agency admitted in 1982 that calls between the two cities had about a fifty-fifty chance of getting through. In our experience, chances were far worse than that optimistic estimate. When we tried to call, we were regularly told that the lines in Maputo were *avariado* (broken down). I looked forward to talking to my family, but we never succeeded in calling them from Beira. My mother often tried to call and repeatedly encountered American telephone operators who had no idea where Mozambique was located. When she explained that it was a country in southern Africa, they would try to convince her that she wanted to call South Africa. One evening in February 1983, the phone rang, and it was Steve's mother, completely surprising all of us. She had also been trying regularly and that one time during our two years there she somehow was connected to us. A month later the phone rang with a different-sounding ring, and on the other end was my mother, with other family members also present. I heard my new nephew, Danny, who had been born in November, babble a bit, but Mercie was asleep, and they missed talking to her. Both of those phone calls were flukes that never recurred and none of us ever discovered the route that had gotten them through to us.[1]

We also celebrated a major event: the arrival, at long last, of our bicycles. When we learned of their appearance at the port, Steve went to an area where customs kept large items under lock and key and he was able to see that they seemed to be in good condition. The Ministry of Health provided transport to get the bikes from the port to our apartment. We attached a baby seat for Mercie to my bike, and she wore protective headgear that looked like a football helmet. My bike was bright blue with several reflector disks on the wheels so that it glowed in the sun. Mercie and I understandably attracted a lot of attention when we rode through the streets of Beira. Children would come up to Mercie calling, "*Piloto, piloto!*" (Pilot, pilot!), inspired by her appearance in the helmet. An unexpected benefit came two months later when a storm shredded the cardboard in the window of the door to the balcony and we were able to repair it with the bicycle shipping boxes which we wisely had saved for just such a contingency.

Figure 8: Steve and Mercie, in her bike helmet, making silly faces, 1983. Photo by Kathleen Sheldon.

While a few Mozambican men had bikes, I never saw a Mozambican woman riding one while we lived there. Men tended to claim whatever bicycles were available, as they were objects of notable expense and prestige. It was difficult for a woman to ride a bike when she wore a capulana that was wrapped around her waist and tied in front. Women often had babies on their backs or small children in tow, adding to the difficulty of riding a bike. There were other European women on bikes, but none of them had a baby seat, so people frequently stopped and stared when we rode past. Once when we were riding bicycles with a group of five cooperantes, we were met by crowds of people, mainly children, gathered by the side of the road and running from adjacent apartment buildings to watch us ride by, calling out, "*Olha, olha,*" (Look, look) and "Look at the child, look at the bicycles!" In our apartment building lobby one day, I came upon a small boy with missing front teeth who was admiring my bike and explaining to a younger child, "This seat is for the child, and this is for the big person. It is really pretty."

It was wonderful to finally be able to move around the city more easily and more quickly. We got into great physical shape, riding to distant areas of the city, and effortlessly carrying the bikes up five flights of stairs when we returned home. A diet with no ice cream or American snack foods probably contributed to our good health as well. The greater mobility brought me a lot of joy and I used to take daily rides downtown or along the beach-front road.

A third improvement was our decision to move Mercie into a bigger bed and into the second bedroom. We wanted to buy a crib, but no ready-made furniture was for sale. After making inquiries we found a carpenter who would build a crib to our specifications. It took a few weeks, but it was a wonderful sturdy bed when it was done. Steve borrowed a mattress from the hospital, as the local factory had no material for making any and there were none for sale in the entire city. We all slept better in the new situation, and she still was cozy under her green mosquito netting.

Mercie played most often with a blue stuffed cotton doll that we had brought from the U.S., which she named Deh Deh (with the accent on the second syllable), and she fed her, put her on the potty, and gave the doll her own pacifier. We knew she was really observing African women when she began putting Deh Deh on her back and wrapping her expertly and tightly with a doll blanket, giving the little hitch with her shoulders that mothers commonly gave to settle their babies comfortably. One day she wrapped Deh Deh next to her chest with a blanket as if preparing to breastfeed and told me, "I woman."

Around that time, I decided to take Mercie to have another formal photograph taken. I dressed her in one of the cute hand-me-down sundresses she had gotten from

Chapter 12

Marika and we went to a studio in downtown Beira. The proprietor was at least seventy years old, a Portuguese man who had remained when so many Portuguese fled, and he clearly eased his situation by drinking alcohol. He had a cat lounging around the room, which was unusual as most people could not afford to keep a pet. He posed Mercie a bit stiffly and she burst into tears when she stood in front of the camera, quite a contrast to her insistence on smiling for her visa photo less than a year before. We did not discuss payment, and I was afraid the cost would be very high, but when I returned to pick up the pictures, he gave me the six prints.

Figure 9: Mercie, April 1983, photographer's name unknown.

Everywhere in Beira we would see people, mainly men, working at income-earning tasks. Some would sit in groups in vacant lots with piles of reeds around them weaving mats and baskets. Others would set up a chair under a tree and post a hand-written sign advertising their barbering skills. Two young men sat outside the post office with label-makers and strips of plastic in various colors, making labels for people. Francisco purchased a label with his name, which he stuck on his Xirico, the locally made transistor radio that everyone owned.

In January someone broke into the little laundry room and stole all of Francisco's clothing, his shoes, and a mat and blanket. He had been at his home in the outlying neighborhood of Manga with his bicycle and his radio, so those valuable items had not been stolen. Francisco's plan was to return to Manga and pay 200 meticais to a *curandeiro* to find the thief. Curandeiros were local healers who often provided herbal concoctions and other remedies. Francisco hoped the curandeiro would be able to cast a spell on the thief, bringing him to justice in a way the police would not.

One morning I walked out onto the back porch and spotted an unfamiliar man. When I approached him, he asked to speak to my empregado but tellingly did not ask for Francisco by name. I was not initially worried or frightened, as I thought he was just one of the people who regularly came around looking for work. But he was holding a large canvas bag, and as I looked from his bag to our clothesline, which was conspicuously empty, I realized that he was a thief. I felt so angry that he was brazenly stealing our clothes in the middle of the day that I walked up to him and said, "Oh, I like your bag," simultaneously reaching for it. I took it right out of his hands even though he was much taller and larger than I was. I looked inside and saw my shorts and a shirt of ours. I still felt angry rather than scared, and I took the bag and lifted it as if to hit him, but suddenly felt afraid that he would hit me back. I began yelling, but I was so distressed I called "Thief, thief," in English instead of the Portuguese, "*Ladrão, ladrão.*" He ran off down the hall and I did not run after him because Mercie was napping inside.

I later spoke with the security men who sat in our building lobby and, though none of them had noticed anything unusual, they laughed uproariously at the image of me confronting the thief. One of the watchmen later carried around the bag I had snatched, hoping someone would claim it, but we never found out who had made the attempt. Since I recovered the items, there was no actual theft. Other

Chapter 12

items were occasionally taken during our stay, and we later realized that we were missing a pair of Steve's Levi's jeans and a T-shirt with Mickey Mouse on the front, certainly desirable items of clothing. Another day I saw a woman wailing in the lobby of our building, as all her children's clothes had been stolen from her sixth-floor clothesline. Her children had been accomplices, because they brought the clothes to the thief, though how he convinced them to do such a thing was not clear.

We learned more regarding the attack on the gasoline storage tanks. There were arrests, mainly of Portuguese men, but also one South African man with a British passport, Finlay Dion Hamilton. It appeared that he was not only involved in the storage tank sabotage but had been importing guns for Renamo. He was the managing director of the import-export company, Manica Shipping, and had acted as a liaison to the British Embassy. At an Embassy reception, he had been introduced as someone who was a resource for British cooperantes. He even had a private plane that he offered if it was needed in an emergency, quite an irony in retrospect, as any emergency that might require British citizens to be evacuated could have been a result of his activities in running guns for Renamo. On the other hand, he presumably would have had inside information if cooperantes needed to flee. When his house was investigated after his arrest, he was found in possession of eight refrigerators, all run on a generator, and three more meat-filled freezers at the airport. We were told that he smuggled weapons for the bandidos through the Clube Nautico, using boxes marked "Peixe para consumo familiar" (Fish for home consumption). Clube Nautico workers thought something was fishy—literally—but there was nothing specific to report to the authorities.

Steve gained further information at a hospital meeting of the neighborhood watch organization known as Vigilância Popular (People's Vigilance). At the meeting, attended by two or three hundred hospital workers, the general sentiment was that Hamilton should be shot, and that feeling was shared at other Vigilância Popular gatherings as well.[2] Mozambique had reluctantly introduced capital punishment and several captured bandits had been executed by firing squad since we had arrived, reportedly observed by crowds of onlookers. A couple of months later the downtown Praça dos Trabalhadores (Workers' Plaza) was the site of a public whipping of eleven people convicted of thieving and speculation. In my journal I simply entered the episode as fact, without writing about our concerns over the introduction of official corporal punishment, which we certainly viewed as cruel and immoral. Unquestionably we felt conflicted, as we were living there because we supported the broad outlines of Frelimo's agenda. Yet we were categorically opposed to public canings, and we were distressed to read newspaper stories about such punishment for black market trading. One report told of a woman in Beira who was fined 1,000 meticais and sentenced to ten strokes with the whip for selling small bread rolls for fifteen meticais, when the legal price was set at two meticais. She had probably paid a black-market rate for the flour and was just trying to cover her costs and earn a tiny profit.

Corporal punishment also evoked bitter memories of the colonial era, when Africans were often subjected to beatings with a *palmatória*, a paddle with holes designed to raise welts on the palms of the victim's hands. The reality of politics in a destitute country engulfed in war did not fit neatly into our ideals of equality and peaceful progress. Though we were politically opposed to the death penalty, everything seemed topsy-turvy in Mozambique. In the U.S., the death penalty was disproportionately imposed on minority communities, and we believed that the state should not be involved in such "legitimized" killing. But in wartime Mozambique, *o povo* (the people), representing a socialist society, apparently wanted those perceived as committing crimes against the community to be executed. It is easy in retrospect to note that we opposed executions and public

Chapter 12

whippings, but at the time, as guests of the country, we did nothing to protest the new aggressive approach to criminals.

February 3rd was National Heroes' Day, commemorating the 1969 assassination of Eduardo Mondlane, though other heroes of the liberation struggle were also recognized in the events of the day. Renamo cut the power on February 2nd, as happened to mark nearly every national holiday. Steve, Mercie, and I were at home that day because there was a tolerância de ponta (a "tolerance point"), meaning that people were given a holiday from work on short notice, on that occasion to enable everyone to attend the public meeting about Hamilton and the bandidos.

Mercie had a bad cold and, when I put her on our bed for a nap, I noticed that she was extremely hot, even though we had just given her a dose of acetaminophen for fever. We both were worried and kept a close watch over her as she slept; then Steve realized that she was breathing oddly, kind of raspy and fast. She appeared to be having a seizure and when he carried her into the living room, she was semi-conscious and toneless, with her eyes starting to roll back. Shivering with dread, we tried unsuccessfully to call the hospital emergency room to get an ambulance and then called Mike Muller at work. He came immediately and drove us all to the emergency room where Mercie continued in her semi-conscious condition. Though she was dazed, she was troubled because she was outside the house and was barefoot. She pointed to her foot, saying, "Shoe?" in a worried voice, knowing that she was supposed to wear shoes whenever she went out.

In the pediatric ward, Steve carried out a series of tests on Mercie. Gama was still in Maputo and there was no other pediatrician that he trusted with our own child. Steve performed a spinal tap on her to rule out meningitis, while I waited impatiently in the next room. He remembers feeling terrified as he performed that tricky procedure. The spinal tap and blood tests indicated that Mercie had malaria, not meningitis, and she was dosed with chloroquine. Within an hour she was much revived and by that evening we were home and eating supper with Mercie singing songs again despite her high fever.

The next day, National Heroes' Day, Steve was back at the hospital, wielding a hoe in the gardens as part of the "voluntary" labor brigade honoring the heroes; it was considered bad form to avoid such tasks. Two days later Mercie was still sick, sleeping a lot and crying from sores in her mouth that made it difficult for her to eat. She was also vomiting her chloroquine, so we went back to the hospital and Steve gave her Fansidar (another anti-malarial drug that we had brought with us, as malaria was increasingly resistant to chloroquine). Eventually her fever broke, and she recovered. But the fright we felt when we did not know what was wrong, or how serious her condition was, traumatized us and remained with us for a long time.

We learned that Mercie had become anemic and underweight, falling into the fifth percentile for height and weight for her age. In a letter to friends back home I commented that, due to the weight loss, she looked "a little older . . . with more clearly defined features." My mother was worried that she was too young to have lost her baby fat. Our friends in Beira became very concerned as well and began helping us. Len Limpus brought us three eggs and a loaf of homemade wheat bread when his family heard that Mercie was ill. Once she recovered, she began eating enormous quantities at each meal and asking for cereal for a snack. Steve Boyle ran errands for us, and he and Jacky brought back supplies from a trip to Swaziland, including hard-to-find batteries, candles, ballpoint pens, hair elastics, cheese, mustard, peanut butter, and even deodorant.[3]

About a week later I fell ill, and I could do nothing but lie around the apartment dozing and suffering from an intense headache. I was in too much pain to read, and I spent three days in a lethargic half-conscious state of mind, alternately sweating from the heat and feeling chilled as the fever ebbed and flowed. Though we never checked

Chapter 12

my blood, we treated it with chloroquine and, since I subsequently recovered, we presumed it was malaria. Steve and I were also losing weight during those months, with mine falling to 105 pounds, excessively low even for my thin build. We never seriously considered leaving, but we were homesick as well as physically sick, and Steve and I both worried constantly about Mercie. I wrote to friends in the U.S. that I was really tired of eating rice and beans and mackerel day after day and, one rainy day while I was ill, "I had a serious craving for tomato soup and a grilled cheese sandwich. Alas." That was a terrible time with all three of us debilitated from fever and worn down in general, though very thankful for the network of friends we had formed in just a few months.

By the middle of March 1983, food supplies were noticeably short, the lowest we had experienced. Pasta was not available even at the Loja Franca, only yellow cucumbers were in the markets, and we relied on rice and beans every day. The beans, bought locally, were heavily bug-ridden, so I soaked a cup or two of dried beans every evening and spent half an hour the next morning removing the bug-infested beans, which were easily spotted once the beans swelled up with the water. But it was not a very appetizing task and half of every batch of beans had bugs hiding inside. Jokes about insects being a source of protein did not really make us want to eat them every day. In a letter home in early April, I enumerated what we had managed to purchase in the local shops and markets over a two-week period. I emphasized to my family that the list I wrote out was the *total* amount of food and represented the *only* items that were available: six bottles of beer, four of Coke (really!), one package of caramel pudding mix, a bag of sugar, a bag of powdered drink mix, a few cucumbers, some tough and bitter green beans, and limes. Other items appeared in the Loja Franca, including a large bar of laundry soap, Knorr soup mix (we bought six packets), Spam-style canned meat

The Mackerel Years

(a real treat, we saved our three cans for weekend meals), one can of sausages, one box of fettucine, baking powder, and chocolate cookies. That small set of purchases added up to over $10.00, which meant it was real luxury food.

We did get more food in the mail from family and friends in the U.S. Steve's mother sent oregano, paprika, and basil that we began to use in the bean sauce to make it more flavorful. She even sent salt. Although we could buy salt locally, it was only semi-processed, remaining gritty and gray in color, so the Morton salt with iodine was a welcome delicacy. Soon after that, Steve asked his mother to send Kool-Aid, thinking that would be a more flavorful drink and a change from soda and beer (there was rarely any fruit juice for sale). We had to bicycle out to customs to claim the package when it arrived, and we could see that she had spent $20 to send $10 worth of powdered drink packets by air. Even though Steve requested pre-sweetened, she sent the regular kind that required one cup of sugar for every batch we mixed up. As the local sugar did not mix well and was often in short supply we did not drink very much of that Kool-Aid.

We celebrated Mercie's second birthday a few days early with friends who came by and shared a coffee cake with streusel topping that I had baked, though the power was cut. We were without regular electricity from March 14th to the 24th, and in my journal I rejoiced that it was "only" ten days without power. Mercie was aware of the regular loss of electricity and, one morning when the power went on, she pointed to the ceiling light and clapped her hands, saying, "Light, yay!" On her actual birthday, March 17th, I made a chocolate cake for her birthday, arranging to bake it during our brief access to rationed electricity. We held a St. Patrick's Day dinner with Niall and Melanie, the Irish cooperantes. St. Patrick's Day was mainly an American holiday, but they were good natured about sharing the day with us.

Chapter 12

We participated in a celebration for Mozambican Women's Day on April 7th by visiting an old people's home in Nhangau, a remote suburb of Beira. Our group included cooperantes from Chile, Canada, Sweden, Holland, and England, accompanied by officials from the national Social Action office. We rode out in a car with a Dutch couple, Peter and Yanne, along a poorly graded dirt road. Along the way we forded muddy patches and gazed on the swampy land dotted with small lily-pad ponds and stretching out in the distance. The settlement in Nhangau had been built as a prison and was marked by rows of little cement huts in the middle of empty land. There were small manioc gardens, banana plants, and orange trees, and an open-sided school with benches marked "*Ass. Hindu*," a gift from the Hindu Association. Children from the school sang songs to entertain us and the old people also sang and danced. We brought along bread, juice, and other treats for the party. Our expedition was reported in the *Diário de Moçambique*, like typical small-town news, quoting an unnamed cooperante that the cooperantes' presence reflected "as always, increasingly, their solidarity with the struggle of the Mozambican people since the time of the armed struggle."

One Sunday afternoon, Steve was called to the home of Provincial Governor Armando Guebuza to see his daughter, who had asthma. Guebuza had been the national political officer for the army after independence, a ministerial position in the cabinet which he continued to hold from 1982 to 1983 while occupying the post of governor, and that dual appointment explained why his official title was Resident Minister (or sometimes Minister Resident) of Sofala Province. Steve recommended that the governor quit smoking to help ease his daughter's asthma problem and advised him on his own minor health issues. The daughter required an injection at the hospital, so the official car with an armed escort took them to the hospital and then brought Steve home to the Mexicana. As he wrote in a letter, that "definitely impressed the neighbors." Steve and Governor Guebuza visited briefly, and Steve enjoyed a pleasant conversation with his wife, Maria da Luz Guebuza, while waiting for the car to arrive. She gave him two young coconuts, and that evening at our apartment we savored the lanho, coconut water with whiskey, reportedly the preferred drink of the governor as well.

Endnotes

1   In a barely believable comment, a traveler through Mozambique just ten or fifteen years later claimed that "Mozambique is blessed with one of the most up to date phone systems in the world. An Australian company installed the network (still in its experimental phase) which runs surprisingly smoothly. All over the north we came upon little cabins where operators could connect you to anywhere on the globe in a matter of seconds and your bill popped up on a computer screen," Justin Fox, *With Both Hands Waving: A Journal through Mozambique* (Cape Town: Kwela Books, 2002), 122. Fox, a travel writer, shares a "boys' adventure" style narrative interspersed with potted historical anecdotes about Portuguese explorers; as a journalist, he neglects to properly cite his sources or even state the year of his travels. A similar account is found in Nick Middleton, *Kalashnikovs and Zombie Cucumbers: Travels in Mozambique* (London: Sinclair Stevenson, 1994); his book emphasizes the exotic aspects of African life, and the sections on Beira focus on his stay at the run-down Dom Carlos hotel, and the prostitutes who approached him.

2   Hamilton was jailed, and eventually released in 1989 as part of an amnesty action.

3   Others have written about the many fears related to having children fall ill in the field, and I have colleagues whose children did not survive falling ill in Africa. Also see, Kelley Sams, "Malaria and Spider Man: Conducting Ethnographic Research in Niger with a Three-Year-Old," in *Mothering from the Field: The Impact of Motherhood on Site-Based Research*, ed., Bahiyyah M. Muhammad and Mélanie-Angela Neuilly, pp. 47-61 (New Brunswick, NJ: Rutgers University Press, 2019). This useful collection emphasizes advice for planning to do research with children, including the additional costs involved, especially for international travel and residence. Also in that collection, see Marylynn Steckley, "'Manman, Poukisa Y'ap Rele M Blan?' (Mama, Why Are They Calling Me a White?): Research and Mothering in Haiti," pp. 201-221; she also addresses the privilege of being favored in a waiting line at a clinic (218).

Chapter 13
May Day in Maputo

April to May 1983

We planned a trip to Maputo in April, where we hoped to gain entrance to the Frelimo Party Congress. Leaders of the Democratic Socialists of America (DSA) wrote a letter to Frelimo naming us as their representatives to the congress, a reasonable request as we had been active members of DSA and its precursor, the New American Movement. Although DSA was small, it was one of the two official U.S. members of the Socialist International, to which Frelimo also belonged. But correspondence was erratic and our situation was unsettled. We thought perhaps if we went to Maputo, we could talk directly to Frelimo authorities and Steve might be admitted as an observer. I intended to pursue my research, visiting people at the university, going to the national archives, and meeting with Rogério Sitoe at the Maputo offices of *Notícias*.

We were fortunate to be able to stay in George Povey's apartment on Avenida Julius Nyerere while he was out of the country getting treatment for back pain. We shared his apartment with another visiting cooperante family, Hans and Liliana and their toddler daughter Marina. They were very international, as she was from Argentina and he was Dutch but had been born in Costa Rica and his parents had also been born outside of Holland, though they retained their Dutch citizenship. Hans was a geologist working for the United Nations. As I commented in a letter to my mother, "Next time we do something like this (ha ha) it'll be through the UN" because the pay and support were so superior. Hans and Liliana had previously worked in Guinea-Bissau, a former Portuguese colony in West Africa that had also undergone a period of anti-colonial armed struggle and subsequent revolutionary transformation. One day we were joined at lunch by the head of the Guinean youth organization, a friend of theirs who was in town for the Frelimo Party Congress. He was about to travel to Moscow, where he had a scholarship to study political economy. In the end we stayed with them for over two weeks, much longer than originally anticipated. We had planned to take a short vacation in neighboring Swaziland but, to our disappointment, our departure was delayed because the international borders were closed for the duration of the congress.

Maputo seemed to be a bustling city compared to the quiet streets of Beira. I usually walked out to the university, though one morning I got a ride with Marc Wuyts, an economist on the faculty, when he saw me walking. I was able to meet with researchers at the African Studies Center, who were mostly not Mozambican, including Judith Head, Colin Darch, Gary Littlejohn, Jacques Depelchin, and Alpheus Manghezi. I made an appointment to meet with Aquino de Bragança, the director of the center, though, when I returned as scheduled later that week, Aquino was not there. I had hoped to get official support for my research, as it was generally considered essential for researchers in foreign countries to be affiliated with a local institution. But in a disappointing discussion with Judith and Gary, they explained that the center was not able to support individual researchers. They simply had no way to keep in contact with me when I was in Beira. Though I never learned the details, they told me that there had been three previous occasions when they endorsed individual research, and all had ended badly. The non-Mozambicans at the university

Chapter 13

were mainly British leftists and I could not help feeling that being an American may have been a disadvantage in that situation. During the Reagan era, anti-American feeling ran high among international leftists and our personal histories and politics did not always mitigate those attitudes.[1]

I did use the main historical archives at the Arquivo Histórico de Moçambique. The staff, including the director, Maria Inês Nogueira da Costa, went out of their way to help me. A key element was the Ministry of Health guia I had, which gave me access to photocopying. Due to shortages of paper, toner, and other supplies, the archive only allowed very limited numbers of photocopies to be made by researchers, but the archive staff was willing to help me because I was based in Beira and had only a few days to go through the materials in their files and on their shelves. At that time, the archives were commendable for their organization and accessibility, a fact noted in an article in the local newspaper, and it was certainly my experience as well.[2] After the disappointing lack of support from the scholars at the African Studies Center, I deeply appreciated the crucial assistance from Mozambican academic staff.

I enjoyed my time there, reading reports from the Mozambique Company, the chartered company that had governed Sofala province for several decades in the early twentieth century. I also found photographs of Beira from a time when white settlers sat in rickshaw-like wheeled benches with two long handles held by African men as they pulled the vehicle along tracks in the streets of the city. I examined numerous sources in the official bulletins and reports that gave me more insight into colonial ideas about racially segregating health care and the role of women in the system. I was also able to read scholarly journals and other materials in the documents room at the African Studies Center at the university, helping ease the intellectual isolation I was experiencing in Beira. I went to *Notícias* one day to meet with Rogério Sitoe, as we had arranged, but he never showed up and I never did gain access to the newspaper archives.³

Our other quest was not progressing very well, as we encountered obstacles in our attempt to go to the Party Congress. We spent an afternoon walking around the city to locate the headquarters of Frelimo's Central Committee. We did succeed in meeting with a responsável in charge of foreign delegations and initially felt hopeful that something would be worked out. However, when Steve returned a few days later, he was told he would not be able to attend the congress. Then, that evening at 6 P.M., we received a telephone call saying that a car would be sent to take Steve back so that he could meet with another person in authority, Secretary of State for Foreign Affairs Valeriano Ferrão, who was directly under Foreign Minister (and future president) Joaquim Chissano. Ferrão (as everyone called him) was very regretful that we could not be admitted, but he explained that they did not have enough information about DSA to allow us in. I do not know if there was any approach that would have allowed Steve or both of us to attend that meeting, but we did try all available routes.

But Steve and Ferrão hit it off personally and enjoyed their meeting, where they talked about politics. They later renewed their relationship back in the United States as Ferrão was appointed as the first Mozambican ambassador to the U.S. from 1984 to 1990. We have continued the friendship, staying as guests in each other's homes and sharing many good discussions and social events. Ferrão retired from public office after his stint as ambassador and in the 1990s was active in support work for the woman-dominated green zones agricultural cooperative (União Geral das Cooperativas, UGC) based in Maputo. He passed away in 2022. Green zones were cultivated areas on the outskirts of the city that were allocated to agriculture and were protected from urban development.

Meanwhile, we enjoyed other aspects of the visit to Maputo, which was deep in preparations for the Party Congress. The city was being cleaned up and we admired

Chapter 13

murals extolling socialism and Frelimo's rule that were being newly painted or repaired. One showed a small child with the slogan, "I want to continue to live in a socialist country." Students at the industrial high school were painting their school buildings, and stores on the main avenues had window displays in support of the congress. We went to FACIM (Feira Internacional de Maputo, the Maputo International Trade Fair), an annual industry and commerce fair. They had displays of textiles and other industrial production, and the agricultural sector was represented by ducks, bees, sugar, and a model communal village with four cows. Despite an effort to showcase Mozambican economic potential, it was a small-scale, dusty affair that illustrated Mozambique's extreme poverty more than its potential wealth.

The radio played the congress proceedings, with Samora Machel's opening day speech lasting several hours. In "Bairro Comunal Polana do Cimento A" (Polana is a neighborhood, this name referred to the "Communal Neighborhood Polana Cement A"), we happened upon a practice dance session in front of the headquarters of the neighborhood organizing group. The neighborhood groups, known as *grupos dinamizadores*, were present in many communities and workplaces and were responsible for organizing people to support local development projects and to support Frelimo. We joined the hundred or so onlookers as women performed, followed by men, their songs accompanied by drums and other instruments. The crowd was surrounded by banners proclaiming, "A Luta Continua!" (The Struggle Continues!), which is Frelimo's best-known slogan. We saw many people marching in preparation for the May 1st parade, including members of the youth organization in red kerchiefs, the police band, and workers singing "O povo organizado sempre vencerá" (The people, organized, will always be victorious). Additional verses referred to "organized women" always winning, and "o plano" (the plan for development) being presented at the congress, also emerging victorious. Truckloads of soldiers and sailors singing revolutionary songs passed by on the streets.

Maputo was better supplied with food and other goods than we experienced in Beira, and we enjoyed substantial meals at some good restaurants. One day at the O Guacalango, newly painted and decorated with café curtains, we dined on rice with a tasty meat and peanut sauce, salad with sausage slices, and beer, while Mercie filled up on pasta and fried chicken. Another day we had grilled shrimp at Taverna del Rei, while Mercie again dined on spaghetti. And we also met Isac, our neighbor from Beira, and ate lunch with him at El Greco after the parade on May 1st.

I had a chance meeting on the street with Merle Bowen one afternoon. We had been graduate students together at UCLA and she was working for the Ministry of Agriculture and doing research on rural political economy at Ilha Josina Machel in Manhiça district, north of Maputo.[4] Eddie Mondlane, the son of Eduardo and Janet Mondlane, lived in the same building where we were staying, and we had a pleasant lunch with him one day. Established scholars such as Allen Isaacman, John Saul, and others were in town to attend the Party Congress, and it was good to have a chance to talk with them about doing research in Mozambique.

The congress met from April 26th to 30th and we listened to portions of the proceedings on the radio and read the daily reports. It was discouraging news in many aspects, as delegates from all regions of Mozambique reported on difficulties in obtaining needed supplies, evidence of increased black-market activities, and the intensifying war. The congress approved a ten-year development plan for increasing industry and especially agriculture, the base of the economy, but economic collapse was starkly evident, and the way forward was not easily seen.

Samora provided spirited leadership, intervening and imparting lessons throughout the sessions, but it was not enough to counter the international isolation and the South African apartheid government's aggression. Around that

Chapter 13

time, Samora had also given a speech at the Conference of Nonaligned Nations in New Delhi where he described apartheid as "the Nazism of our time." The brutal racial oppression in South Africa was well known and thoroughly documented and his comment seemed to us to be clearly inviting international support in ending apartheid. Though international efforts were increasing, the Reagan administration continued to ally itself with the apartheid regime and to isolate Mozambique, and the consequences for Mozambicans were dire.

Sunday, May 1st, we rose early for Dia Mundial do Trabalhador (International Workers' Day), so we could get to the meeting point for international cooperantes who would be marching in the parade. There were only nine Americans in the group and though we gathered at 7:30 A.M., we did not actually march until noon. Waiting in the heat and dust in a side street was exhausting, so halfway through the morning Steve took Mercie back to George Povey's apartment, climbing up the long hill from the downtown site of the parade.

I had little experience of May Day parades. Even though the day commemorates American workers' successful struggle to gain the eight-hour workday (among other things), it has been perceived as a socialist holiday in the United States, and celebrations remain small to non-existent. In 1980 in Portugal, however, Steve and I had attended a huge May Day parade with an estimated one million people still celebrating their recent emergence from decades of fascism. Crowds and crowds of communist and socialist workers and their families had filled the streets of Lisbon in a wonderful, lively parade and afterwards adjourned to the parks to picnic and relax.

The news media in Mozambique reported that 200,000 people marched in the parade in Maputo in 1983 and tens of thousands more lined the streets in support. First in the march were workers from the various industries, wearing their *batas*, the heavy cotton jackets or jumpsuits that protected their clothing—air transport workers in bright orange; health workers in white or blue; forestry workers with tree branches stuck into their belts; textile workers in green, waving small red paper Frelimo flags and chanting "Viva, viva, viva"; representatives from various government ministries; and workers from the beer factory, with giant beer bottles on their float. Entire work forces went by, singing revolutionary songs, followed by the mass organizations. OMM was represented by thousands of women carrying posters of Josina Machel and many banners and slogans, exhibiting enormous enthusiasm as they chanted "O-M-M, a luta continua!" Members of the youth group followed, then athletes wearing their sporting uniforms—golfers, boxers, bicyclists, basketball players, even boaters with a yacht wheeled by! Many neighborhoods and cooperatives also participated.

We spent part of our time resting in the shade to escape the oppressive heat, thus missing the military and some other sections. The participants were lined up, tightly organized in the side streets leading into Avenida 25 de Setembro, and there was a strict order of march as each group joined the main parade which went past the viewing stand. While we were waiting our turn to join the parade, other groups who were also waiting sang and entertained us. We especially appreciated watching the African National Congress and the South African Council of Trade Union participants. The march was so large that it fell behind schedule, and many marchers wearing batas, unsuitable for such a hot day, were urged to run the entire route in order to keep to the timetable. I finally marched near the end with our small group of Americans and, though we moved quickly, we did not run.

After May Day, and still in Maputo, we went to a variety show one evening, one of many events held in honor of the Party Congress during those weeks. The entrance charge was just 100 meticais for two hours of music and dance.

Chapter 13

The acts included a jazz band that played on water buffalo horns and mixed traditional styles with modern lyrics, such as a song that proclaimed, "There is no place for racism or colonialism in Mozambique." A group of traditional dancers wore red, green, and yellow, the colors of the flag. A dance series included a cross-section of Mozambican society—older, heavyset women with OMM capulanas, exuberant youth, workers in hard hats and coveralls who performed a wonderful *makwayela* (a dance style created in the mining compounds of South Africa), and soldiers in uniform. The finale brought everyone together to march through the audience with flags flying. The socialist politics was not subtle, and it was thrilling to share the excitement and sense of purpose and possibility.

Endnotes

1 Much of my analysis of why I had difficulties gaining support from scholars at the Centro de Estudos Africanos (CEA) is confirmed in later reports, though at the time I knew little to nothing of their political and intellectual conflicts. For a critique of the internal politics in the early 1980s at the CEA, see Christian Geffray, "Fragments d'un discours du pouvoir (1975-1985): du bon usage d'une méconnaissance scientifique," *Politique Africaine* 29 (1988): 71-85; and see two reports by Carlos Fernandes, "History Writing and State Legitimisation in Postcolonial Mozambique: The Case of the History Workshop, Centre for African Studies, 1980-1986," *Kronos*, no. 39 (2013): 131–157, and "Regional and Local Dynamics in the Shaping of the Centre for African Studies in Maputo, 1976–1986," *Journal of Southern African Studies* 41, 3 (2015): 581-597. Observations about the center, the scholars working there, and their research program can also be found in Manghezi, *The Maputo Connection*, 89-94.

2 Kathleen Sheldon, "Creating an Archive of Working Women's Oral Histories in Beira, Mozambique," in *Contesting Archives: Finding Women in the Sources*, ed. Nupur Chaudhuri, Sherry J. Katz, and Mary Elizabeth Perry, 192-210 (Champaign-Urbana: University of Illinois Press, 2010).

3 Sitoe worked as an editor at *Notícias* for many years, and in 2021 was appointed to chair the national watchdog committee, Conselho Superior da Comunicação Social (Higher Mass Media Council, CSCS); *Club of Mozambique* (10 May 2021).

4   Merle Bowen, *The State Against the Peasantry: Rural Struggles in Colonial and Postcolonial Mozambique* (University Press of Virginia, 2000).

Chapter 14
Hamburgers in Mbabane

May 1983

We were able to travel to Swaziland (later called Eswatini) after the end of the Party Congress. It is a mountainous, land-locked nation that had fewer than one million residents in the 1980s. Though an independent kingdom, it was economically dependent on South Africa, its much larger and much wealthier neighbor that surrounded it except for a seventy-five-mile border with Mozambique. An official slogan, in marked contrast to that of Mozambique, was "Swaziland and Private Enterprise Together." We arranged a ride in a car belonging to Captain Starck, a Swedish pilot who worked for the United Nations. He told us, "I've worked in various parts of Africa for the past forty years, and this post in Mozambique is the most difficult." The four-hour trip was uneventful and, despite a lot of anticipatory apprehension, we had no trouble at all at the border, where the crossing was facilitated by Captain Starck's experience and position. The roads, which were in poor condition in Mozambique, became downright dangerous once we were on the remarkably twisty unlit route through the mountains of Swaziland, which had one of the worst car accident rates on the continent.

We stayed in Mbabane, the capital, a pleasant town of about 20,000 people, with ample hotels, restaurants, and well-stocked shops—all novelties to us after the months in

Mozambique. Our hotel was the centrally located Tavern Hotel and for the first time in months we enjoyed taking regular hot showers, eating three big meals each day, and browsing through the stores along Mbabane's main street where we enjoyed using our Mastercard to buy supplies and food.

Visits to the local OK Bazaar shopping mall were a special treat. I felt some ambivalence when faced with so many consumer goods, as the stores presented a stark contrast to the barren shelves just across the border in Mozambique. And although I appreciated the chance to stock up, I was anxious about the money we were spending. It was not excessive, but it was more than we had spent for nearly a year. That was even noticed by our bank back in California, which called my mother to let her know that after nearly a year of inactivity, high credit card charges were suddenly appearing from Swaziland.

Lunch was sometimes hamburgers at the local Wimpy's, though we had a greater appreciation for the choices at Italian, Indian, and French restaurants. We snacked at the Indingilizi Gallery, a craft shop where they served pie filled with sweet crisp apples and covered with creamy custard, and Mercie had vanilla ice cream with real strawberry sauce. No doubt seeking to compensate for the limited diet in Beira, Mercie ate huge quantities, especially from the buffet breakfast at the hotel, which included juice, cereal, cheese omelets, toast, sausage, bacon, and grilled tomatoes. Most mornings she had three pieces of toast (cold from sitting in the British-style toast rack), two or three scrambled eggs, plus juice, a notable meal for a two-year-old. We reveled in our ability to choose how we wanted our eggs prepared, and that there were two kinds of meat set out each morning.

For supper one evening we went out to the Likhaya Restaurant, which was located in a Holiday Inn and was reputed to have a "Swazi" atmosphere. But we found it to be very western, complete with electronic music and a Portuguese singer. The "Swazi" ambiance was provided by the waiters, who wore the traditional piece of cloth tied at

Chapter 14

one shoulder. We had observed that Swazi young people not only wore traditional dress, but usually spoke Swazi, in contrast to urban young men in Mozambique wearing slacks and shirts and speaking to each other in Portuguese. On another evening out, in an Italian restaurant, we noted two older men in a booth near us, both wearing the typical red cotton cloth knotted at their shoulders. The next morning, a photo of one of them was on the front page of the newspaper, as he was the minister for foreign affairs. Still, it felt strange to be eating lasagna and cannelloni in Africa, with "Saturday Night Fever" blaring in the background.

We rented a car and drove through the modest Mlilwane Wildlife Sanctuary. Though it was small enough to occasionally see the fence that kept the animals inside, we welcomed the opportunity to observe antelope, Cape buffalo, wart hogs that ran across our route, zebra, and even a rhino (which was mostly hidden). At a rest camp inside the preserve, we spotted a hippo and a crocodile in a pool, plus tame blue cranes wandering around. On the return to town, we stopped to admire the twin Matenga Falls. Mercie missed most of the sights because she fell asleep in the back seat. It was funny that in an English-speaking country Mercie displayed her increased Portuguese vocabulary, saying "*pato*" for shoe (*sapato* in Portuguese) and exclaiming "*mashibonja!*" for *machimbombo*, the Mozambican word for bus, when she spotted a parking lot full of buses near our hotel. One of my favorite words, machimbombo was supposedly derived from the English for machine pump, though an equally likely explanation suggests the word's root is from the Zulu word *ibhomba*, which signifies the direction in which a traveler is going.

We went on a scenic drive through Swaziland's mountains, though we did not go to the highest summit, which was over six thousand feet. The road traversed the Usutu Forest, a pine forest planted in evenly spaced rows as a source of lumber and pulp. Though some sections were lovely, we also saw many cleared patches and drove by the unlovely pulp mill. In the middle of the woods, close to nothing but trees, we were stopped by a Swazi police officer who was doing vehicle inspections on a road where our car was the only one in sight. Just as he waved our car to the side of the road, Steve remembered that his wallet with his driving license was in a jacket he had left in the hotel room. The officer spoke little English, but he managed to indicate with gestures that we should activate our turn signals, which was when we discovered that our rental car's left front light was out of order. With visions of a prolonged bureaucratic encounter at best and remembering stories of people spending time in foreign jails for similar offenses, we began to try to talk with the officer. We did not make much progress with his meager English and our non-existent Swazi, so in the end he just waved us on, and we felt we had experienced a narrow escape.

Our trip back to Maputo was a day-long odyssey by bus. Swazi buses often had slogans and names painted on the front, such as "Choose Yours" and "Love Him," though ours was sloganless. We left Mbabane at 10:00 A.M. and first stopped in Manzini, where Mozambicans returning home from shopping trips loaded the roof of the bus with sheets of corrugated tin roofing, window frames, and even lumber for a house. The bus was filled with people bringing back fifty-kilogram sacks of cornmeal and all sorts of other goods, as we were ourselves, having stocked up on canned tomato sauce, a case (twenty-four jars) of White Rhino peanut butter, dried beans and lentils, two kilograms of rice, mosquito coils, and toothpaste. We even bought Mercie a new bathing suit and splurged on a Rita Marley cassette tape.

The ride was long, much of the road was unpaved, and Mercie sat on Steve's lap most of the way. At the border, the entire bus was unpacked, checked over, and repacked. The passengers were mainly African, though we met two British female cooperantes who had bought supplies in Swaziland. We stopped at periodic roadblocks, and young soldiers walked the aisles of the bus checking everyone's papers.

Chapter 14

Mercie figured out the routine and amused the soldiers by offering her photo identification for inspection though they had not requested it.

When we reached Maputo, we were not sure where to disembark. The bus stopped at various places throughout the city, and people would get off the bus and load their goods onto the two-wheeled handcarts that could be hired. Our situation was further complicated because the phone at George Povey's apartment was out of order, so we could not call Hans and Liliana to meet us at one of those regular bus stops. We rode to the end of the line, thinking we could call someone from the terminal, only to discover that the bus company phone was also out of order. It was dark already at seven in the evening, and we feared we would be stranded. Eventually one of the bus company managers, a Frelimo member, took pity and gave us a ride in his truck to the apartment, saying it was the least he could do to thank us for coming so far to help his country.

The next day we flew home to Beira, where we were met by Steve Boyle and by a driver from the Ministry of Health. Being welcomed back by two people reinforced our sense that Beira was becoming our home. And everything was fine at our apartment, as there had been no problems while we were away. A lot of mail had arrived, including two Christmas packages; one from my sister Barbara had been en route for seven months! Jacky and Steve, the Brazilian cooperante Juarez, and our neighbor Isac all stopped by to say hello, and we caught up on the news with Gerri and Murray Dickson. They left Mozambique two months later, in July 1983, though they remained active with Mozambican issues and returned with other development projects in later years.

We did learn that Francisco had been caught without his identity documents when a bus in Manga was stopped at a check point. Since we were away, there was no one to wonder where he was or what had happened to him. He spent eight days in jail, emerging with close-cropped hair and looking a bit thinner. When we asked how the food had been in jail, he would only say, "Era muito confusão" (There was a lot of confusion), a sentiment we often heard to describe a variety of situations.

Chapter 15
Health Care for the People

May to July 1983

Steve was feeling overwhelmed by the waves of malnourished children at the hospital and arranged to work one or two days a week in neighborhood health posts in Inhamudima and Munhava, where he knew he would see many more children but hoped they would be healthier than those who arrived at the hospital. Those small clinics served a huge number of patients; an average morning brought in over one hundred children, who were mostly seen by the nurses. Steve often saw more than thirty children in four hours, sometimes as many as seventy, and one morning he faced over eighty children waiting to be seen in a few hours, an unimaginable patient load from the perspective of the United States. When he worked at a Los Angeles County clinic in La Puente, he never saw more than seventeen patients in a morning of work. In the last month or two of our stay in Mozambique, Steve worked at the Ponta Gêa health post, an easy walk from our apartment and in much better condition than the decrepit state of the little posts in Munhava and Inhamudima. At Ponta Gêa he had a floor fan to cool the air and the doctor's chair was not broken, both major upgrades in standards.

Access to child health care was expanding in a remarkable manner. We were told that in Beira in 1981, just two years earlier, there were only one thousand child visits to a health care provider, including vaccinations, illness, and all the other reasons for a visit. By 1983 the number had grown to ten thousand, mainly a result of strenuous Frelimo government initiatives, including a massive program to vaccinate every child. But that rapid growth explained some of the shortages of medicines and supplies.

I accompanied Steve one morning to observe his practice at the small clinic in Inhamudima, a neighborhood about two miles past the governor's house and an uncomplicated bike ride from our building in Ponta Gêa. We took a round-about route that morning so we could see more of the surroundings, but as Steve described his usual route, writing in his journal, "I ride through the neighborhood along narrow dirt paths with a few zillion kids running behind yelling 'cooperante' or 'mzungo' (white man). I go past the open drainage canal used as a communal dump and toilet (wonderful aroma) and turn left at the third trash pile."

The area was densely packed with about fifteen thousand people living in mostly substandard housing. Though there were a few cinder-block homes, most were mud-and-wattle, with walls built from wooden strips fitted with stones and mud; all sported tin roofs and were surrounded by reed fences enclosing small courtyards. In the yards we could see tables fashioned from odd sticks and boards and women tending cooking fires. I saw little evidence of gardens with vegetables growing, though some flowers appeared. Children drew in the dirt with sticks, and families sat in their yards eating breakfast. Women with large tins gathered around the communal water faucet. Tiny twisting lanes went off in all directions, and though I could not see any order to the residences, every door had a number painted on it.

The health post was in a small mud-and-wattle building, a counterpart to the homes in the area. Steve saw a succession of children accompanied by their mothers and, in only two cases, their fathers. An older male nurse, Gimo, assisted him. Gimo had about thirty years' experience, spoke several Mozambican languages, and was indispensable. He was extremely proud of his daughter, who was a medical student in Maputo. We learned a few years later that his

Chapter 15

daughter was killed in an automobile accident in Maputo. Gimo was devastated; in his loss he turned to alcohol and became incapacitated himself.

Figure 10: Steve with nurses at the Inhamudima clinic, 1983.

The primary problems that Steve saw that morning were malnutrition (in mothers as well as children), asthma, diaper rashes, allergic reactions, and a lot of ear infections. One boy was deaf due to a high fever he had suffered the previous year, possibly from meningitis. A mother brought in a newborn with a sixth finger that had not dropped off on its own accord. Gimo helped not only with treating the patients, but with translating between Portuguese and Chisena (spoken locally) or Bitonga (spoken by people from the Inhambane region south of Beira). The last family that Steve saw that morning had just moved to Beira from Inhambane four months before. The daughter had kwashiorkor, a result of the limited diet. The mother said they had been eating only massa, and she could not answer when asked how she would manage to feed the child over the next few weeks. The irony—and mystery—was that she should have had access to a more varied diet, as her husband worked for Pescom, the government fish distribution and marketing company.

Several months later, Steve was again on a schedule of seeing patients at various health posts. One woman came to see him at the Inhamudima clinic with her eight-month-old infant, and she was pregnant again. He learned that her husband had passed away before the birth of the eight-month-old, and his brother had come up from Maputo planning to follow the custom of levirate, in which a widow is "inherited" by her deceased husband's brother. There had been some flexibility in the way that families handled widow inheritance in the past, and often a woman had a right to say "no" to initiating a relationship with her brother-in-law. However, in the patrilineal societies of southern Mozambique, children "belonged" to the father's family and kin, and if the widow distanced herself from her husband's family, she risked losing access to her children. Widows generally entered marriages as strangers and outsiders to the clan, though over time they could become integrated into the daily agricultural work of the women in their husbands' families. A woman who had lived in a community for many years might therefore prefer to remain there if she were widowed, with her children as well as female co-workers and access to land. For certain women, marriage to a brother-in-law might be a desirable way to maintain their position in the village.

It was a custom that was easily abused and was one of the traditional practices that OMM criticized. In the case that Steve saw, it was clear that the family was no longer entrenched in the rural agricultural society that supported the levirate, as the brother had come to Beira simply to lay claim to his brother's widow. Once he had relations with her, he returned to Maputo and left her pregnant, with a tiny infant from her marriage, and with no easy source of support. A female nurse working with Steve was very angry about that unfortunate woman's situation, telling him that was an old custom that needed to end, saying, "It is continued by men so that they can get a little extra." The practice has decreased over time, as women's organizations work to educate women about their rights.

Steve was asked to give a talk about health and sanitation at a militia training camp located on the Golf Club grounds.

Chapter 15

There were about two thousand militia members gathered on the old fairways under the sun, mostly men except for about eighty to one hundred women. I had observed that as younger people were recruited into the militias, the percentage of women appeared to be much larger. One group we saw running along the road bordering the Golf Club looked like teenagers, and they were almost half women (or girls). Steve spoke without a loudspeaker about health and hygiene and answered people's questions. When he raised the issue of birth control, there was a lot of interest from the men there. It was more common for women to learn about family planning when they attended pre-natal clinics, though it was not always easy for women to bring that information back to their husbands or to convince them to use contraceptives. But the men were very interested in learning their options, and felt comfortable asking questions of Steve, who enjoyed the opportunity to do some teaching.

Steve had also been teaching in a more formal setting, leading a pathophysiology course for nursing and physician-assistant students. He enjoyed that task, despite the struggle to teach in Portuguese and without regular textbooks or other supplies. The students had a mimeographed book with some of the material, but Steve used his own English-language textbooks that he had brought from home.[1] He prepared for class by making extensive notes in Portuguese and then writing out the lessons on the blackboard.

Steve was also involved in an immunization program that targeted measles and other childhood diseases. As part of a national effort, neighborhood leaders and clinic staff met to plan the project, and then went together door-to-door to check each child's vaccination card and verify that they were up to date. Most were not, so the injection was administered at a table that had been set up in the middle of the neighborhood. They had organized procedures to keep the vaccine cold, and by administering the vaccine immediately they did not have to worry about making appointments and revisiting children. Measles in Africa is a serious and often fatal disease, and though Mozambique had an extremely successful nationwide immunization program, it needed to be continually monitored as new children were born. It was also one of the programs that was severely disrupted by Renamo attacks on health posts in the rural areas. Steve was especially pleased to participate, commenting that, though there were problems, "it is the ideal program you always read and hear about taking place in a country like Mozambique where health care and the government exist to 'serve the people.' At least in this little tucked away corner of the world it actually seems to work."

Figure 11: Vaccination clinic in Inhamudima, 1983. Photo by Steve Tarzynski.

A few weeks later I accompanied Steve when he was seeing patients at the health post in Munhava, which was more like a health compound, with maternal-child offices, a pharmacy, a laboratory, and a small maternity hospital. I spent most of the morning watching him care for an endless line of small children and their mothers. Steve had learned a few key phrases in Chisena; "Mwana asatapika kangazi lero?" (How long has your child been vomiting?) and "Na panza?" (And

Chapter 15

diarrhea?) were typical examples, though not exactly useful in daily conversation. The mothers were always highly amused to hear the mzungo doctor speak their language, but the African nurses would scold the mothers, telling them to stop laughing and answer the doctor's question.

Many babies were weighed in a cloth scale fashioned like a sling hanging from the ceiling. Dehydrated children were fed the oral solution right there, poured from a recycled Coke can into a small plastic spoon to put into their mouths. One child with severely advanced meningitis died at the hospital that afternoon. It appeared that the parents had taken their child to a curandeiro before coming to the health post, and the father blamed "demons" for the death. But curandeiros were able to understand psychological and cultural issues that might be underlying community members' physical illness and they often were familiar with local herbs and other treatments that were effective. Steve saw one child, the son of the head of Public Works, who had severe eczema that had been helped by a paste made from a root that his mother had obtained from a curandeiro.

Steve also began making weekly visits to the health post at RENAB (Reparações Navais da Beira), the naval dry dock and repair yard, where he monitored some of the occupational safety and health problems. That was interesting for him because it was completely different from pediatrics. The opportunity to go to RENAB was part of a Ministry of Health plan to expand their program in occupational safety and health. At a provincial meeting to inform physicians in Beira about the project, they were told that each of them would be allocated responsibility for one factory. Steve immediately volunteered, claiming rights to the beer factory, much to everyone's amusement. But transportation to that factory could not be arranged, so he was assigned to RENAB.

Figure 12: Steve with workers at RENAB, "Independence or death, we will win," on the wall, 1983.

At the ship repair yard, he would see six to eight workers on each visit, most of them complaining of stomach ailments, aches and pains, pulled muscles, colds, or minor cuts and bruises. He also did inspections of the worksite. He made one request for improvement, for soap and a towel for the RENAB health post, hoping that he could at least initiate regular hand washing in between patients, but after six months there was still no towel or soap on site. One case he handled successfully was a senior manager's addiction to tranquilizers, brought on by the high stress level of the work, a management problem around the world. RENAB also supported Mercie's creche, which was unusual as it was a primarily male workplace and most creches in Mozambique were affiliated with workplaces that had many women workers. As sponsors of the creche, RENAB helped acquire needed supplies and workers had priority in placing their children in the center.

Another workplace that established a creche was the hospital, which inaugurated the space on the first floor of a guest house on the hospital grounds. It had taken the workers only three months to get it organized, and it served sixty

Chapter 15

children. Steve attended the opening ceremony, which was reported in the *Diário de Moçambique*. A red ribbon was cut by a pediatric nurse who was there with her own newborn, and the carpenters who had worked on the modifications were introduced. Toys and other supplies were to be made by patients in occupational therapy, though initially the Swedish and Dutch cooperantes brought donations.

Meanwhile, the war continued. We learned that South Africa had bombed Maputo, which on first hearing was a very frightening event, though it turned out to be a single raid by a squadron of Mirage and Impala fighter jets. They tried to attack Mozambique's only oil refinery, Petromoc, as well as a key bridge over the Matola River on the road that connected Mozambique and Swaziland, presumably the road we had just ridden over. But at both of those sites, Mozambican anti-aircraft installations prevented any damage and drove the attackers away. Other jets attacked residential areas in the Maputo suburbs, where three people were killed, including a five-year-old girl playing outside her home. Three more Mozambicans, including a woman worker who was eight months pregnant, were killed at the Somopal jam factory. Miraculously, no children were injured in the factory creche, though all the creche windows were broken. But life continued, as I walked Mercie to day care in the morning in lovely crisp autumn weather in May. We stopped to listen to the children at the local elementary school sing the national anthem one morning and watched as three companies of new militia recruits jogged past the post office singing and chanting revolutionary slogans.

The government underwent one of its periodic shifts, where mostly the same individuals were moved around to different posts, intending to improve the deteriorating situation. Marcelino dos Santos was appointed as the new governor in Sofala, while Armando Guebuza was moved to be Minister of the Interior, an office he held for only a few months, though he remained one of the eleven members of Frelimo's Political Bureau, the inner circle of the party. The same ten men had been in the Political Bureau since independence, with an eleventh added in 1983. Guebuza continued to be prominent on the national political scene, serving as president of Mozambique for two terms, from 2004 to 2014, and becoming one of the wealthiest men in the country.

Dos Santos was generally considered to be number two in the government and, as he was one of several Central Committee members assigned to posts outside of Maputo, his placement did suggest that the government wanted to improve its relations with the more distant regions of the country. Though it appeared to be an attempt to decentralize, I thought it was even more centralizing, as top national officials were placed in the top provincial positions and Samora Machel personally took over the Ministry of Defense as well as continuing as president. The Central Committee had been enlarged at the Fourth Party Congress, from 67 to 130 members, who were elected at the congress. The new numbers added many women, peasants, and workers, expanding the committee in terms of the members' background as well as in number.

Hope that the situation in Mozambique might improve was evident at the huge rally held at the railway station to officially welcome Marcelino dos Santos. There were about ten thousand people attending, drawn by the desire to see Samora Machel. Many sang and danced in groups before the speeches began. I went with our Irish friend Niall Crowley and Steve stayed home with Mercie. Jacky went with a group from her school where she taught English. But early on she pulled out her camera and was immediately taken off to the side for questioning. The fact that she had neglected to load film into the camera made her situation even worse, as the police wanted to know just what she was up to. Her Steve had been questioned by police a few weeks earlier because he had his camera out and was seen standing too close to the governor's home, so she should have been more aware of the scrutiny from authorities. As it was, she was questioned for three hours, and missed the whole event. I had brought along a camera, but fortunately I never took it out of my backpack, though I did regret that I was not able to photograph Samora Machel.

Samora spoke at length, and I edged my way close enough to see his expressions. He was as dynamic and amusing as his reputation foretold, and the audience responded with great warmth and good feeling. He talked about the importance of Beira to the well-being of the whole country. He pointed out that though the bandits targeted the government when they destroyed schools, health posts, and electric pylons, the real victims were the people. Those who believed that Renamo was only attacking the government had "uma cabeça da galinha" (the head of a chicken), a phrase we adopted for family use to refer to stupidity. He began with a call and response, initiating "*A luta*" (The struggle) and the crowd replying "*continua!*" (continues), as he urged the gathering to yell loud enough to be heard in Maputo. And he frequently broke into song, especially "Kanimambo, Frelimo."

Endnote

1   The mimeographed text was Manual de Patologia Geral para Enfermagem e Agentes de Medicina (Ministério da Saúde, Direcção Nacional de Formação de Pessoal, 1981).

Chapter 16
Mexicana Life

June to August 1983

We were promised that we would be able to move into an apartment on the floor above us that was slightly larger and in much better condition. The existing occupants were the Brazilian physician, Iris, and his wife and three children. His contract was ending, and he was reluctant to return to Brazil. A slight, dark-skinned man with a carefully trimmed beard and warm temperament, he was very cultured and sensitive, and he did not want to contend with the racism he had experienced in Brazil. He was trying to get a contract in Zambia but had a lot of difficulty reaching anyone by phone. After a week of failed attempts, he managed to reach someone in Harare, Zimbabwe, who was supposed to help him make the contact in Zambia. As his English was poor, he asked me to assist in interpreting over the phone, but after forty-five minutes of discussion we still had not managed to connect with Zambia.

One Sunday at the end of May, our neighbor Isac arrived in the early morning to tell us, "Iris está morte" (Iris has died). We thought we misunderstood Isac's Portuguese at first, in a strange reminder of my confusion about the words for dead and bitten. We simply could not believe what he was telling us. Sadly, we finally comprehended that during the night Iris had jumped from the balcony of his apartment on the floor above ours. His efforts to get work elsewhere in Africa had not been successful, and he did not want to return to Brazil. His death left his wife a widow and three small children partly orphaned. It was awful for her as she struggled to make the arrangements to return home without him. Just the day before his death one of his children had seen a thief take Steve's best blue jeans from our clothesline. The child had followed the man and reported back to us but was too small to stop the theft in progress. We were deeply grieved by the loss of our neighbor, friend, and fellow medical cooperante, and we felt so sad for the children.

We moved into their old apartment in June, as had been arranged before the tragedy when we all thought Iris would have a new job outside of Mozambique. We really appreciated the new space, with two balconies on the front of the building, two bathrooms, and a more workable kitchen. Not only was it larger, it also boasted a functioning stove, a better refrigerator, and usable cupboards. We were helped in our move by several of our neighbors, including Nicolai, a Soviet physician who also brought us milk, Isac, and a Cuban couple, Roberto (an internist) and Marta (a dentist). Though most of our friends who were helping us move were considerate, a couple of visitors wanted to go and look over the balconies, and one person (not anyone mentioned here) even asked me, "From which balcony did Iris jump?" I had no idea and would not answer such a tactless question in any case.

Our lives were beset with a variety of mostly minor troubles during those months. We got a letter one day from our friends Bob and Peggy, who were caring for our cat, Thika. They had found her unconscious under a bush and though she had no obvious injuries, she died soon after. They felt terrible, and had a veterinarian perform an autopsy so they could let us know the cause of death, but it appeared that she had simply been hit by a car. That was very sad news for us, we missed her very much, and once again it emphasized our distance from home, family, friends, and everything familiar.

Chapter 16

We left our bicycles in the front lobby of the Mexicana one day while we had lunch. They were locked on chains and there was a *guarda* always present at the door, but when we went down to retrieve them our lovely lights that ran on pedal power had been stolen. None of the men standing around admitted to seeing anything, including the man who was paid to watch the building. The thief took only my front light but had stripped off the entire assembly of dynamo and wires from Steve's bike.

One evening we found Francisco in a confused state of mind. He was with a friend in the small room he sometimes used in our building, and we left them overnight, thinking that he was drunk (unusual for him) and would sleep it off. But in the morning, he was still in bad shape and was hallucinating, so Steve consulted with Joseph, a neighbor who was a mental health technician from Zambia. On his advice, Steve took Francisco to the emergency room for treatment. We eventually learned that he had drunk *nipa*, a local brew that he bought from a curandeiro. When Steve found the juice bottle used for the *nipa*, it held a foul-smelling clear liquid with what looked like bits of tree bark floating in it. Francisco remained in the hospital psychiatric ward for several days recovering from his experience, while we took over the cleaning and cooking and hired a neighbor's empregado to help with the laundry.

Francisco and his friend Horácio were waiting at a bus stop in Manga on a Sunday evening a few weeks later when they were picked up again by the militia, who were overzealous in their sweeps of the streets for vagrants and potential recruits. Young men were especially vulnerable. Francisco had all his papers in order, having learned his lesson from his previous encounter, but he and Horácio were both taken to police headquarters where they languished for a day or so. We did not know what had happened to him and could not locate him until eventually we heard through the grapevine (perhaps from the Swedes who might have had the news from their own empregado) that he was in jail. Steve went out to the police station, found both friends sporting bruises from the rough handling by the militia, and succeeded in getting them released.

The markets suddenly had food in June that we had not seen for months. We never really comprehended the erratic supply of food that apparently depended on how the agricultural season intersected with Renamo incursions on rural roads, though June was the season for harvesting fruit and vegetables. Oranges, lemons, and grapefruit were for sale and, one day, when I found avocados and a big zucchini at one of the Indian-owned vegetable shops, I marveled that I could buy two different items on the same day. Another day I found a Muslim store selling eggplant. In the course of a single week, I bought squash, tomatoes, cucumbers, turnips, cabbage, and grapefruit. Everyone was buying coconuts, shaking them to check for freshness, and carrying them home by the long cords still attached to the rough outside husk. The feeling of a new plenitude was substantiated by dozens of white egrets that stopped over at the swamp behind our apartment building, spending a few days there before continuing their migration.

It did not last for long. Francisco waited nearly two hours for sausage at the cooperative in a line so big he called it a *bichão* (the "-*ão*" ending indicating large size). Just as he reached the front, a group of people he described as "Portuguese" pushed their way to the front counter and bought up the remaining supplies, and he came back empty-handed and distressed. The father of one of Steve's patients connected us to an egg supplier, and we acquired more eggs when a group of medical *cooperantes* were awarded a special authorization from the Ministry of Health that allowed us to purchase eggs outside of the ration system. Several of us went on a shopping expedition to the egg distribution warehouse. The managers were all away when we arrived, however, and we waited around for most of the afternoon until someone in authority came along. Then we had to repack the eggs we purchased, removing them from

Chapter 16

their protective egg cartons and placing them helter-skelter into used boxes for the trip home. That was a successful venture, as I scored sixteen eggs that day, and we were all grateful for the protein.

Steve and Jacky made a trip to Zimbabwe to stock up on necessities and luxuries. They brought back a large steak—actual tender meat!—which we all shared at a dinner to mark the halfway point of our stay. With the grilled steak we had crisp-edged scalloped potatoes, and chocolate mousse made from a packet for dessert, with copious amounts of gin and wine to accompany the banquet. As I commented in my journal, it was very much a divisas meal, as everything had been bought with foreign exchange.

Packages came in June with food and gifts from my parents, one for my June birthday, and the other with Easter candy and plastic cars for Mercie. The Easter box had been sitting at the customs office for weeks, but we had never been notified of its arrival. When I asked the agents why we had not been informed, they decided we should pay an extra fee as a holding charge, since they had had to keep it there! My Portuguese had improved to the point that I could argue my way out of paying the fee, and they let me leave with my goodies.

The following month a lot of mail came, including letters from my mother, a T-shirt from Barbara for Mercie, and letters from other family members and from friends. My dissertation advisor, Ned Alpers, was traveling in Mozambique with his son Joel. He had been doing research in Maputo and was supposed to have a stopover at the Beira airport, but by the time I got his itinerary the date had passed. He was arranging to send me some publications, which I was desperate to receive.

My parents had sent large square six-volt flashlight batteries, and I made three trips out to customs to free the batteries from custody. As the batteries were nearly five inches long and over two inches square, the customs workers believed that they were not simple batteries, but

The Mackerel Years

were voltage regulators that I was shiftily trying to import. They wanted to charge an import duty of 425 meticais (over $10.00) and no one wanted to take responsibility for releasing them without collecting the fee. But every time I rode my bicycle out to their offices the chief was not there. Finally, someone believed me when I insisted that they were simply *pilhas* (batteries) for a flashlight and let me take them home.

We more easily retrieved a luxury item that arrived—a hot water shower head, ordered from Brazil through our Brazilian friends. It was only $7.00, and it was a miraculous invention. We attached it to the showerhead where it worked like an immersion heater, with a wire running along to the electrical outlet. It seemed enormously dangerous, but when properly installed and grounded it was fantastic, directly heating the water that was used for the shower. We no longer had to heat pots of water on the stove for a lukewarm bath, which never succeeded in truly cleaning any of us.

Months later I received, by registered mail, a third notice informing me of a box being held at Encomendas Postais, an office of postal packages that was separate from customs. That turned out to be the parcel of photocopied articles and the book on *Women and Work in Africa* that Ned had sent to me from Maputo in July, held hostage by the post office for the intervening months. Encomendas was an unpredictable office. One morning, I was unable to collect several packages they were holding. One that was addressed to me was in a locked cabinet and the person with the key was not there. Another that was addressed to Steve could not be retrieved because I needed to have his identification papers with me. On another visit, an old man behind the counter, who I described in a letter to my mother as "somewhat loony," claimed they were closed even though the door was open and there were minutes to spare before the 5:00 P.M. closing time. As he spoke to me, he reached under the counter and placed the Encerrado (Closed) sign on the counter. I was saved by the arrival of another worker who recognized me and sharply told the old

Chapter 16

man, "Give *a senhora* her packages!" Later during our stay, I received a notice about a package they were holding for me at Encomendas, and when I went to pick it up, I was told that the person with the key had left. When I asked, "Why didn't he leave the key with someone else?", I was told that they did not trust each other! By that time, we knew about the big scandal involving the theft of overseas packages, so apparently the man with the key was aware of what was going on.

That same week there was an article in the Sunday paper, *Domingo,* about chefes e responsáveis que nunca está (chiefs and responsible people never being available). The article listed a selection of the usual phrases, which had become very familiar to us: Já saiu (He has already left), Ainda não chegou (He has not arrived yet), and Está numa reunião (She is in a meeting). Often people would equivocate, saying, "It seems that he has left," or "It appears that she is in a meeting," thus avoiding the problem of outright lying. The drawing accompanying the article showed an empty desk with a sign on it saying "Não estou aqui" (I'm not here).

On June 1st, International Children's Day, children were out in the streets enjoying the day that focused on them. It appeared that every child in the city had a balloon. There was a small party at Mercie's creche also. She was very happy there and got bored on the days I kept her home when she seemed a bit ill, or if the electricity was cut, making the creche less safe. On those mornings, after what felt like hours of playing, reading, building with blocks, going for a walk, and coloring, I would check my watch to discover that it was only 10:00 A.M. and the whole day stretched out ahead of us. For several days in July, wintertime, Mercie had a cough and stuffy nose, so I kept her home. The weather was beautiful with a deep intensely blue sky, crisp air, billowing navy-blue sea, and all the clouds swept away after several days of rain. After the rain passed, a woman extended the *machamba*, a cultivated plot of land behind the apartment building, hoeing away the weeds and turning the soil, getting ready to plant maize and manioc. Men dressed in ragged shorts appeared in the swampy area and cut the reeds, tying them in bundles to carry off for housing and fences in the bairro do caniço.

Mercie was learning adult behavior by watching the Mozambican women around her. She would hold her Tiny Tears doll to her chest and say, "Eat, eat." She often wrapped her dolls and carried them on her back, telling Steve, "Meesie carry baby back." And she copied us, taking her plastic Mickey Mouse music box that only played "It's a Small World" endlessly, and twisting the dial saying, "I can't find BBC!", mimicking our own daily effort to get a good connection on the short-wave radio. She hit her toy phone against the wall, as she had seen us doing to try to make our regular phone work. When talking on her play telephone, she would say "estou sim," the typical Portuguese greeting of "I'm here," and she liked to sit on our balcony and greet passersby by saying "boa tarde" (good afternoon). Her English vocabulary was also increasing, including "pe-oh" for peanut butter, and "bees," which took me several days to realize was "please." She would also shape toys out of her blanket, pretending that it was a dog and making it say "Woof, woof."

Mercie had more opinions as well, declaring "It's good!" about a meal of rice and vegetable sauce, and pleasing Mozambicans by saying "wogo" for "até logo" (until later). She learned a new song at creche about "Todos os patinhos, sabem bem nadar, Cabeça para o baixo, rabinho para o ar" (All the little ducklings, they know how to swim, head down, little tail in the air) and she was walking around the apartment like a duck, saying "Qua, qua, qua." For a long time, we could not figure out what the words were supposed to be, as she sang them "Sabe bem verdade cabeça da galinha!" (He knows the truth chicken head!). Another animal song was "Somos pintos, piu, piu, piu" (We are chicks, peep, peep, peep), with many verses (We

Chapter 16

are chicks, little chicks... we all go into the yard... we all run to get the peas... let's eat, peep, peep, peep). Later she sang "Vamos brincar" (We're going to play)—her version was, "Mommies bring car." She liked to play creche with her dolls and stuffed animals, having them perform creche activities, including the frequent game of going to the bathroom. She often had to change the clothing on a doll when it "fez xixi" (made pee pee). Sometimes we would play a post office game in which she would deliver pieces of paper to us, and we would make up a letter to "read" to her. One day I pretended to read a message that said, "Write and tell us all about your creche," and she proceeded to talk in great detail about eating *pão* (bread), playing with other children who she named, and singing songs about "qua qua qua," birds flying, and planting a garden.

For a while we were the only ones who could understand her funny mixture of English and Portuguese and her odd pronunciations. She had trouble with "s" in combination with other letters, so sweater was "fetter," slipper was "fitter," and spoon was "foon." She was becoming very particular about how her blocks were stacked and how blankets were wrapped around her dolls. She would cry from frustration, and then ask us to dry her eyes by saying "Tears on cheeks." She began treating her dolls for illness, a precursor of her desire to become a physician like Steve. And she would "read" books to her dolls, telling them animatedly that Scuffy the Tugboat was a "Nice boat!" She also enjoyed the Portuguese children's books we had found, a favorite being *Os Três Macaquinhos* (*The Three Little Monkeys*). She mixed her languages, saying "I bebbing água" when she was drinking water (correct Portuguese would have been "Eu bebo água"), or when we played with her, she would call out, "Be careful, I fall on my cabeça!" (cabeça meaning "head").

One day when I collected her at her creche and all the children were yelling "Ta ta" to her, she turned around and in perfect Portuguese said, "Vou para a casa com mama, ouviu?" (I'm going home with my mother, you hear?). She also picked up the habit of saying "macaco" (monkey) when she was annoyed about something or somebody. We guessed that the teachers at her creche called the children monkeys when they were misbehaving, or maybe the children called each other monkeys; in any case it did not seem to have the connotation of cuteness that we sometimes meant in English when we said, "You little monkey!" Mercie would mutter "macaco" under her breath like a swear word. Like toddlers everywhere, she also started ignoring us when she did not want to do what we asked. She would just close her eyes and stand there, as if we were out of sight, out of mind, out of reach.

Chapter 17
Talking with Nurses

June to August 1983

My research was advancing, though it was frustrating to see how little I had accomplished in one year. Dr. Rui Bastos introduced me to his wife, Balbina dos Santos, a historian who had a short-term job with the national historical archives. She was sorting uncatalogued books and papers at the Municipal Library and determining what should be stored in the national archive in more permanent and secure conditions. She invited me to join her on the second floor of the library and have a look for myself before the items were sent to Maputo. That was a wonderful opportunity for me, as the large open room was filled with shelves and boxes of old books and files that were not catalogued or otherwise available to library users. Balbina further assisted by setting aside material she thought might particularly interest me such as booklets and reports about the chartered Mozambique Company. That floor of the library also housed various historical artifacts, including one of the wheeled benches that had once run along rails through Beira, pulled by African men, and which I had seen in photographs at the national historical archive in April.

I went out to the hospital and arranged to interview a midwife and a nurse who worked in the blood bank. I was able to sit with each of the nurses at a table and position the tape recorder for comfortable use. They arranged to take time off from their work and spend an hour or so answering my questions, and I began to feel more competent in my pursuit of women's history. Laura Saraiva, the midwife, was a good choice for one of my first attempts, as she was chatty and interested in talking about her work history. She had entered nursing training in the 1950s in Maputo and had always had the goal of practicing as a midwife. After twenty years of moving from one clinic to another throughout southern Mozambique, she settled in Beira. She described a busy day of delivering thirty-four babies, commenting, "We didn't have time to rest." She was pleased that the expansion of health services under Frelimo had brought more women to the maternity centers for proper care before and during their deliveries: "Now everyone comes here and we are always busy, though some women have to sleep on the floor because we don't have enough beds."

I spent part of one morning with Lucinda dos Santos, a fifty-six-year-old midwife at the clinic in Ponta Gêa who had worked in the colonial health service for the railway company. She told me about the indignity of the segregated system of that time: "When a white woman came in, I could not give that white woman an injection. The bed—there was a sheet where a white woman would rest when she had the injection. When a black woman came in, wasn't it so, when a black woman rested there, we had to take off that sheet for another, because we could not mix them." After independence she was promoted, though she tried to say that the head nurse should be a man. She was told "No, the people chose you to be chief," and so she remained as head nurse at the railroad, Caminhos de Ferro, a place she described as being "the center of racism" in the colonial era.

When I asked how conditions had changed following independence, Lucinda particularly cited the new opportunities she had for continuing education. She regretted the years lost when she could not extend her knowledge, and she was enjoying the seminars and other courses where she could learn about new medicines and improved treatment methods: "Now we always study, always learn." But she

Chapter 17

was not happy about the problems everyone was facing, mentioning that sometimes there was no food for breakfast, and everyone was spending so much time waiting in line to buy food that work was paralyzed. As a working woman, she faced difficulty in finding the time to stand in line, explaining that, "Food is very difficult now, we who work, who don't have a household worker to wait in line for us—hunger. Hunger! I leave here at mid-day, the store is already closed. I leave here at 5 P.M., already there is no food. I arrive home, there is no food." She explained that she was Muslim, and it was especially hard during Ramadan, as she could not eat during the day but at night could only find tea, and that was not enough to sustain her.

Lucinda was a member of OMM, and she said the group's main problem was a lack of materials for organizing. Any project that was suggested faltered. "They wanted to make food to teach other women how to make that food. There were no supplies. They wanted to crochet, no supplies. They wanted to embroider, no supplies." Often the projects that OMM sponsored, as with the macramé bags for the Party Congress, were typically female activities. They did not meet any western feminist ideals about revolutionary women and production, but that was not a concern in Mozambique. Women leaders there wanted to involve women in developing a socialist society and they had greater success if they recruited them with schemes that relied on skills women already had or were interested in learning. With the relentless deterioration of the economy, however, even those limited plans were doomed to fail.

I accompanied Steve once again to the health post in Munhava where he saw patients one morning a week. I had arranged an interview with Gilda Amony, a midwife at the Munhava maternity center that was adjacent to the health post. Gilda was ready and waiting for me, a short robust woman dressed in a navy-blue knit dress, bright red kerchief, and gold-colored necklace, clearly indicating her respect for the meeting with me. She was happy to talk with me and we covered a wide range of topics in the interview. She was the daughter of ministers in a Protestant church near Inhambane and her mother had been trained at Chibute, a well-known mission center. She told me that her mother preached when her father was away visiting outlying districts. But her mother did not read Portuguese, so she would read the service in Landim, a term sometimes used for southern Mozambicans also known as Shangaan. The Portuguese did not consider a person to be literate unless they could read Portuguese, but Gilda's mother was clearly an educated woman though she was not recognized as such by the colonial authorities. As Gilda commented, "It was only Portuguese that she did not know. In her language, our language, she knew how to read and write."

Gilda also described in detail the course work she had undertaken in the colonial nursing program in the 1950s, when she had trained in obstetrics. She had been transferred frequently, working as a nurse-midwife in a dozen different maternity centers across southern Mozambique before settling in Beira where she married and had five children, four of whom had survived to adulthood. She left work during the years that the children were very young, returning once they had grown.

She told me how much her work had changed since independence, as the health service was reformed and developed new ways to reach out to the African population. Corroborating Laura Saraiva's observations, she mentioned that under colonialism very few African women had come into the maternity centers for pre-natal care or to deliver their babies, in part because they recognized that they would not receive the excellent health care they deserved in a system that was strictly segregated by race. But in the few years since independence, Gilda said that there were many more patients, and experienced nurses were happy to begin taking the initiative in treating patients. For instance, in a case where a woman was hemorrhaging, they would still call for a physician, but now, "We don't wait until the doctor arrives to resolve the problem of the bleeding. Sometimes when the doctor arrives, the problem is solved, and the patient is already recovering."

I asked if she and her husband, who worked in an office in Beira, pooled their income, and she said that though she knew some people did, she did not. "Men don't think about the future. I have my child; I have my mother who is widowed without family or skills. And the man in our race does not think about the parents of his wife." After a bad experience early in her marriage, she did not give her earnings to her husband, but saved it herself, so she had it available when her daughter married. She was telling me that her worsening arthritis was making it difficult to continue working when she was called away to see a patient just as my tape was ending.

On another visit I interviewed an older midwife at the maternity center in Munhava, but it was a disappointing experience as we simply could not understand each other. With each interview I used a questionnaire to gather background information that included the question, "Como encontrou o seu marido?" (How did you meet your husband?). I had not had a problem with that phrasing, as the topic arose sequentially in a series of questions about the woman's life history and the story of courtship was one that most people liked to share. But *encontrar* in Portuguese could also be interpreted as "to find," and that midwife answered, "Bom"—she found him to be a "good" husband, or perhaps simply in good health! That sort of miscommunication was typical of the entire conversation. I knew that my fluency in Portuguese was improving, but my confidence was briefly undermined by that interview.

The anxiety I felt was seen in an intense dream I had around that time. In the dream I was pregnant and trying desperately to get to a doctor's office. The doctor kept not showing up, and I repeatedly checked my watch. Then there were explosions that we learned were planes bombing Maputo. As Steve, in the dream, went to find out what was happening, I woke up. We deciphered the symbols in the dream to mean that I was waiting for my doctorate, and the dream pregnancy was the dissertation. The obstacles I faced were clear, as wartime conditions continued to make my research and everything else difficult.

Chapter 18
Day-to-day in Wartime Beira

August to September 1983

More and more militia companies were jogging in formation through the city, singing songs. One day Mercie and I watched as ten companies of about one hundred members each went across the bridge over the Chiveve, many led by women. Most had no uniforms and were participating in their work clothes, including one man in blue overalls and a yellow hardhat. All were singing and all were armed, though with ancient rifles that Steve thought might be World War I vintage. I was becoming accustomed to the constant presence of soldiers and weapons throughout the city, and I even felt some reassurance, undoubtedly a false security, that factory workers were trained, though it was obviously a very minimal level of self-defense.

The war continued to ravage the countryside. We were frightened to learn of an attack on a Soviet mining installation in Zambézia that resulted in twenty-four workers being kidnapped and several deaths, including two Soviet engineers. More than once when Steve was covering the emergency ward, he treated people who had been injured in attacks near Gorongosa, including workers for the safari company Safrique. Gorongosa had formerly been a game

The Mackerel Years

park for tourists, but in 1982 it was captured by Renamo and used as their base camp. We heard, and it was later confirmed, that Renamo members were killing the animals for food. It would be many years before Gorongosa could operate as a game reserve again. One night, Steve treated a truckload of twenty-five farm workers who were brought into the emergency room, all suffering terrible wounds to their feet and legs that resulted from their vehicle running over a landmine buried in the road near Gorongosa.

That same emergency room shift brought in an elderly man from the outlying rural areas who had a large tumor, probably a muscle tumor (myosarcoma), in his upper arm. He had never been seen by western-trained medical personnel and, without proper care, the tumor had fungated, meaning it had grown to the size of an American football, had grotesquely deformed his upper arm, and was fed by an array of small arteries that supplied blood to the tumor. A nurse on duty in the emergency room, with good intentions, tried to clean the mass with the ubiquitous Savlon topical disinfectant. But the Savlon dissolved the numerous blood clots that had formed across the surface of the tumor, and the exposed blood vessels started pumping blood all over. For the first and only time in his career, Steve applied a tourniquet to the man's arm above the tumor to stop the bleeding. The patient did not like that very painful procedure, and he fought back. Several nurses jumped on him while Steve knelt on his chest trying to get a sure grip on the tourniquet and secure it tightly to the arm. Everyone was shouting and slipping on pools of fresh blood, as steel trays and other equipment went banging and crashing around the treatment room. Meanwhile, the patient was screaming in his local language and trying to bite Steve. The old man was strong and wiry from decades of manual labor, but, by sheer numbers, members of the hospital staff eventually subdued him and were able to control the bleeding. He was then sedated and the Soviet surgeon who was on call that evening came in to amputate the man's arm. As was so often the case, Steve never learned what happened to that man,

Chapter 18

though he probably simply returned home, either being cured by the loss of the arm along with the malignancy or facing eventual death if the cancer had spread, as there was no possibility of chemotherapy or radiation treatment. In any event, there were no more serious concerns in those pre-AIDS days, and it made for a memorable evening.

Steve had a twelve-hour shift in the emergency room two or three times each month. One evening when he was at the end of his shift and completely exhausted, he was summoned to the pediatric ward to check on a problem. As he felt his way through the hospital, with no lights due to the bandidos sabotaging the electricity yet again, and having left his pocket flashlight at home, he hoped he would not stumble into anyone or anything. And he hoped it would not be a critical problem, as he just wanted to go home. When he got to the ward, he found a nurse at wit's end because he had not been able to start an intravenous line on a small child who was deathly ill with measles. Steve wrote, "In the stinking heat and humidity, with only a smelly kerosene lamp held close to my face, several dozen species of Mozambican insect life crawling over my face and neck, a worried mother holding her gravely ill child, and several student nurses watching, I got that damn I.V. started. And the kid eventually got better days later." Sometimes the outcome made the struggle and hardships worthwhile.

Our nostalgia for a more varied diet was marked by my perpetual journal notes about what we ate, especially when we contrived to have a treat or something unusual. Steve once cared for the wife of the director of Comércio Interno or Internal Commerce in the emergency room and noticed that the director and his wife were both obese. It appeared they did not suffer from the food shortages that the rest of the city confronted. But we received more good fish (not carapau) from our Soviet neighbors Nicolai and Tamara, and that same week we enjoyed a gift of potatoes from the father of one of Steve's patients, a man who was the head of the municipal Department of Public Works.

As the value of the metical fell slightly, Steve was earning a bit less in dollars, making us anxious about even getting food at the Loja Franca, where we had been able to find wheat flour that was not available elsewhere (we stocked up, buying twelve kilograms, about twenty-five pounds). We went one Sunday to the Clube Nautico and had a simple meal of beef slices, potatoes, rice, and beer, even more pleasant because we were with friends, Juarez, Pascal, and Yacine. The Limpus family put on a big party to celebrate Inalla's third birthday, and I particularly noted that three cakes were served. The Limpuses also had trucked in topsoil to their sandy lot and cultivated a garden. They often shared their homegrown lettuce and squash leaves, and we planted a small section for ourselves as well. Another Sunday we had lunch with our Brazilian friends Liziêt and Júlio, where we enjoyed potatoes and more "good" fish. I again suspected they were buying such items on candonga, which we still avoided, though we understood that others felt they had no other option for obtaining enough food for good health. Mercie especially enjoyed playing with Liziêt and Júlio's son, Swahili, who was a bit younger. They kept exchanging little kisses and Mercie acted more babyish to bring herself to his level. That same evening, we were invited to dinner with Swedish medical cooperante Anders Hellstrom and his wife, Marie, but Mercie fell asleep after lunch, so I remained at home with her and Steve went and had a Swedish dinner to complement his Brazilian lunch. It was difficult to take Mercie out in the evening on our bicycles in any case. After Inalla's party, my bike, which had Mercie's seat attached, had developed a flat. We walked most of the way home, carrying her and pushing both bikes.

We found that Francisco was again taking money from the household fund and not buying items for us on our ration card. We missed out on a chance to get rice and cheese, especially annoying when our rice supply was dwindling. Steve had to tell him that he had to get us the money or the

Chapter 18

food, or we would fire him, and while he managed to repay us, we never did get that ration of rice or cheese. We were reluctant to fire him, as the problems were minor and there was no guarantee that a new household worker would be more reliable. And we continued to feel ill at ease about our role as employers. We did not want to slip into a role as harsh demanding bosses, yet it seemed that our good-natured leniency contributed to what felt like abuse. And the lack of food was not Francisco's fault, as there were ongoing organizational problems at the cooperative. One day he waited in line for five hours to buy sausage and two bottles of beer, and another time one of the clerks was injured by a metal can that was thrown when those waiting in line got rowdy.

The medical cooperantes set up a complicated system to obtain a regular supply of milk and cream. Each Sunday morning one family in the group accepted the delivery of a three-foot-high old-fashioned milk tin from the dairy, and over the next several hours other members of the group came with their own bottles to collect their allotment. We typically received two liters of milk and two liters of cream. I began using the cream to make ice cream, which was fine when we had electricity. We all boiled the milk ourselves, being uncertain about the pasteurization process at the dairy. After it cooled, I would beat the cream with sugar and whatever flavoring we had around (cocoa powder was popular) and then freeze it for a great treat. We had not had any ice cream since our trip to Swaziland several months earlier.

The health cooperantes also organized special Friday afternoon excursions to a variety of food warehouses. In late September I was amazed to realize that our refrigerator was almost filled with eggs, tomatoes, cabbage, and fish, though it was the dreaded carapau. The following month the cooperantes group went to Pescom, the fish company facility, and also bought green bananas at the fruit distribution center, which was a huge, dark, and empty warehouse except for one corner piled high with bunches of bananas. When bananas were available, we tended to get too many at one time, but I discovered a recipe for banana cake in the *Joy of Cooking* that was delicious and used up the excess fruit.

Food arrived from Steve's mother, who sent a box with canned food and bags of dried beans by sea. The cans tore all the plastic bags of beans, and they arrived all mixed together in a single plastic bag marked "Provided by Deutsche Bundepost for damaged package," a little clue to the route that mail took to reach us. I sorted the five kinds of beans into their own bags to make it easier to cook them. In another box she sent a lot of tea bags, which was a major export from Mozambique and one of the only items we could find in the shops—it was exactly analogous to sending tea to China.

In October, two more boxes came from our families, with pudding mix, dried fruit, cereal, dried soup mix, and granola bars, which were a special treat. It felt like Christmas, with so many goodies. We were able to buy shrimp from time to time, but they were not the large prawns which we had enjoyed during our first weeks in Beira. Steve became the expert shrimp deveiner, a tedious and disgusting task that involved stripping out the greenish vein down the back of each shrimp. One weekend we made a big pot of spaghetti and shrimp sauce for lunch with Steve and Jacky and Manuel Julien, a visiting Mozambican physician from Cabo Delgado. We had substantial leftovers, which we expected to eat during the week, but Francisco ate half the pot by midday on Monday. After my initial irritation, I knew I could not begrudge him a chance to have an atypical and tasty meal, and to be fair I had not told him that it was off limits. I was simply tired of worrying about food and rations, and Francisco.

One night at dinner with Mike and Ruth Muller, their daughter Marika kept telling Mike to stop drinking his beer. It turned out that the childcare teachers were teaching the children little homilies related to family behavior, such as,

Chapter 18

"Papá não bater mamá, mamá não bater papa" (Papa does not beat mama, and mama does not beat papa). Mike and Ruth sometimes had access to food we could not find on our own. The first time I ate goat was in a stew at the Muller's, and another time they had starfruit, which was shared among a large group of us as a special delicacy. We stood around a table in their backyard and watched as the deeply ridged fruit was sliced crosswise, revealing the reason for its name. I found it a bit tart, and we agreed that it was an acquired taste, but not bad for a change of pace in our limited diet.

Mike was about to be transferred to Maputo, once housing issues were sorted out, and while he and Marika would stay there, Ruth planned to return to England with their baby, Seán, where she could complete a training course in library science.

At a party at the Muller's before they left, I chatted with Steve Gloyd while my Steve stayed home. We had originally met him when we arrived in mid-1982 just as he was leaving at the end of his contract. On this trip he was briefly visiting his old posts just outside of Beira at Mafambisse and Nhamatanda and had traveled to both towns with no problems. Back in the U.S., he established the Mozambique Health Committee, and my Steve served on the board of directors from the beginning. Later called Health Alliance International, it is a highly regarded non-governmental agency based at the University of Washington that organized several successful community health projects in central Mozambique and continues to implement new projects.

I was getting desperate for fiction to read, as I had finished nearly all the books that we had brought with us, everything that family and friends had mailed to us, and many more that we borrowed from English-speaking friends. While I read a lot of mysteries, I also finished *War and Peace* and a huge collection of John Cheever's stories. Steve Boyle read as avidly as I did, and we decided to visit the Golf Club, located in a mostly deserted building on the abandoned colonial golf course near our Ponta Gêa neighborhood. Steve B. negotiated our access to the library with a caretaker, and we found shelves of English-language novels, a legacy of the days when much of Beira's business was in the hands of British Rhodesians. We did get permission to borrow books, and that was a much-welcomed supplement to our reading list, though many of the books were of little interest.

We spent weeks in August without regular water, but that time it was the result of a broken pump in our building rather than sabotage. Under normal conditions such breakdowns were common, and it was always a problem to find the necessary parts and someone with the expertise to make the repair. They attempted to install a new pump and, although it made a terrifying racket and shook the whole building (giving Mercie a nightmare that night), it was not successful. We were able to shower around the corner at Liziêt and Júlio's, who kindly tolerated our intrusion every couple of days. A new pump was installed the following week.

One day I was robbed while waiting in a bicha for oranges at a shop near downtown Beira. Even more frustratingly, the oranges had already sold out and the shop owner was pushing the crowd to make them leave his store. I was holding my nearly empty backpack in my hand in front of me, as I never put it out of sight on my back in a crowd like that. But nonetheless a pickpocket managed to unzip the small outside pocket and lift my wallet and glasses case. The case had my sunglasses, as I was fortunately wearing my regular glasses, but even the sunglasses had prescription lenses. Since my right eye was legally blind, I amused myself by imagining someone thinking they had gotten a great pair of shades that they were then unable to see through due to the lens distortion. My wallet was probably equally disappointing to the thief. I had only about 200 meticais, plus a five-rand note from South Africa. It was a tiny amount of money even in impoverished Mozambique, and I was sure it was quite a bit less than the thief expected to

Chapter 18

find in my wallet. But I did miss the family photos I carried there. In what I assumed was a futile gesture, I reported the theft to the police. I later returned to the police station to file a formal report of the theft. The office matched familiar stereotypes of Third World police stations, with a ceiling fan slowly circulating, numerous flies buzzing at the windows, and people dozing on wooden benches placed along the wall. Two men, one in rags and one well-dressed, told and retold their versions of a bicha altercation. The young police officer who took my report struggled to type up the information, and he listed me as being Latin American and included a calculator among my losses. I sent a copy of that report to our insurance company, which eventually reimbursed me in the amount of $50.00. They showed great faith in accepting that letter as evidence, as there was no letterhead and it was submitted on plain paper, though it included the usual official rubber stamps.

Rob Davies, a researcher at Universidade Eduardo Mondlane in Maputo, visited Beira and gave a talk one evening about regional politics.[1] His specialty was the role of South Africa, and he explained that South Africa had previously planned to have a "constellation of states" in the region, focused on South Africa and including the Portuguese colonies. The constellation idea had been undermined by the independence of Angola and Mozambique in 1975 and, more recently, Zimbabwe in 1980, though in 1983 Namibia (also known as South West Africa) was still under South African control and the small landlocked nations of Swaziland and Lesotho were geographically hostage. Malawi, which bordered Mozambique but not South Africa, was led by the conservative President Hastings Banda and could not always be relied on to be an ally to Mozambique. The Frontline States, comprised of the black majority-ruled countries that bordered South Africa, had formed the Southern African Development Coordination Conference

The Mackerel Years

(SADCC; later known as SADC, the Southern African Development Community) to harmonize their development projects and to counter the "constellation." South Africa's attacks on its neighbors and its support for UNITA (União Nacional para a Independência Total de Angola, the National Union for the Total Independence of Angola) in Angola and Renamo in Mozambique were, according to Davies, largely a result of the apartheid regime's frustration at the collapse of their constellation. We appreciated any news and analysis, as we were surrounded by rumors and it was impossible to sort out real information from speculative gossip.

We did not know that talks were then taking place between Mozambique and South Africa at the Nkomati River near the border between the two countries. Eventually, in March 1984, Mozambique and South Africa signed the Nkomati Accord, an agreement that emphasized Mozambique's dependent status. Seemingly balanced, it stated that neither country would provide backing for armed action against the other from their own territories. That clause should have meant the end of South African support for Renamo, which nonetheless continued for many more years. But Mozambique did limit the African National Congress presence, in a wasted attempt to appease South Africa.

A few months later, Jacky Boyle and I had lunch at the Embaixador with Joe Hanlon and a couple of British journalists. Joe was an American journalist who was based in England. He later wrote several books about Mozambique, edited the informative periodical *The Mozambique Peace Process Bulletin*, and established a network of emailed news stories about Mozambique. I had hoped to learn more current news about the war in Mozambique from the journalists, but none of them were very forthcoming, or perhaps they knew as little as Jacky and I did. They clearly hoped to get new information by asking us a lot of questions about the situation in Beira, but I knew by then that those of us living

Chapter 18

in the middle of events were the least knowledgeable about what was going on.

In early September 1983 we were struck by the news that the Soviets had shot down a South Korean commercial airliner with Americans aboard. We heard the story in a very sketchy form in a BBC radio report, and both the news and the lack of detail heightened our anxiety and reinforced our feelings of loneliness and distance from home. What if a world war ensued, what would happen to us? But that attack also made it clear how small the world really was, as the Soviet workers around us were equally troubled in the following days when it was not clear in what direction U.S.-Soviet relations would turn. One evening we joined our upstairs neighbors, Anatoly and Luba Zaitchouk, for an impromptu supper. They were both Ukrainian pediatricians in their thirties, and we shared a further bond, as they had a daughter about the same age as Mercie and a son aged six, whom they had left in the Soviet Union with family members while they worked in Mozambique. We sat in their darkened living room with a shared sense of sadness and concern, eating canned sardines, sugared nuts from Greece, other delicacies that were flown in by the Soviet government, and drinking vodka toasts to a peaceful future for our children, "Mir, paz, peace."

The following month we were further distressed to learn of the U.S. invasion of the tiny Caribbean island of Grenada. There had been a forcible takeover of the government by a Marxist military officer. The Reagan administration feared that the addition of a new pro-Cuban leader would shift the balance of power in the Caribbean and used the excuse of the presence of one thousand American medical students to plan the incursion. From the U.S. government perspective, it was a successful mission, as the students were rescued (though some later said they had been in no danger and resented having their education disrupted), the loss of life was minimal (nineteen American soldiers, though many more Grenadian and Cuban military were killed in the fighting), and a pro-U.S. government was installed. From our position, living in a poor socialist nation, we found the entire event reprehensible and frightening, and our determination to contribute to international socialism and improved international relations was further fortified.

Endnote

1. Rob Davies is profiled in Manghezi, *The Maputo Connection*, 89-94.

Chapter 19
Talking with Cashew Workers

August to September 1983

I went to the OMM headquarters and spoke with Maria das Dores, one of the provincial leaders of the women's organization, about arranging interviews with women at the cashew factory, called Caju. Given the importance of cashew exports to the Mozambican economy, it was a key workplace to investigate. There were officially about 550 workers at Caju, and 250 of those were women, making it one of the major industrial sites of female employment. Maria das Dores was very supportive and set up a meeting with three women from the factory at the OMM office for later that week. She also said, "They want to talk with you, as they believe that American women are more advanced than women in Mozambique. Mozambican women still think that men are superior." On the appointed day none of the cashew workers showed up, but I did talk with Nalia Ana dos Santos Leão, the OMM secretary for Cheringoma, a town outside of Beira. It was a depressing but informative story.

Nalia had moved out to Cheringoma a year previously, when her husband was transferred there with the railway. She had not expected that she would spend months watching conditions deteriorate. She described machambas of manioc and potatoes, but the *mapira* (sorghum) had died in the drought. She commented that, "The green zones give us nothing, we don't have enough water, and it is not worth the effort" to continually plant crops that never grew enough to be harvested. She told about a bandit attack on June 9 at 4:00 A.M. when five people were killed, including her OMM assistant and that woman's six-year-old child. About thirty soldiers and militia were stationed in Cheringoma, too few to stop the overwhelming Renamo force. The victims included a soldier and a militia member. None of these casualties had been reported in local newspapers.

Nalia also talked about the problems OMM had organizing women. The OMM center was too damaged to use, so she kept the sewing machine in her home. She had samples of baby clothes with her, but she doubted that they could continue that project, as they could no longer obtain cloth or thread. There were internal problems also, as she reported that women used OMM funds to buy food for their families and there was a lot of what she called "intriga," gossip and conniving. She remarked that the enemy blocked all their efforts because people were afraid to go to meetings or do any work for Frelimo. OMM members in Cheringoma were trying to carry on with their projects in prenatal care and children's education, but her statement that "Não temos nada" (We have nothing) summed up the experience of a community just a short ride outside of Beira.

I had a series of mixed-up communications with the women at OMM. First, I went to the office one day thinking that they had transport that I could take to the cashew factory, but they had not been able to arrange that. I returned another day expecting that the cashew workers would meet me there, but that time the OMM women thought thought I was going out to Manga to do the interviews at the factory. On that visit the women in the OMM offices gave me a pile of baby clothes, which they expected me to sell. When I was reluctant to take on that responsibility, they asked me to bring the clothing to a nurse at the maternity ward who would sell the clothes to that ready market. OMM's politics

Chapter 19

were often troubling to me, as I did not see how making and selling baby clothes was a feminist activity, since it combined two of the most conventional roles for women, as mothers and seamstresses. For their part, they saw a way to make a bit of money by filling a need, and they put a lot of energy into sewing children's clothing.

I arranged to hitch a ride on the Health Ministry shuttle (an old Land Rover) out to the cashew factory in Manga, only to learn that the responsável who was supposed to help introduce me at the workplace had gone into town to the OMM office. My frustration was intense, as it seemed I met with crossed wires and obstacles with every attempt to further my research. After one or two instances where I had missed connections, I was extremely careful to spell out the day, time, and place where I planned to meet with someone, but the clearest instructions were subject to misinterpretation. I sometimes complained to Steve that I was there to try to investigate their history, living with unanticipated hardships and barely enough food to get us to the end of the week, and I was stymied at nearly every turn. But I simultaneously felt guilty about my frustration. After all, I had appeared without invitation and inserted myself into everyone else's schedule. Not only were Mozambicans living with many of the same unforeseen hardships, they would remain in Beira while I would be staying only for another twelve months.

But I finally had some success in the cashew interviews. The day that I was told that the cashew responsável was at the OMM building, the Health Ministry driver, Miguel Chifenya, was truly kind and drove me back into the city, where I found Raquel Fernando at the OMM office. I taped an interview with her about her work, with occasional translation help from Maria das Dores. Raquel was the daughter of a man who had worked in the mines in South Africa and a mother who had been a peasant farmer in Inhambane. She married at seventeen and her parents paid bridewealth of a bull, some fish, one sack of rice and one of cornmeal, a five-liter can of cooking oil, and a few other items. But her husband had not paid his taxes to the colonial government and, though they had two children (only one survived childhood), he left Mozambique to find work in one of the neighboring countries in order to avoid the Portuguese authorities. When Raquel did not hear from him, she decided to move to Beira to find work, leaving her child with her parents in Inhambane. In 1967, under Portuguese colonialism, there were very few options for a nineteen-year-old woman with only two years of formal schooling. She found a job doing domestic work for a Portuguese woman in Beira.

When the cashew factory opened in 1973, she heard that they were hiring women. She walked out to the factory on her own and was one of the first to be hired. Over the years since then, she had worked in various departments in the factory. She told me about the separation of male and female work and said that the workers had never discussed the pay rates. But she was glad to talk about the improvements since independence, as she had completed two more years of classes at the factory and was active in OMM, which she described as responsible for the newly implemented maternity leave and the day care center at the factory. When I asked if there was any memory she particularly wanted to share, she remembered how when she worked as a domestic servant her food was not the same as her employer's, "I did not eat with the woman. The food of the woman and the food of the servant were different. The food was not the same. Now, it is the same food," she said approvingly about the end of colonialism and the onset of socialist independence.

On the walk home along the unpaved roads, Raquel asked me if there were women's organizations in the United States. I responded that there were, but they were not part of the government structures as OMM was, and in fact the president at that time, Ronald Reagan, was opposed to issues related to women's rights. Raquel suggested that perhaps when I returned, I could bring my experience in Mozambique to help organize American women. I agreed

Chapter 19

that I had a lot to learn from Mozambican women, though I did not say that I was unsure just how I might transfer the lessons.

As I walked home through Matacuane neighborhood, a dozen children began tagging along, pleading for food and toys, and asking who was I and what was I doing? Then rain started to pour down and I got soaked. I held out my thumb in the international request for a ride and a small old black car stopped to give me a lift. The driver was a middle-aged man of Portuguese descent, and he immediately commented, "So, you are going to the Mexicana?" He also knew that I had a connection to the hospital, a reminder of what an insular town Beira was, where the Americans were known to nearly everyone. As Steve and I rode our bicycles downtown one day on a regular trip to the shops and the post office, a small boy called out "O casal americano!" (The American couple!), confirming that we were recognized around town as the only Americans. Another time Steve Boyle and I were in the local INLD bookstore (Impresa Nacional de Livros e Discos, the National Book and Record Company), where I collected my *Tempo* magazine, and Steve overheard the clerks talking about me after I left. They knew that I was American, that my husband was a doctor, that I had a child, and other details about my life. Though I stopped in every week to pick up my subscription, I did not recall ever having a conversation about those topics with them. The constant attention and sometimes rude stares were tiresome, but there was nothing that could be done about it.

I continued with the cashew factory interviews, with major support from Miguel, the driver for the health workers. If there was room in the truck, he was happy to take me along, and I traveled the whole circuit with him as he dropped physicians, nurses, and medical technicians off at the health posts and maternity centers in Chingussura, Manga, and Inhamízua, the most distant. Sometimes people in far flung suburbs would climb in for a lift back to town. I enjoyed the ride despite being bounced around in a Land

Rover with worn-out shock absorbers on mostly unpaved roads, as I was able to simply observe more aspects of life in Beira. Women wrapped in faded capulanas were out hoeing their machambas and crowds of people were walking along the verge, balancing bundles on their heads as they carried supplies to the market or back home. Wild grasses and spindly papaya trees lined the route.

Figure 13: Cashew workers at the Beira factory, 1983. Photo by Kathleen Sheldon.

The next time I went out to the cashew factory, there was no sign of Raquel. I went to the management offices, but there were very few people around because the factory had been closed. The war had interrupted the transport of cashews, which were mostly from trees owned and tended by individual farming families. With no cashews, there was no work at the factory in sorting and packaging the nuts. Even though there were no nuts to process, a few women continued to come by the site where they had planted a small plot of sweet potatoes. The factory was being managed by the government, as cashews were a major source of foreign exchange, amounting to one-third of all foreign exchange income during the best years in the 1970s. The government plan was to keep some workers on the payroll in the expectation that cashews would return and workers would be recalled. The cashew workers were still drawing a salary while they worked on factory fields. One small field adjacent to the factory had sweet potatoes and tomatoes struggling in sandy soil; women also were transported to a field in Dondo in a work rotation.

Eventually, Regina, who worked at the factory creche, and Alexandre, from the grupo dinamizador, came by and they arranged for me to interview a couple of women. I had asked to speak with older women who had worked at the factory for at least several years, and Regina and Alexandre brought along two women in their early forties. As I was thirty-one years old, these women did not seem particularly aged, though they did have a few years of work experience. Regina and Alexandre sat in on the interviews and helped a bit with translations. Both Luisa Monteiro and Cristina Fanduco, who shared their stories with me, spoke Portuguese. But as was common, it was their second or third language. I usually found that my own command of Portuguese was about equal to the women I was interviewing, as I misused verb tenses and forgot some of my vocabulary. The cashew workers were often nervous about talking to me and intimidated by the presence of the tape recorder, and their tongues froze. In general, the cashew workers had much briefer responses to my questions than other women I interviewed.

Both Luisa and Cristina had come to Beira as children. Luisa and her mother had farmed a machamba in the Beira suburbs. Cristina's husband had died, and she had sought work in the cashew factory when it first opened. They recalled the difficult days of working during the colonial period, when their daily pay was 25 escudos (about $1.00 a day), but they only were credited for having worked a day if they filled a twelve-liter tin with properly cleaned cashews.

If the tin was not satisfactorily filled, it was carried over to the next day and they were not credited as having worked the first day. If they were successful in filling a tin every day, they would be paid 700 escudos at the end of a month (approximately $25.00), a rate that was rarely achieved. They remembered exactly how the wages had risen after independence, so that by the time of our interview they were receiving a much higher pay rate of 3500 meticais a month (just under $90.00).

That first day I was also shown around the factory, which was a series of large, open-sided, nearly vacant, cinder-block sheds. I was told that 531 workers were still on the payroll, mainly doing cleaning and maintenance or cultivating in the machambas, but they were not at the factory that day. One woman who had left the factory had opened a small restaurant nearby to serve the workers. Luisa, as a responsável for one of the sections, explained the work done in her area, while Alexandre described what kind of work normally occurred, repeatedly saying, "When we have cashew nuts," and lamenting the impact of the war with the "bandidos." When they did have nuts, they would even work through the weekend to finish processing all the cashews.

Cashews are unusual, as each individual nut grows at the base of a fruit that is used for an alcoholic beverage that many women brewed in their own homes. The nuts arrived at the factory still inside a tough outer casing, which was removed after the nuts were heated in an oven. Removing that casing released a corrosive liquid that burned the skin of anyone handling it, reflecting the plant's botanical relation to poison ivy. All the women I spoke with commented on the discomfort of dealing with that stage of the processing with bare hands and no protective gear. The nuts were also sorted by size and by whether they were whole or broken before being placed into cans of various volumes for shipment. I gained a new appreciation for the work behind the cans of cashews in American supermarkets.

Chapter 19

Figure 14: *"Let's harvest all the cashew nuts; harvesting the nuts develops Mozambique." Poster from Ministry of Information, 1980s, in my possession.*

In addition to the processing sheds, I was shown the machine repair shop, the carpentry shop, a stock room, the warehouse, the creche, a first aid room, and the machamba just at the edge of the factory grounds. The carpenter's room was also being used to store some drums, and they explained that they had an active cultural group that performed on official occasions, most recently when Samora Machel was in Beira. They also remembered how the Portuguese had discouraged and even forbidden such dancing under colonialism, and they were especially proud that they had revived that activity. The creche was quite small and the supervising teachers were retired cashew workers. The children were playing on a dirt floor and their lunch was cooked over a charcoal fire, but the workers saw it as an advance, as there had been no creche at all previously. A large field in front of the buildings was dedicated to soccer games, played only by the men.

That day there was only one class in progress in the corner of one of the large processing rooms. On a later visit I observed classes in session, some simply meeting in corners of the factory building, while others were in small newly built sheds. The Portuguese language was being taught by a man who worked in the statistics department. When I peeked in, the students were discussing which words they had found particularly difficult in the reading assignment. Math was taught by Alexandre, and a blackboard had simple equations such as $3+2=\underline{}$ written on it. There were about fifteen pupils in each class, and almost all were women. The supplies were very basic. Students sat on benches or used upended crates for desks. They had course books from the National Education System and workbooks for their writing and math problems. Two other rooms were set up with benches and blackboards, though they were empty when I looked in. One was prepared for a history lesson with events from Mozambique's struggle to end Portuguese colonialism written on the board: "Mueda," the site of a massacre of Mozambicans by Portuguese authorities in 1961, and "luta para dez anos" (struggle for ten years).

On my first visit, Alexandre made a somewhat formal speech before he returned to his other tasks, expressing gratitude to me for doing research at the factory: "I say 'thank you'!" Then I sat with three women and chatted until my transportation appeared. We sat around a table in a large dim meeting room decorated with political murals. Posters reminded workers that the State Plan for export crops depended on cashews, and commemorated Mozambican Women's Day. Painted murals of Eduardo Mondlane and Samora Machel nearly filled the walls and, in recognition of the importance of women in that workplace, the OMM symbol was painted on the wall as well.

Chapter 19

The women and I talked about the many different languages in Mozambique. The radio in Beira broadcast not only in Portuguese, but also in Chisena and Ndau, the most common central Mozambican languages. I had decided not to worry about learning any of the local languages, as I could not expect to learn more than one, which would have been a different kind of restriction, giving me access only to Mozambicans who spoke that language. As I discovered, many of the cashew workers spoke Bitonga or other languages from southern Mozambique, so Chisena or Ndau would not have been helpful. I determined early on that it would be best to focus on improving my Portuguese. At the same time, I regretted that I had to rely on a language that was often not the first language of anyone involved in the interview or the conversation. Though we usually managed reasonably well, it was a barrier to more nuanced exchanges.

The cashew workers and I also discussed the problem of hunger in the city. The tomatoes they planted were not growing well in the sandy soil, and the sweet potatoes they planted had rotted in the unseasonable heavy rains. They all complained about the long lines to purchase food and the skirmishes that broke out while people waited. One woman said, "Sometimes I take a blanket and wait overnight in front of a shop," so she could be sure to buy whatever was being sold. I talked about my experience with the theft from my backpack while hoping to buy food. They admired my nylon backpack, and one asked, "Is that kind of cloth made by women?" We talked about the attack on the Soviet engineers also, alarming news that signaled the expansion of the war. Such conversations helped me feel more a part of the life of the city, as we could all commiserate about the impact of the war and the difficulties of life in Beira.

I explained that Steve was a doctor at the hospital and that my daughter was going to creche. They had thought I was just a *menina* or schoolgirl, and initially they refused to believe me when I admitted to being thirty-one years old and were amazed to learn that I had a daughter. They were pleased that I had my own child in a Mozambican childcare center, and when I mentioned that she was learning to sing "Kanimambo, Frelimo," they all began to sing it with me.

I made several more trips out to the cashew factory in Manga. One morning I interviewed four women in quick succession, and a few days later I spoke with three more workers. These women were quite nervous in my presence and the tape recorder really made them shy. Because so few women were actively working at the factory, my pool of possible informants was restricted. Some of the women who came to speak with me had only been working there for one or two years and could not narrate the kind of work history I was hoping to collect. Their responses were so abbreviated that they amounted to an outline of their lives. I usually ended the interview by asking a more open-ended question, inquiring if there was any memory that they wished to share, or other information that I had neglected to inquire about. On more than one occasion the women conveyed greetings to their family members, in the mistaken assumption that the interview was destined for the radio, and perhaps believing that the recorder was itself a radio. That misunderstanding, suggesting that they believed their comments were destined for public consumption, undoubtedly dampened their willingness to speak openly to me.

Most of the cashew workers who spoke to me had moved to Beira from rural families in southern Mozambique. They had usually spoken Bitonga as children, though they also mentioned other local languages such as Chuabo or Chitswa. They typically only had a year or two of formal education and none of them spoke Portuguese at home, though most were willing to try with me. As Gloria Humu commented, "I speak a little (*um bocado*, literally a bite), I will try," and proceeded to tell me how her father had cut cotton for the Portuguese, and how her mother had died three days after giving birth to her, so she was raised by her stepmother. Her father had twelve children, of which only five survived, and he could not afford to send them to school. She had married,

Chapter 19

but her husband had problems that she did not specify, so she returned to her father's house and finally left there to find work in Beira, following her brother who lived in the Munhava neighborhood. Later she remarried in Beira. She talked about her work for the previous eleven years in the factory, "Shelling, shelling, shelling (*cascou, cascou, cascou*), until now, when I work in the sorting section."

A couple of the women shared very personal stories about their lives. One woman related how she had been married at age sixteen in her home area near Inhambane. But her husband beat her, as she said, without any justification. One night he beat her from eight in the evening until three in the morning, until she lost consciousness. She then realized that enough was enough and she returned to her father's house. But they did not have the funds to repay the *lobolo* or bridewealth, and when her husband kept bothering her family for the money, saying "I want my money from the bridewealth of the marriage," she traveled to Beira to find work. She earned the necessary money, which she sent to her father so that he could repay her husband and officially end that marriage. The need to repay bridewealth in order to dissolve unhappy marriages was a common motivation for women to seek waged work and was a factor in the work histories of several of the cashew workers with whom I spoke.

I was beginning to gain a sense of how their experiences as cashew workers were shared, and how they differed from the nurses whom I had already interviewed. Many of the cashew women had married young and unhappily, and their desire to escape from the desperate poverty of their rural villages and from their forlorn home lives was their incentive for moving into the city and going to work at the cashew factory. Most had had lobolo exchanged when they married. Bridewealth was usually a sum of money along with household goods and food given by the groom-to-be to the bride's family. Historically it had consisted of cattle or hoes, which were integral factors in rural, family-based production.

Frelimo intended to end the practice, which was officially regarded as being oppressive to women. A common slogan at the time was "Abaixo com lobolo!" (Down with bridewealth!). The cashew workers' experience seemed to corroborate that attitude, as they had to earn the money through low-waged factory labor to repay the lobolo and formally end their marriages. But it was not simply a repressive custom that could be ended by government decree, as the Frelimo analysis implied. When I sat waiting for my transportation to return, the cashew workers stayed to keep me company on several occasions. Our conversations usually turned to such topics, and they told me that "the government wants to end lobolo, but they won't be able to." The women explained that only the lobolo exchange gave value to a relationship and brought the families together. A legal paper did not accomplish those goals, only the events surrounding lobolo fulfilled that need. They commented that many fathers would not be happy unless they acquired lobolo when their daughters married, and a trend in some areas to give a smaller token, called a "gratification" or thank-you gift, was not sufficient. They had similar views about polygyny (sometimes called polygamy), the still common practice of men marrying more than one wife. Again, Frelimo saw polygyny as oppressive to women, but the cashew workers told me that men will have two or more wives, and it was not likely to end because of new government policies. The official position opposed to polygyny made me hesitant to ask women directly if their husbands had a second wife, and no one volunteered such information during my interviews.

We also talked about the immense difficulties they faced. They appreciated the opportunity to take literacy classes at their workplace, but they had a hard time studying because when they were in class, they were constantly worrying about the work facing them at home. Their domestic work took them all day to accomplish, beginning

Chapter 19

at dawn with work in their machambas, then returning to their homes to prepare breakfast for the family, clean the yard, get water, and care for small children, before going back to the machamba, then home again to prepare food by pounding it in the mortar, cooking lunch, and then back to the machamba again. They did not even have *caril*, as curry-flavored sauces were called. They needed to get water at the neighborhood tap and carry it home on their heads. Wood for the cooking fires also had to be collected, and there were woodlots around town where young men chopped up the logs and women waited in line to buy their supply. The cashew workers agreed when I observed that a woman frequently did those chores with a child tied on her back and while pregnant. Sometimes a neighbor would watch their children in exchange for food or clothing. Once children were old enough to attend school the mothers had to wash their clothes at night by hand with little or no soap, leaving them to dry overnight. The following morning, they would iron the clothes using old irons that were heated by filling them with hot coals, so the children would be clean and fresh for school.

I was constantly impressed with the ability of people living in incredibly dilapidated housing to prepare themselves day after day for work and school despite the many obstacles they faced. The women at the cashew factory generally wore old capulanas wrapped around their waists and blouses that were ragged from being washed roughly by hand. No new clothing was coming into the shops to replace their worn-out clothes. Rita Laquen, one of the cashew workers, showed me a special red and blue capulana that had not appeared in the shops, but was only sold by the government to women workers through their workplaces. In general, though, capulanas were a basic yet scarce item and women resented wearing their old and worn cloths until they were completely tattered. I only bought two capulanas during the two years we lived in Beira. Francisco bought one of those, a commemorative capulana sold at our cooperantes' cooperative. It was a colorful cloth with a lot of red and green in the design, specially produced for Frelimo's Fourth Party Congress. The cashew workers also talked about Operação Produção (Operation Production), a new nationwide government program to move people deemed unproductive out of the cities and into more fruitful work in the rural areas. It was a controversial issue, though there were plenty of city residents who approved of the plan to clear loiterers out of the downtown areas. Registration cards issued by the central government had just been introduced in Beira in October 1982. As the cashew workers commented, women were particularly vulnerable because they were less likely than men to have their documents in order. A single woman who had a machamba but no waged work faced real problems, as she might not have anyone to speak up for her. Men in authority often considered such women to be prostitutes, simply because they were not married or otherwise under male control. But the cashew workers decried the confusion that followed in the wake of the poorly organized program and, as one woman explained, "No one has all of their documents in order." Even those who did, such as Francisco earlier in the month, could be caught up in the sweeps and held by authorities who themselves were not always clear about which documents were legitimate.

We did not see a lot of Operação Produção activity in Beira until the end of August, when there were suddenly police and military personnel on many street corners, checking people's identity papers. Large groups of people were held along the road waiting for the arrival of trucks that then took them away, though I was never sure where they went. Perhaps the first stage was just to take them to the local police station or *postos de verificação* (verification points) for further checks. One truck outside of the library had benches in the back for twenty or thirty people. I was never questioned, though Steve was briefly stopped in Munhava. *Tempo* had carried a story of a sweep in a nightclub in Maputo that had caught some cooperantes out

Chapter 19

for the evening. But it was obvious that the police were mainly stopping people based on racial assumptions, which may or may not have been explicitly stated to them.

During that period of more visible seizures, Horácio was picked up again, though we never learned what the reason was. He worked for our neighbors Juarez, the Brazilian pharmacist, and Yacine, the French nurse, who had gone to Maputo to sort out her contract. She had tried to change one clause in her contract and the bureaucratic response had been to end her contract entirely, so she then had to struggle to get it reinstated. Horácio had no papers at all, but when he claimed he was working for a household at the Mexicana, a military man brought him around to our place. Francisco nearly collapsed when he answered the knock on the door and saw the uniformed man outside and came trembling into the living room to get me. But we were able to vouch for Horácio as being employed by a cooperante household and our word was accepted as sufficient proof of Horácio's work situation. Horácio went before a tribunal, was issued an identity card, and was released.

I continued a schedule of visiting the cashew factory and interviewing women workers. But it was difficult to find older women. Two of those I spoke with were only eighteen and nineteen and did not have a lot of history to share. Luisa, who had been helping me all along, was there, but she was exhausted, a result of hard work and not enough food. On another visit to the cashew factory I spoke with Candia Share, who worked in the personnel office. She had gone to work after her husband was killed in the war "many years earlier" and she needed to find a way to support her family. Her mother cared for her small children, ages seven, four, and one (and presumably from a subsequent relationship as they had apparently been born after the death of her first husband).

A man in the administrative offices who spoke with me about production goals and the possibility of earning foreign exchange from cashews told me that they needed the divisas "*para engordar Moçambique,*" literally, to fatten Mozambique, an image that resonated in that time of hunger. While I was in the offices, I copied down information from work assignment sheets posted on the bulletin board. I was on a constant search for any small piece of useful data, which occasionally showed up in unexpected locations. On another visit, I was able to copy a two-page document about the nationalization of the factory (any sort of government intervention was referred to as "nationalization").

On one of my last visits the women told me, with dismay, that the cashews stored in their warehouse would be shipped north to a factory in Angoche that was still processing nuts. Caju, the Beira factory, was later damaged by a mortar attack by Renamo, and never reopened as a cashew factory. A news item in 1999 reported that the factory was rehabilitated under private ownership to manufacture fruit juice. During the conversion, many machambas were damaged when workers drained a tank of cashew oil that had become rancid and "highly caustic" in the intervening years.[1]

Endnote

[1] "Africa: Beira Factory Spill Turns into a Hazard," *AllAfrica* (1 February 1999), https://allafrica.com/stories/199902010098.html.

Chapter 20
Tea and Bread at the Provincial Women's Meeting

September 1983

I had a special opportunity in September to observe a provincial meeting of the women's organization, in preparation for the OMM Extra-ordinary Conference planned for the following year (initially set for April 1984, it was postponed until November).[1] OMM rarely met at the national level, and planning for the event included gatherings in villages, workplaces, and urban neighborhoods leading to larger provincial meetings and then finally the national conference. I went by the OMM headquarters to seek permission to attend, but Maria das Dores was waiting for the arrival of the OMM secretary-general, Salomé Moiane, and could not see me. The next day, the second day of the meeting, I went to the Assembleia Popular, the provincial legislative building, to again try to get permission to attend. Just as I walked up to the entrance, I met Balbina and another acquaintance who worked as a secretary in the OMM office. The woman from OMM went and found Maria das Dores, while I sat outside the main meeting room waiting for approval to enter. Maria das Dores returned with *senhora protocolo*, the woman in charge of protocol, and they told me I would have to wait to enter until a break in

215

the proceedings at 10 A.M. I could hear the people inside singing, and I thought I would have a morning of frustration, hearing only random pieces of the deliberations. But other delegates also arrived late, and very soon they let five of us in at once. I found a seat next to the wife of the director of the ship repair yard, RENAB, who knew about Steve's work at the RENAB health post.

The room had desks and chairs for 110 people, set in rows, and I counted 100 attendees. There were about half a dozen men, including Provincial Governor Marcelino dos Santos. There were very few white attendees; in addition to myself I saw only Signe Arnfred, who was the Danish researcher working with OMM, Marcelino's wife Pamela dos Santos, and the RENAB wife whose name I never did write down. All the women wore western dress and, though a few had headscarves not one of the attendees was wrapped in a capulana. Delegates were given folders with the themes for discussion. Due to a shortage, I did not get a complete folder but collected some of the papers later in the day.

The first part of the session, from 8 to 10 A.M., was devoted to listening to people read the themes aloud, to prepare us for the later discussion. When the women reading the papers made grammatical mistakes, Marcelino interrupted them to correct their Portuguese. When Maria das Dores said *relatório* (report) instead of *relato* (account), he gave her a little lecture about the distinction, which clearly annoyed her and threw her off her stride. Such interventions were embarrassing to others in attendance, and I was distressed to see a women's conference under such patriarchal control. In fact, Marcelino was the dominating presence, as the reports published in the local newspaper focused on his opening speech, his closing speech, and his other activities, almost completely ignoring what the women themselves were doing and saying.[2] Coming from a western socialist feminist perspective, where we had been trying (not always successfully) to develop non-hierarchical political processes and women's spaces, it was troubling to attend a "revolutionary" meeting that emphasized hierarchy

Chapter 20

and male leadership. The meeting in Beira seemed to me to represent a throwback to old-fashioned, Soviet-style, top-down leadership. The papers that were read that morning addressed divorce, family relations, and women's work, as well as reiterating the formal call for the women's conference that had been issued during Frelimo's Fourth Party Congress. Papers on such themes as prostitution, adultery, promiscuity, and traditional practices including initiation rites, polygamy, bridewealth, and premature marriage had been read the previous day, which I had missed. Small groups were organized for later discussion, and then Marcelino spoke for nearly an hour about the goals of the conference. He emphasized that the reports that had been read aloud were not directives but were a starting point for further debate and elaboration. I was especially pleased with his comments about the importance of knowing women's history to understand their current conditions.

The morning tea break offered a snack of white bread with cheese and margarine. There was one functioning women's bathroom, but given the attendees at the meeting, the men's bathroom was soon commandeered by the women as well. After the break we met briefly in our small group, where the group leaders tried to recruit someone to be secretary. Everyone demurred, claiming that they had no experience, but when we returned in the afternoon several women took extensive notes. The attendees represented a range of backgrounds, including urban professional women and a representative from rural Gorongosa who had walked one hundred miles to Beira for the meeting. As we left for lunch a youth dance group was entertaining people outside, but they were dismissed by Salomé Moiane so that the delegates could go home for lunch in a timely manner.

My discussion group had several men and, to my dismay, they talked a lot, though for the most part the participation of the men did not seem to bother the Mozambican women. As I was there as an observer, I simply sat and took notes and did not offer any comments about the issues that arose. When one of the men said that these topics were not only about women, but were also about men's problems, I noted sarcastically to myself, "How feminist!" But we did rearrange the tables so that we had a circle rather than all facing forward classroom style.

One of our first tasks that afternoon was introduced by Matilde, a nurse, who requested that we begin with a song. We sang

> Pai Machel
> Nos já vamos
> Difundir suas orientações
> Na realidade
> Para todo o lado
> Dinamizaremos
> Suas orientações Machel

The song tells "Father Machel" that we are going to deepen his orientations and political messages on every side in the real world, and we will carry out his objectives. Then we sang the OMM song, a rousing anthem:

> Levantam todos, mulheres moçambicanas
> Tendes a vida, filha de Moçambique --
> (Stand up everyone, Mozambican women,
> Take care of life, daughter of Mozambique).

Our small group talked about initiation rites that afternoon, with national leader Salomé Moiane helping to direct the discussion in an open way that moved the conversation forward without being restrictive. Several people spoke about the common practice of massaging and pulling on the labia to elongate them (using the term *puxar labios*), a custom across southern Africa that resulted in longer labia. Unlike the better-known rites in other parts of Africa that sometimes included cutting women's genitals, the Mozambican rites involved a group of girls of similar ages stroking and enlarging their own labia. The rites could also

Chapter 20

include adding tattoos to a girl's face or body via a process of scarification.

More than one delegate voiced the opinion that uninitiated women and women with no tattoos were not real women, as they were not properly prepared for adult sexual activity. Participants mentioned that instruction about regular washing as part of sexual relations was imparted during the rites and referred to bad odors that occurred when people did not learn proper conduct. One woman wanted to share her experience but had difficulty expressing herself because she did not have the words in Portuguese and the presence of men inhibited her.

A woman from Gaza province gave a graphic description of the process of tattooing, a form of scarification in which small cuts were made in a design on a girl's belly, chest, or shoulders and then rubbed with lotions and ashes to ensure that the cuts were raised and dark. The designs were considered a beautification practice as well as an erotic adornment that helped attract men. Many girls looked forward to the procedure and would choose the decoration they preferred, but according to members in the group, sometimes children would flee from fear as the cuts were made "in cold blood with no anesthesia." Another woman in the group had facial scars as well as a less common physical embellishment, as her front teeth were filed to points. She was from the north, and she believed that the procedures would "little by little" fall into disuse, without the need for official actions to discourage them. Others complained that urban children, who were less likely to undergo the rites, did not have proper respect for adults, as they always played and never studied, and their parents did not have control over them. The implication was that continuing the initiation rites would give parents more control.

The reality was that people wanted to continue the rituals and they were not going to stop performing rites that were an integral part of their identity just because the government wished it. The group generally agreed that the rites were less likely to be pursued in the cities, and that many fewer girls went through the procedures than in earlier decades. But some women commented that a girl who had not been initiated would have trouble finding a husband, or the husband might not like his uninitiated wife and would go to other women.

Nearly every delegate made at least one comment, and the repartee was open and often entertaining. Salomé Moiane tried to bring closure to the discussion by saying that there were good and bad aspects to the rites and people needed to decide which factors were worth retaining. It was clear that the much-quoted revolutionary slogans calling for an end to the rites had been too simplistic and indicated a cultural distance between the government and ordinary Mozambicans.

It was not until years later that I more fully realized that there was value in some of the traditional practices. At the time of the OMM meeting, I agreed with the Frelimo analysis that initiation rites trained women to be subservient to men and that they were obscurantist and detrimental to developing modern women. I thought the men were dominating the discussion in our group, and when one of the men commented that he thought it was alright for women to pull their labia, I considered that a completely sexist comment. Later I came to understand the rites as profoundly female-centered, with a positive focus on female sexuality.

Another man in our group stated that he wanted lobolo or bridewealth for his daughters, raising a similar issue of conflict between a traditional practice and official judgment and corroborating what I had learned from the cashew workers. He said that people were still exchanging lobolo, but they were doing it clandestinely because they knew that the practice was opposed by Frelimo. Marriage that was just between the two "children" was not a good thing, the families needed to be involved, and many believed that lobolo was a legitimate way to ensure that involvement.

A further theme for discussion was the issue of premature marriages. In addition to the obvious problems

Chapter 20

with sexuality and potential pregnancy for young girls, people were troubled because girls' education was disrupted when they married at a young age. One man spoke up to say that he believed that girls provoked men to have sex with them, though that comment was refuted by Balbina dos Santos and other women, who reminded everyone that we still lived in a patriarchal society that placed women in certain categories and gave them few options. Others blamed co-education, as boys and girls met and began relationships without their parents' knowledge. Several delegates waxed nostalgic for the old days when mothers had control over their daughters; "Daughters were afraid in those days," as one commented. And they discussed polygyny (sometimes called polygamy), the practice where a man could marry more than one wife. A marked gender division of perception emerged, as the men in our group thought it was decreasing while the women felt it was increasing, though they believed that second marriages were often secret and were not given the same formal recognition as they had when polygyny was accepted.

When Marcelino dos Santos stopped by our group briefly the next morning, he greeted Salomé Moiane by saying, "Oh, the grand lady is here." We also had a visit from Alda Espírito Santo, the noted anti-colonial leader and poet from São Tomé, a small West African island that had also been a Portuguese colony. She spoke about the family law they enacted there, and we sang a song for her. The song, in Ndau, was about how Samora had gone to Tanzania, how the liberation war had expanded into different provinces, and how the current fight with Renamo was not a real war but only bandits (not a *guerra bem bem* but only *ladrões*). In the middle of the song the group hummed as backup as Antonia, a neighborhood leader from Beira, read a poem she had written. And we sang "Levantam todos" again, adding a verse about the conference: "At the Conference women are going to analyze social problems that affect women, what are the obstacles to her emancipation—Viva viva Mozambican women."

Everyone went home or back to their hotel for lunch. In response to Salomé Moiane asking, "How is the food at the Hotel Mozambique?", the women admitted that it was inedible, which was certainly no surprise to me. The delegates staying there reported that they had squid that was badly cooked and that there was no salt. The organizers of the meeting were upset, as they knew that people had to eat well and be well rested in order to participate in the discussions.

I took the opportunity during breaks to talk to people about my research. I approached Beatriz, a woman who worked at the Belita garment factory. When I explained that I had already done interviews with nurses and cashew workers, she was very enthusiastic and invited me to come to Belita and interview women there as well. Signe was involved in a similar project in Maputo, where she interviewed ten women at each of seven workplaces, including a cashew factory. She had not included nurses or other professional women, and she gave me verbal support for what I was trying to do. She was also constrained because she was doing her research under OMM auspices, and they had not released her report. In fact, OMM never did release her research and eventually they lost their set of the research results, so that Signe's copy and the photocopy I made later in Maputo were the only ones available. Though Signe published other essays and articles about women in Mozambique, including reflections gleaned from her participation in pre-conference meetings all over Mozambique, her material on working women in Maputo was never published.[3]

The discussions continued for two more long days, from 8 A.M. to noon, and then from 2 P.M. to 7 in the evening. The initial reports were revised by members of our group, and we spent time reading the revisions, while we also moved forward in discussing other themes, such as divorce. Delegates were concerned that the people's

Chapter 20

tribunals, where many divorce cases were heard, did not counsel women or try to reconcile couples. There was some sentiment for getting OMM more involved in the tribunals. Prostitution was analyzed as a new difficulty related to capitalism, and soldiers were also seen as a problem. One commander had been publicly flogged for raping a woman during the Operation Production sweeps. There was criticism of cooperantes who had relationships with Mozambican women, with the opportunity to buy goods at the Loja Franca viewed as a temptation for young and poor women. In conditions of such scarcity, it was certainly understandable that there were women who would approach men who had foreign exchange and access to that legendary source of luxury items. I couldn't help wondering whether shopping at the Loja Franca was that much of a benefit, for instance, when local salt, only partially processed and still gray, appeared there for sale for divisas. But I knew that long-term committed relationships were also occurring between cooperantes and local women; not every such partnership was exploitative.

In the discussion about family relations, the women complained that men never helped with any household chores. A man from Chemba drew laughter when he told the group, "I don't do any of that work myself, but I support the men who do!" But there was consensus that even when a woman was ill, she could not expect her husband to do any housework; rather, the man would sit and wait for her to serve him. Balbina and some others worked on the last night until 3 A.M., typing up final versions of the reports, which we then read and corrected in our group. At one point the written version stated, "There are men who help" (Há homens que ajudam) with housework, and our group leader wanted to make that, "There are *very few* men who help" (Há *muitos poucos* homens que ajudam). The group compromised with "There are *some* men who help" (Há *alguns* homens que ajudam).

On the last day we each paid a token sum of 100 meticais to help cover the costs of the meeting, finalized our small group discussion, and practiced our songs before going to the plenary session at 11 A.M. While we waited for Marcelino to arrive (which he did at 12:20), we all sang, and some women danced. When he arrived, he immediately observed that it was almost lunch time, and he requested a dance, so the women reprised a dance they had performed a bit earlier. We then sang, "Frelimo sings with us, you can't sing alone" (or study alone, walk alone, and so on). After the lunch break, the plenary session finally got underway at 2:00 in the afternoon. In a process that lasted several hours, each small group read every report they had generated, before the floor was opened to more discussion and clarification.

One interesting response was from a soldier, attending the meeting in civilian clothes. He felt the people should not criticize the Forças Armadas (Armed Forces), as was done in the discussion about prostitution, but should support them. Several women said they were simply reporting on real events, and Marcelino intervened to explain that "The army must have exemplary behavior. If they are the same as the enemy, then what was the point of the revolution?" The soldier then rose again to apologize and agreed that it was a problem that needed to be addressed. The whole process, though long and at times tedious, represented what I thought was an admirable democratic practice, with issues brought out for debate rather than covered up and ignored.

Chapter 20

Figure 15: My small group performing at the OMM meeting in Beira, 1983. Photo by Mariano Maonera.

Each group performed songs or made another presentation. Our group danced up the aisle singing "Machanga," sang "Samora" and "Levantam todos" at the front and retreated to the tune of "Pai Machel." Another group enacted a skit about initiation rites. The play contrasted a modern family who sent their daughter to school and had a scientific talk about menstruation and ovulation, with a family who took their daughter out of school so that she could undergo the rites. The godmother exclaimed, "Keep it secret, Frelimo's here!" When the modern girl came looking for her friend to see why she was missing school, the traditional father said, "Oh oh, here comes OMM!" The performance concluded as the second girl decided to end the process of the rite before it was completed and returned to school with her friend.

Other performers included a group of women who had been in the anti-colonial armed struggle, and a final group that sang "A wile mukolonhi" (Colonialism has fallen) and gave floral bouquets to Salomé and Marcelino. Greetings were conveyed to Samora for the occasion of his fiftieth birthday at the end of September, and a woman read the final document of the conference. The final event was Marcelino's closing speech, in which he observed that none of the reports about initiation rites had talked about how those practices benefited men, though I thought that was implicit in the portrayal of the rites as keeping women oppressed. He noted that Mozambique was in a time of transition with the "shock" between old and new values, between traditional, capitalist, and socialist beliefs. He told the women that "Our job is to create as much stability as possible in the circumstances." He also included a forceful attack on the bandits and called for military training for all workers.

He marked part of his comments as off the record, directed only at those in the organization so they could know what was happening. He described how in Maringué, a locality with many difficulties, a company of fifty men was enough to defeat the bandits, if those fifty went in and trained others in a forty-five-day program that was being implemented. Ten local people would be chosen as *commandantes*, and everyone was called on to be vigilant twenty-four hours a day. Referring to the anti-colonial struggle, he claimed, "This is nothing new, we've done this before, and it can be done." He said that information would only be published when the bandits were liquidated. In hindsight those comments seem both incredibly optimistic and pitiable, as the war continued until a peace accord was negotiated in 1992, and innumerable small communities like Maringué were devastated in the intervening years. In 1983 few of us realized how much aid Renamo was getting from South Africa, or how tenacious they would prove in their struggle to topple Frelimo and institute an anti-socialist government.

That last evening ended at 10 P.M., following lengthy discussions, Marcelino's two-hour speech, and the Frelimo party anthem, "Somos soldados do povo marchando em frente da luta contra a burgesia" (We are soldiers of the people, marching in front of the struggle against the bourgeoisie). When we emerged from the building, we were

Chapter 20

greeted by two performing groups, one in yellow and orange from Mobeira, a local biscuit factory, and one in blue from the Belita garment factory. I was impressed and encouraged by all the rhetoric and display, as indicated by a comment in my journal, which now sounds impossibly naive: "These people are revolutionaries—it is easy sometimes to forget when dealing with daily hassles." We were willing to overlook or ignore a lot of adversity and policies that made us uncomfortable. We had a two-year commitment to stay and support Mozambique, and we needed to believe that our undertaking was based on politics that were being realized, not just pie-in-the-sky ideas. Forty years later, it is hard to recapture those heady youthful feelings of hope for a better future. I may have a more pragmatic view of the world, or maybe I am just more cynical, but I still have some hope that we can make the world more fair and just, as elusive as that goal sometimes seems.

Steve was quite ill with malaria again in October, debilitated and taking over a week to slowly recover. He sat around the apartment feeling lethargic and unable to rouse himself, which was common enough with malaria, though to me it seemed that once the worst of the malaria attack had passed, he should stop moping and snap out of it. I was frustrated, as he was certainly ill but was also disheartened. Despite my best efforts, I could not raise his spirits, which I believed was a necessary first step to recovery. As he wrote in his journal, "I walk a thin line between emotional breakdown and emotional inertness to avoid pain and anguish." Both malaria itself and chloroquine could act on the central nervous system to make a person depressed. Eventually the infection ran its course, but Steve continued to have an especially difficult time dealing with life in Beira. His work involved direct responsibility for people suffering from terrible illnesses and the ravages of war, including far too many children dying from malnutrition, from diseases that would have been easily cured in the U.S., and from injuries. With that daily reality, his "thin line" was a fragile margin of survival.

In contrast, my own work brought me into contact with women who told me about specific improvements in their lives since independence. Despite the many complications and hindrances, I was collecting information and developing my analysis about women, work, and politics in Mozambique. It is clear from Steve's personal journal that progress in my work was one of the factors that allowed him to continue to hold on until our two years were completed. Despite our illnesses and the shortages of food, electricity, and other necessities, my experience of Beira allowed me to have a more hopeful view of our own situation.

Endnotes

1. I discuss this meeting further in Kathleen Sheldon, "'Down with Bridewealth!' The Organization of Mozambican Women Debates Women's Issues," in *Women's Political Communication in Africa: Issues and Perspectives*, ed. Sharon Adetutu Omotoso, 9-26 (Springer, 2020). Another source of information about OMM during the early years of independence is Elizabeth Banks, "Sewing Machines for Socialism? Gifts of Development and Disagreement between the Soviet and Mozambican Women's Committees, 1963-1987," *Comparative Studies of South Asia, Africa and the Middle East* 41, 1 (2021): 27-40.
2. For two examples, see "Moçambique: Frondosa Arvore com Variedade de Flores," *Diário de Moçambique* (*DM*) (9 September 1983), consisting of the text of dos Santos's speech opening the meeting; "Aprofundar e Alargar Debate sobre a Mulher," *DM* (14 September 1983), describing dos Santos's closing comments.
3. Many of her articles were published in Signe Arnfred, *Sexuality and Gender Politics in Mozambique: Rethinking Gender in Africa* (London: James Currey, 2011).

Chapter 21
Guinea Fowl for Dinner in Zimbabwe

November 1983

We began arrangements in October for a two-week vacation in Zimbabwe with my parents. They loved to travel and were happy to have the opportunity to see southern Africa. At that time Zimbabwe was a successful and peaceful country, just emerging from a terrible war that had ended decades of white-minority rule. In 1966 the white colonial settler government under Ian Smith proclaimed a Unilateral Declaration of Independence for Rhodesia (its colonial era name) from the United Kingdom, in a reactionary attempt to undercut international plans to end colonialism and introduce government by the majority. The country had suffered a devastating guerrilla war until 1980, when independence was finally negotiated between the mainly British white Rhodesians and two rival African liberation movements. The 1980s and much of the 1990s were years of apparent peace and economic stability for Zimbabwe, and we were fortunate to visit during that period. Eventually, unresolved problems with land reform together with President Robert Mugabe's growing tyrannical behavior led to a new round of rural violence, the extreme curtailment of political freedom, and a ruinous economic crisis that extended into the twenty-first century.

The Mackerel Years

Because we had such limited ability for communication from Beira, my parents made the travel arrangements from the U.S. Their travel agent was very apprehensive about their plans and insisted that they stay at the Meikles, an opulent hotel in downtown Harare (the capital city), despite the availability of many less expensive and perfectly comfortable lodgings. In mid-October I received a telegram from my mother with their arrival dates and other information. When I went to the post office to send a reply telegram, I was accosted by an elderly drunk man who was a bit crazy as well. He came up to me and touched my arm and my watch, and when I roughly ordered him, "Go away!", he refused. Instead, he began to remove mysterious objects from a filthy bag he was carrying, moved a disgusting rag from his head to mine, and began shaking items in my face. I was increasingly frightened because his actions were so unpredictable. Several people were present in the post office, but at first no one else intervened, although eventually other customers approached and managed to lead him out of the building. Throughout his performance the postal worker was trying to get my information and could not understand that I wanted to send a telegram to the USA. She thought EUA (Estados Unidos da America) was a different place than USA and that I wished to send two telegrams. My mother never got that telegram from me. I went home and mixed myself a pre-lunch gin and Coca Cola.

We learned that my sisters Barbara and Carol were expecting babies in April, and I felt very sad and alone, so far away from people I loved and missing the arrival of new family members. But we enjoyed the support that my family gave to us, both material and psychological. In contrast, Steve had written to his father to ask for a loan of $750 to pay for a pediatric review program scheduled when we returned the following year. Steve wanted to take a refresher course after two years away from American medical practice, but the deadline to register was before our return, and we could not afford to pay the fee from Mozambique.

Chapter 21

As Steve read his father's refusal to make the loan, he began to fume and crumpled the letter. His father outlined his reasons for saying no and asked if Steve was planning to settle down to a steady job. By then Steve had already heard about a couple of job possibilities, including as a full-time staff pediatrician at the Kaiser Permanente facility in West Los Angeles, the post he did take as soon as we returned. But his father seemed to think that, by asking for money, Steve was demonstrating his irresponsible and unreliable character. It was agonizing to receive such a chastising letter at that point in our stay in Beira, though his father regretted it in later years when he and Steve were reconciled and became very close. Nearer to the end of our stay Ned Alpers wrote to me that there was a new research center at UCLA, the Center for the Study of Women. He had put my name forward for a research assistant position, so to my great relief I also had a job waiting for me back in Los Angeles.

But all of that was set aside while we traveled to neighboring Zimbabwe. We arrived at the airport at 7 A.M. to catch the 9 A.M. flight to Harare on LAM (Linhas Aereas de Moçambique, Mozambique Air Lines). After we boarded the plane, Mercie began to rub her eyes and complain that her eyes were bothering her. We also felt irritation in our eyes, and very soon the attendants had everyone disembark and we heard that a container of formaldehyde in the cargo hold had somehow ruptured. As we waited in the passenger lounge, we met a man from Chicago who sold airplane parts. He could not believe that we were living in Beira, and promised to call Steve's family when he got back to the U.S. Just before noon another one of LAM's three planes landed, filled with passengers traveling from Maputo to Quelimane or somewhere further north. They were made to disembark and wait at the Beira airport until we were all flown to Harare. When our plane returned to Beira later in the afternoon, those other passengers were allowed to complete their own journey.

We easily went through Zimbabwean customs and took a taxi into downtown Harare, where we were left at a curb about a block away from the Meikles. As we struggled up the street with our toddler and suitcases, bellmen from the hotel spotted us and ran down the street to meet us and take our bags. We were exceedingly grateful for that attentive service, which continued throughout our stay. Though we did worry about the cost of the very luxurious Meikles, it was a wonderful place for rest and relaxation, and we especially appreciated taking regular hot showers and baths.

My parents arrived the following morning and we settled into a pleasant routine of sightseeing, shopping, and eating at gourmet restaurants. Or not even gourmet, we were thrilled with lunch at a pizza place, and enjoyed a delicious Indian meal in another restaurant. My parents brought a lot of books and supplies with them, and we bought more in Zimbabwe's well-stocked shops (though camera film and flashlight batteries, on our list of necessities, were not to be found). We especially needed bigger clothes and shoes for Mercie, who was now growing rapidly. We realized that we had left our camera, including exposed film we had hoped to develop in Zimbabwe, in the closet of our apartment. It all worked out for the best, as we were freed from snapping shots during the entire vacation and my father was happy to be designated official trip photographer. Mercie charmed my parents, though we had to translate her Portuguese for them and, after my mother kept asking, "What did she say?", we made a list of her words to help them understand their own granddaughter.

The food was memorable, not least because we came from scarcity. I tried guinea fowl (tasted like chicken) and Steve ordered warthog one evening (tasted like pork). We loved ordering late-night cucumber sandwiches from room service, as the combination of white bread (crusts removed) and refreshing green and crisp cucumbers was simply delicious. That was one of the first hotels where

Chapter 21

I experienced evening turndown service, as young men in colonial-era uniforms (white shirts, shorts, and knee-high socks) performed their tasks under the watchful eye and clipboard list of a supervisor. It seemed the height of luxury and decadence. We keenly felt the contradiction of enjoying such service amid so much poverty, though we did appreciate the opportunity to recover our health and our spirits.

It was exceptionally hot, as it was the middle of summer in the southern hemisphere, and we kept our sightseeing to an easy schedule. It was also jacaranda season and downtown Harare was bathed in a lavender glow as trees bloomed on every street and public square. We rented a car and drove to the Evenrigg Botanical Gardens, admired the flowers and birds, and ponds with goldfish and lily pads. There were no other visitors there, the heat emphasizing the large shining silence and the small buzzing of insects. And we drove out to the geological curiosity of the Balancing Rocks, with its acres of boulders piled awkwardly on top of each other.

We took excursions out of Harare as well. We flew to Victoria Falls, where we sat by the hotel pool, admired the Falls, which were spectacular despite the drought that had reportedly diminished the water flow to only 10 percent of normal, and ate lunch to the sounds of a local marimba band on the patio. One evening we took a cruise along the Zambezi River, and we reveled in our location as we drank sundowners and watched the birds and hippopotamuses along the riverbanks. Back at the fire-lit hotel grounds we attended an African dance program, and delighted in seeing stilt dancers, pole climbers, and spirit masks performing tourist versions of traditional dances. The next morning as we ate breakfast on the patio, a large troop of baboons, including a mother with her baby clinging to her back, went racing through the yard, pausing in the outdoor bar, and stopping to cavort on the swings and slide in the children's play area before continuing on their way to the nearby mango grove. And we visited a crocodile farm, where Steve held a ten-inch baby croc that proceeded to pee on him, to Mercie's glee.

From Victoria Falls we flew on a tiny airplane to the game preserve at Hwange National Park. The small crew did everything, from checking our tickets and our bags, locking up the one-room terminal as we left, and then flying the plane! But it was a choppy flight and, as we approached our destination, Mercie threw up all over me. We could have gone on a game drive as soon as we arrived at the Safari Lodge, but I needed to clean up and so we missed out on that. When we went for cocktails at a small animal blind by a waterhole at the hotel that evening, we discovered that it was possible to see herds of elephants and other animals without leaving the grounds. Nearly thirty elephants of all sizes ambled close to join us for a drink.

We did go on a successful early morning game drive the next morning. The driver took our minivan into a grove, saying sometimes giraffes could be seen there. As we all peered to the right of the vehicle, a family of giraffes approached us on our left, startling my mother when she turned around, suddenly spotting a gentle-eyed giraffe gazing at us through the van windows. Twice we stopped to watch large herds of elephants cross the road and there were birds of all kinds, various antelopes (waterbuck, steenbok, impala, and kudu), zebras, ostriches, and jackals. I loved the grace of the various antelopes, with distinctive markings and imperious bearing. Then we returned for a fabulous buffet breakfast. Mercie had a wonderful time. She especially enjoyed swimming in the pool, which she had greeted by calling out, "Mommy, nice ocean!"

On a second game drive we went to a hidden platform at a more distant waterhole and watched a herd of nearly one hundred elephants file in, taking turns to drink at the water's edge. Then we drove up the road and our spotter saw some distant lions, which we were able to approach, observing the heavily maned male and four golden females sunning themselves on a small hillside. We saw two rhinoceroses early on the drive and later came across three more, a family

Chapter 21

group of mother, father, and baby. The mother was blocking the road, and our driver gunned the engine to try to get her to move out of our way. Then the big male began pawing the ground and seemed interested in charging our little bus. Our driver did not waste any time, driving away quickly, as none of us really wanted to wait around and see what Father Rhino had in mind. Steve, riding shotgun with Mercie on his lap, felt that was a more dangerous encounter with nature than he desired. We saw more animals while relaxing on the grounds of the hotel, as baboons played around on the thatched roofs and birds were everywhere, including an eagle that swooped down and stole food left on a patio table. A gorgeous herd of sable antelope came by, their sentinels standing ready at the edge of the group.

After a couple of days back at the Meikles in Harare, we rented a car again and drove south to see Great Zimbabwe, the majestic stone palace and enclosures built by local people as early as the thirteenth century. It flourished until the sixteenth century, when it entered a decline for reasons that are still debated by historians. When first seen by European explorers in the nineteenth century, they refused to believe that the ancestors of the Africans living in the region could have built such a monument, and for many years Europeans insisted that it must have been constructed by Arab invaders. It is a huge complex of ruined buildings and walls, covering many acres, and the style of building as well as symbols such as birds and snakes carved into the walls offer vital clues to life in southern Africa centuries ago. The word "zimbabwe" referred to a settlement of stone buildings and enclosures, and the stone bird figures found there have been adopted as a symbol for modern Zimbabwe with a bird emblem on the national flag.

My father and I immediately went to the Hill Complex when we arrived. That site was an historic center of human settlement that retained a sense of spirituality and peace, reminding all visitors of the power of the past and the continuing strength of our ancestors. I felt an intense connection to the people and the place and could have wandered around endlessly. The next morning Steve and my father climbed up to the Hill ruins, and Steve and I returned later in the day with my mother.

Peacocks wandered around the grounds of the hotel, startling us by squawking and walking right into our rooms if we left the doors open. Months later Mercie was still talking about the inquisitive peacocks that were at her eye level, though her strongest memory was being stung by a bee as she paddled in the pool with my father. She would mention the baboons in the bar, the baby crocodile that peed, peacocks entering the house, or ask after Grandma and Grandpa, saying "Memba dat?"

We perceived a greater tension between black and white Zimbabweans than we experienced between the races in Mozambique. Mozambique had an official policy opposing racism, and most of the whites who were there had chosen to remain after independence to assist the Frelimo government or had arrived later as political supporters. In Zimbabwe, where independence had come just three years before, many whites who owned property had remained to see what would happen, though they were often suspicious and wary or even overtly racist. We found that when casual conversations revealed that we were working in Mozambique as cooperantes, black Zimbabweans immediately became friendlier and began calling us "comrade." Many of them had family members in Mozambique or had lived there themselves, as the border between the two countries was long and porous. Zimbabweans also knew how difficult conditions were just over the frontier and we felt the warmth of their concern for us.

After two weeks of living like rich tourists we had to return to Beira, though my parents stayed for a few more days in Harare. We met Niall and Melanie, our Irish friends, at the airport as they arrived for their own vacation. Once we were airborne, I began to think again about my work, as Aquino de Bragança sat in front of us on the plane. I had finally met him briefly in Maputo in April, so I re-

Chapter 21

introduced myself and told him about my research. During our flight back he generously wrote a letter of introduction to help me get into the archives in Beira, and he addressed it to Pamela dos Santos. She was a South African exile who as a young woman had to flee after a police raid caught her in an apartment where people of different races were staying, which was not legal at that time. While living in Tanzania she had met Marcelino dos Santos, and they eventually had a daughter and married.

I did not have a chance to see Aquino again. In October 1986 he was on the plane carrying President Samora Machel and other government officials that crashed under suspicious circumstances near Mbuzini, South Africa, killing thirty-four of the passengers, including Samora and Aquino. The cause of the crash remains poorly explained. Many observers hold the South African government responsible for employing a false beacon to divert the plane off course until it crashed into a hillside. Whatever the specifics, the death of Samora Machel and the circumstances of the crash itself had a lasting impact on regional politics. It was a major event in the campaign of terror that South Africa's apartheid government waged against Mozambique in the 1980s.

Chapter 22
Talking with Garment Workers

December 1983 to February 1984

I renewed my efforts to interview the garment workers at Belita, riding my bike along the unpaved roads to the factory, located in the Maquinino neighborhood, just inland from the downtown area and up the street from the Assembleia Popular building. One morning I ran into a chicken that careered into my path. It lived, which I thought was more than it deserved for its stupidity.

I wanted to include women working at Belita in my study because, like the cashew factory, it had a high proportion of women workers. At the time I began visiting the site, there were 320 workers, of which 103, or about one-third, were women. On my first visit in October 1983, I met Beatriz, my contact from the provincial women's meeting, at the factory office. She showed me around briefly and I arranged to return to meet with members of the management. The factory was much brighter and cleaner than the cashew factory, with the sewing machines clattering away on the second and third floors. It was not as easy as it first appeared to set up interviews at Belita. When I returned at the appointed time, no one was there, and Beatriz was very apologetic. They were all at a special meeting to organize production councils, known as Conselhos de Produção, which were the precursors of trade unions.

The Mackerel Years

When I went back to the factory again, I learned that Beatriz was out in the districts organizing for OMM. I was sorry to miss her and, as matters transpired, I never did have an opportunity to interview her because she became a traveling organizer for the newly formed trade union and was constantly on the road. I admired her for getting paid to do feminist and union organizing. I went to the OMM headquarters to learn her schedule and spoke with Maria das Dores again and temporarily left my letter for Pamela dos Santos there as well, as Maria thought that OMM might be able to intervene. She suggested I just go back to Belita and approach other workers there and, when I did that, I met Ana Maria Helena dos Santos (who was no known relation to the others named dos Santos). Ana Maria Helena was interested in helping me, but she wanted a letter from OMM confirming my identity and giving her permission to talk to me. So, back I went, riding my bike to the OMM offices and, surprisingly quickly, obtained an OMM letter and took it back to Belita.

I was still expecting delays, so when I returned to Belita with my OMM permission letter, I did not bring my tape recorder or even paper and pen. But they immediately set up a meeting for me with half a dozen women representing various sections in the factory. We gathered in a conference room, sitting around a huge heavy wooden table, a table so large that it was an obstacle to conversation. Most of the women sat there and did not speak. I suspected it was the first time many of them had even been in that room and they probably felt as intimidated as I did. I was able to explain that I wanted to interview women workers about their experiences. One woman commented that before independence, "Somos escravos" (We were slaves), but by 1983 she felt there was more respect for working women. "When I return home after work," she explained, "I sometimes find my husband bathing our child. He understands that I also work and need help in the house."

I returned for a tour of the facility later that week. The bottom floor held the management and accounting offices,

Chapter 22

the warehouse, and a small shop displaying samples of the clothing they produced. The warehouse was empty, though Ana Maria Helena told me, "It used to be filled with material imported from Hong Kong, Japan, the United States, and all over." By 1982 they were relying on cloth from Textafrica, a textile factory in nearby Chimoio. The third floor was the main work area, with the cutting and pattern sections. I watched as one man drew a pattern onto a large paper and others prepared to cut stacks of cloth. The center section of the floor was filled with sewing machines organized into groups of twelve, men and women all working together, some hemming white sheets, others sewing red skirts or military caps. Most of their inventory was destined for government or other official workplaces. The second floor had a small health post, a repair workroom, and a lounge where the workers could eat lunch. At that time, it was possible for workers to contract with the Fabrica de Refeições, the Meal Factory, to have a cheap lunch delivered, though they complained that the meal was usually only rice with a watery sauce. Belita subsidized half the per-person cost of the meals and each worker paid the other half, which totaled 48 meticais (about $1.20).

The Mackerel Years

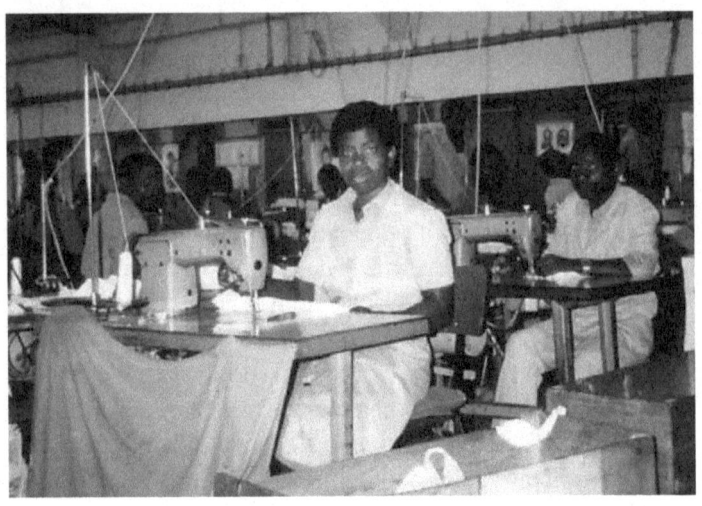

Figure 16: Belita workers, 1989. Photo by Kathleen Sheldon.

The working conditions were viewed as unusually good. They had a month-long vacation, taken collectively when the factory closed from December 19 to January 19 each year, though excluding workers in the packaging section and the main offices. The factory would lend money to a worker who faced an unexpected expense such as a wedding or funeral. And if a worker died, a family member would have first option on a job in the factory. I was told that after one man had passed away his son came to work at Belita. As provided by law for all working women in Mozambique, women at Belita could take sixty days maternity leave. When they neared the end of their pregnancy, they could move to less strenuous work areas. I spoke with one very pregnant woman who was folding the sheets being hemmed by her section, and she pointed out her usual sewing machine, covered with a dust cloth while she worked elsewhere. Belita was considered a model factory, with good production levels and a high proportion of workers in the party cell and in the women's and youth organizations. The workers also participated in an annual discussion about their production goals, though the increasing problems in maintaining electricity and obtaining cloth made it difficult to meet the production targets. I admired the high level of organization, which seemed to present a notable example of a socialist workplace.

On another visit, I toured the creche where workers at Belita could enroll their children. It was in a building just down the street from the factory and workers from several businesses in the neighborhood could send their children there. Nighttime literacy classes for the workers were also held in that building. The creche was on the second floor of the building. While I was waiting to be taken around the creche, I chatted with Ana Maria Helena and Rita Bacare, two workers who were accompanying me and who had also shown me around the factory. They told me that they found the night classes very difficult. Rita said, "I would rather have classes in the morning when my mind is more alert." Women workers had a lot of trouble in the adult education program due to what were called PPFs (perder por faltas) or failing the course because they missed so many class meetings. While we were sitting there a group of five-year-olds marched by after *ginástica* (gymnastics), shouting out the song "Kanimambo, Frelimo!"

Dona Lena, the creche director, gave us a tour. There were ninety-six children in their care and they were watched by twenty-four workers, including cooks and other support staff. The building had previously been a suitcase factory and had just opened as a childcare center in September 1983, so the rooms were still fresh and clean. But all their water had to be carried up in buckets from a ground-floor tap. They had no propane gas for cooking, so all the food was prepared on charcoal stoves on an outside porch. That day I saw little bread rolls and green peppers. Both Rita and Ana Maria Helena had enrolled their children there, whereas previously they had left them at home with an empregada, a worker who cared for the child at home and may have been

The Mackerel Years

also responsible for cleaning the house and cooking some of the meals.

I had a pleasant interview with Rita, who was about seven months pregnant with her third child. She was exactly my age, had been educated at a mission school near Tete, and was married with a five-year-old daughter and a son who was just over one year old. Her husband drove a truck for the long-distance transport company Rodoviário. He was often away on his route from Beira to Tete, at that time a perilous highway under attack by Renamo bandits. When I asked about her marriage, she commented that lobolo had been exchanged when she married. She laughed a bit about it, "I was loboloed, two contos five hundred. It is the custom, isn't it? He paid lobolo to my parents; my in-laws along with my parents made a traditional ceremony . . . the family made a little food to eat."

In apparent contradiction to the exchange of lobolo, her parents had been known, in her words, as "conscientious churchgoers, my father was very religious, so the Father of the Murraça mission came to take me to the mission when I was eight." She learned to sew in the mission school and later took a course in Beira where she earned a certificate in sewing. When she first moved to Beira, she worked at a different factory but applied to work at Belita because she believed it would be more stable after independence in 1975. The owner of the other factory was a white man and she feared he would flee, as in fact many thousands of Portuguese did. Belita had been owned by a Chinese family who had fled immediately after independence, forcing the government to intervene, and when Rita applied to work it was already in the hands of Mozambicans.

She had worked until the day she gave birth—not just once, but twice! With her first baby, she worked her usual Saturday morning shift, returned home in the early afternoon, and by 8 P.M. she was in the hospital giving birth. With the second pregnancy, she had worked a regular Wednesday shift, went home around 5:30, ate dinner, rested a bit, and realized she did not feel well. She got a ride to the hospital from a friend, as her husband was away. As she told me, she "went to the hospital, the doctor arrived, and so on, baby in hands." She called the factory the next morning to say she was not skipping work without reason, as her baby had been born the previous evening. Many women tried to take part of their sixty days of maternity leave before the birth, but Rita just kept working and had a full two months paid leave once the baby arrived. In response to her questions about American workers, we talked about the lack of a legal right to maternity leave in the U.S. and the poor working conditions of many garment workers in California.

I returned a couple of days later and interviewed two more women who were working at Belita. Aurora Soares was a bit older, having been born in 1940. Her father had been a teacher and then trained as a nurse. When I asked if she had been "loboloed," she responded, "No, my father did not accept lobolo, it was a civil marriage and in the Catholic Church. All of us, not just me, my whole family does not accept lobolo." Though Aurora's attitude seemed more logical than Rita Bacare's, Rita's family's expectation of lobolo was a good example of how such cultural practices continued in the face of religious and political censure. Aurora had also learned to sew in a mission school on a manual machine, first encountering an electric sewing machine at Belita. She had twelve living children, ranging in age from twenty-five down to four years old. The oldest who were still at home watched over the younger ones, helped with the housework, and assisted with the cultivation of rice in her urban machamba. She had begun to suffer from pains in her legs, so her doctor had told her to stay out of the water in the rice field. That year she expected to harvest three or four sacks of rice, a yield that was much reduced from her output in previous years.

When we were talking more informally after the interview, I commented that the Belita workers all seemed to know each other well, and they replied that they did. Ana Maria Helena said they had held a workplace party to

The Mackerel Years

celebrate April 7th, Mozambican Women's Day, and the workers had come with their spouses. And they had also sponsored a family party for Children's Day on June 1st. Such activities reinforced the image of Belita as a pleasant place to work.

I returned a few more times to do more interviews, but it was sometimes hard to set things up. Ana Maria Helena was ill for a while, and one warm day when I arrived, she was wearing a heavy sweater as she had chills and was obviously not well. More than once I would ride my bike out to the factory, only to find that it was closed because there was no electricity in that neighborhood.

In mid-December Mercie got sick again. She had a very slight fever, and no appetite, so she was napping while we ate lunch. When Steve went to check on her, he found her in the throes of a convulsion. We plopped her into the bathtub to cool down her fever. The tub was already filled with lukewarm water, as we were in the middle of another power cut and following our regular precaution, we had run the water into the tub as soon as the electricity went out. While Steve went to call Gama, I held Mercie in the water. She had a second convulsion in the tub, but I refused to get flustered. I needed to embrace her slippery little body securely, leaning awkwardly over the tub edge and holding her head above the water line.

Gama arrived, took control of the situation, and drove us straight to the hospital. Gama was able to do the spinal tap and a blood test for malaria, so Steve was spared. All the tests came back negative, and it appeared that Mercie had a common benign childhood condition that brought on febrile convulsions in response to high fevers. The seizures typically cease when the child reaches six or seven years of age, but obviously can be a source of extreme anxiety for parents. By evening Mercie was back to normal, doing her new trick of walking around the apartment on tiptoes.

In addition to worrying about Mercie and keeping her home when she was ill, I had more bureaucratic hassles

Chapter 22

regarding getting research permission. I was frustrated in my attempts to contact Pamela dos Santos. She was never in her office when I stopped by, and I finally left the letter that Aquino da Bragança had written for me on the flight from Zimbabwe. On a Friday evening a few days later, Sr. Ramos, from Pamela dos Santos's office, called to tell me that she had just left for Maputo and so could not meet with me. He made no suggestion about arranging a meeting when she returned. He relayed her advice, which was that I should go directly to OMM. I suspected that was somewhat devious, that he would only call me when Pamela had left town, so that I had no possibility of talking to her directly.

I returned to OMM to ask for a guia to do research in the local archives. I spoke with Maria João, whom I had met in the OMM offices previously. She asked that I return when the provincial secretary was there, as only the provincial secretary could make such a decision. Yet when I rode back out to the OMM office several days later, I was informed by the staff that they had decided that the OMM secretary could not issue a guia, only the minister could—only Marcelino dos Santos, minister-resident and governor of the province! I immediately went upstairs to the office of the provincial first lady, Pamela dos Santos, to see if I could work something out via that route. Her assistant, the above-mentioned furtive Sr. Ramos, told me, "No indeed, you should approach OMM and if the OMM provincial secretary thinks that the minister should make the guia decision, then she herself should address Marcelino about taking the next step." But the reality was that the OMM staff did not want me to meet with the OMM secretary until I had approval from Marcelino. It was a classic "Catch-22" situation, as each office refused to take responsibility and simultaneously requested that I not circumvent them to find someone who would make the decision. I felt like screaming, "Somebody just take responsibility!!"

As I commented at the time, "You'd think they'd have better ways to spend their time," faced with a growing war, worsening hunger, and generally depleted conditions in the city and in the province. I amused myself by imagining a state governor in the U.S. worrying about such trivialities. I did not believe then that OMM and the government were deliberately trying to keep me from my research for political reasons, though that was not an unknown experience for researchers in some African countries. In retrospect, it seems that there might have been some apprehension about trusting an American researcher with open access to archives, meetings, and other sources. Mozambique was a new nation still trying to develop its own ideas about its history, and the United States had policies that opposed Mozambique's own development plans, including support for apartheid South Africa. But at the time it felt like a combination of overwrought bureaucracy along with a legacy of timidity, where no one wanted to be the individual who gave the "okay." It was enough to turn someone down by sending them to another office or asking them to return another day, while never actually saying "no"—a procedure that was not directed exclusively at non-Mozambicans. A cartoon that ran in the weekly magazine *Tempo* in 1983 showed a man at a desk saying to another, "Ah, Sr. Carlos. Your document has not been signed yet, come back tomorrow." Then the second box showed the same two men with long white beards, and the bureaucrat was saying, "Ah, Sr. Carlos. Tomorrow you will have everything resolved."

While waiting for some resolution to the stalled bureaucracy, I just kept going to places where I was known and my presence was already accepted. At Belita one day the office staff gave me their annual reports to look at and, while I was sitting at an out-of-the-way desk copying out the reports by hand, the director of the factory came along. He talked to me for a while about women's work, remarking that, "There are women who are heads of sections in the factory who are still ordered around by their husbands at home." He felt that Mozambican society did not have a good appreciation of working women and, while the situation was changing

Chapter 22

for the better with laws supporting women's rights, in general Mozambique was in a bad position because of underdevelopment.

He also found a report in the files that he thought would interest me, an account of an incident from 1979. It contained a lot of intriguing information that I found invaluable. The report mentioned that only five women worked at Belita at independence in 1975, none of them at the sewing machines. The process of hiring women had accelerated rapidly after that. But during the late 1970s, women in the garment factory were still a new phenomenon and there were several cases where women were perceived to be malingering, claiming they were not well and could not do their regular work. As I had seen, pregnant women were allowed to work away from the sewing machines, and the report was not critical of pregnant women or of women who had other legitimate claims. Rather than simply fire those who frequently requested lighter work without a legitimate reason, the factory leadership organized a series of meetings and discussions that included representatives from OMM and the Ministry of Health. They set up a protocol for confirming that women who were hired were physically able to do the work. It was a fascinating document, an internal memo that illustrated how the new socialist management was dealing with women workers through involving workers in the decision-making. I was thrilled that it had been made available to me and greatly appreciated that they allowed me to write out my own copy for my files.[1]

I continued with an interview schedule at Belita. I had hoped to include an interview with Ana Maria Helena's grandmother, one of the first women to work at the factory, but there were intervening events. When I tried to arrange a time, I learned that Ana Maria Helena's uncle had passed away and her grandmother had returned to Inhambane with the body, as her family was always buried in their home village. But women who were working in the factory were available and we had many wide-ranging discussions.

Joana Madeira was another garment worker who had been educated to the fourth grade in the mission schools and had taken further training in Beira. She told me, referring to a specific training manual, that she "had taken a course in patterns... that olive-colored book, I took the olive course." Her father bought a sewing machine for her, and for several years she had a successful home-based small business as a dressmaker. She was one of the first women to come to work at Belita, so I asked her, "What happened in 1979, when women were possibly malingering?" She avoided speaking of individuals by telling me that "where a lot of women work, there are always problems... because no one can understand another person's situation. I can understand my own illness. Another person's, I cannot understand. ... But now we are fine, there are no more problems."

Ana Maria Cristina told a story of how the new laws supported women. Her first pregnancy had ended in a miscarriage, so, when she became pregnant a second time her doctor ordered her to rest in bed from her fourth month. He did not want her to climb the stairs at the factory or be involved in other physical labor. She stayed home and, as she recalled, "At home also I did nothing, I did not pound in the mortar, I did not go to my machamba, nothing. Until the ninth month, when I had the baby, I had a normal birth." In the poorest nation on earth at that time, she had benefited from paid medical leave for the entire five months that she was away from the factory and was able to return to her former position, an indication of the important legal provisions for women that had been introduced by the socialist government.

After the interviews, Joana Madeira turned the tables and commented, "You ask a lot and you are learning about us, but can you tell us something about women in the United States?" Many issues were common to women in the U.S. and Mozambique, as we discovered in discussing the problems of getting men to do housework. Ana Maria

Chapter 22

Cristina said she found it easier to get her children to help with housework than to count on her husband, although she thought men were more likely to help with childcare. For instance, her husband was willing to change their baby's diapers, but resisted doing other work around the house. Steve and I had divided housework as evenly as possible, taking turns cooking meals and sharing other tasks, but we recognized that it was not usual for couples to make the effort to arrange household responsibilities like that.

Regarding abortion, the garment workers I interviewed were uncomfortable with expanding access. They feared that women would then go walking, walking, "*andava, andava,*" from man to man if they no longer faced the consequence of pregnancy. They also believed that their children were learning too much about sexuality in their biology classes, with the result that they wanted to go "practice" what they were learning about. Some of their attitudes could be traced to the influence of the Catholic Church in Mozambique, as they had all been educated in Catholic mission schools and the Church was especially strong in urban areas. But local African attitudes also encouraged motherhood. Most African women expected to become mothers many times over and ending a pregnancy by abortion ran counter to their most fundamental ideas regarding female adulthood. The high rate of infant mortality was also a factor. Women wanted to have children who would provide for them when they were elderly, and it was already difficult to successfully raise their offspring to adulthood.

Local herbal abortifacients were known and used at times but improving legal access to safe medical abortions was not a vital concern of Mozambican women or of the women's organization. Ironically, it had been an apprehension of mine while we were there, as my menstrual cycle had been disrupted by the move to Mozambique. When I experienced the first month or two in Beira with no period, I feared I was pregnant. I did not want to go through a pregnancy while living there, so I investigated my options, and considered having an abortion though it was not legal in Mozambique. As a cooperante, I could have found a way, but it was a false alarm for me, though an enduring anxiety for many women.

Divorce was viewed as a problem as well, as there were many cases of men abandoning women and leaving them in a difficult situation. In a traditional non-registered marriage, abandonment was a de facto divorce that left women without support. One approach was to improve women's access to legal assistance for maintenance and child support. The garment workers who were conversing with me all agreed that, in the new justice system of local tribunals, women often had a chance to get support, whether the marriage was official or not. Women who served as judges on the tribunals were willing to listen to women who had a complaint. And the workers discussed changes in women's work opportunities. I commented that the expansion in women's work options was a recent change and that most women still worked in their machambas, and Joana responded, "Like slaves"—the second time a Belita worker had compared women's work to slave labor.

I always enjoyed these relaxed conversations where the women were more willing to comment on current politics. Once the tape recorder was turned off, they dropped their guard. They were invariably interested in how American women lived and were surprised when I told them that though living conditions were better in the U.S., they had more legal rights in Mozambique. They even had a constitutional provision for equal rights for women and significant supports for family leave, that women in the U.S. continued to struggle to achieve. The Equal Rights Amendment (ERA) would have amended the U.S. Constitution to include wording that made women the legal equals of men, a proviso that was already in the Mozambican Constitution. The ERA had apparently lost a long and hard-fought battle in 1982, though attempts to finalize its passage were revived in the 2020s.

My time at Belita was coming to an end. When I returned for more interviews in mid-February, they were working hard to meet their production goals and could not spare any women from the sewing machines. I interviewed a young woman from the packaging sector who really was too young to tell me very much and, with better results, I spoke with Castigo Bie Bie, a man who had worked at the factory for twenty years and had a lot of information about the history of the factory. But as I was leaving that day Ana Maria Helena said, "So, Dona Caterina (the Portuguese version of my name), I guess you are about done here." "Well," I thought, "not really, but I guess I am if you say so." I suspected my visits were becoming an imposition and, since I was asking the same questions of each woman, it must have seemed to them that it was unnecessary to collect more interviews on the same topic.

When I looked at the series of interviews I had completed, I could see the shared experience of the garment workers. Mozambique under colonialism had an extremely poor record of educating girls, with the result that only 7 percent of Mozambican women could read and write in Portuguese at independence. African men also fared badly in the colonial education system, though in 1975 the male literacy rate was twice that of women, with 14 percent able to read Portuguese. Yet at Belita I had found a group of women who had been educated in mission schools during the colonial era, where they had learned to sew. The irony was that Belita had been an almost entirely male factory until after independence, so the current garment workers had been trained in the colonial era for jobs that did not exist until years later, when the provincial Labor Ministry along with the women's organization had devised a plan to hire more women. As with the nurses, jobs that were commonly associated with women in much of the world had been reserved for men in Mozambique. Women's job opportunities had expanded only when a socialist government came to power.

Endnote

1. I returned to Beira in 1989 and went back to the Belita factory. I gave them a copy of my newly completed dissertation, and they showed me another document related to the one described here. Those reports and my analysis were published as "A Report on a 'Delicate Problem' Concerning Female Garment Workers in Beira, Mozambique," *Signs* 16, 3 (1991): 575-586.

Chapter 23
Bureaucracy and Shortages

December 1983

I went to the OMM headquarters to meet with the provincial secretary and was told that she had gone for the week to Marromeu, a town north of Beira on the Zambezi River. I asked the women who were there if I would be able to attend a city-wide OMM meeting that was planned for later that week, and they told me there would be no problem, but I should go to the city OMM office for permission. The next morning, I went to the OMM municipal headquarters and learned that the meeting would in fact begin that afternoon at the Escola Comercial Amílcar Cabral. (Amílcar Cabral was the highly regarded revolutionary leader of Guinea-Bissau who led that country to liberation from Portuguese colonialism.) I asked again if I could attend as an observer and was taken to meet Alice Meigos, the OMM secretary for the city of Beira. She seemed pleased and reiterated that it would be fine, I could attend.

I went to the school after lunch and found about fifty men and women waiting for the doors to open. We chatted about the usual topics that occupied everyone, especially food. People said there was a lot of food in the outlying districts, but there was no transport to bring it into the urban markets. It was a lively gathering, banners flying with

The Mackerel Years

slogans, "Vamos apoiar as vítimas da seca" (Let's support the victims of the drought) and "Viva o Presidente Samora Machel Dirigente Querido do nosso povo" (Long live President Samora Machel, Beloved Leader of our people). The cultural group from the cashew factory was drumming and dancing, the women wearing light green shirts and green plaid skirts. I knew several people there, including Lília, the nurse I had interviewed, who was staffing the first aid room, and other women I had met at the provincial meeting in September.

Then a woman I recognized came up to me and greeted me warmly, kissing both my cheeks in the usual way, and said, "I'm sorry, but your name is not on the list of invitees, so I can't let you enter." I explained about all the verbal arrangements, and she checked around with some others, but the result was that I needed a written document to attend, and it had to be from the provincial level as they had made the initial order about holding the meeting. I went home, called the OMM provincial office, and arranged to go out there to get the necessary document the next morning. In the end it was all fruitless, as the provincial secretary was the only individual who could make the decision, and she was in Marromeu for the week and had not delegated any responsibility to others on her staff. I had made four bike trips out to the OMM provincial offices about attending this one meeting, but with no results. Maria João explained that there were four people in the office, but none of them could make any independent decisions. I must have looked disappointed, as she went on to tell me that I shouldn't feel sad: "We like you and we think you are doing good work, but we must follow regulations." In the end, however, I did not observe the city OMM meeting.

In early December we experienced another power outage that continued for ten days. I complained in a letter to my mother that the refrigerator was like any old storage cupboard, as we could not use it to preserve food that needed to be cold. Around that time, we got a phone call

Chapter 23

from a small vegetable shop where we occasionally had found items. The shop, a storefront a few blocks away from the downtown area, was owned by a family of South Asian descent. I used to stop there every week on my way to the bookstore where I collected our *Tempo* magazine subscription. When the vegetable bins were empty one week, I asked the owner when he would be getting more supplies. He replied, "Write down your phone number and I will let you know." I did that, leaving our phone number in a moment of foolish optimism, as I honestly did not expect that we would ever hear from him when he had something to sell. But several weeks later he did call when he had vegetables, so we rode our bikes to the store and bought five kilograms of cabbage and ten kilograms (over twenty pounds) each of tomatoes and green peppers. That was, as I wrote in my journal, "a hell of a lot of peppers!" We had Francisco cut them into chunks and bag them, and we stored them in a freezer at the hospital that was connected to a generator that continued to function during the frequent power outages. Steve would stop by the freezer when he left work and break off a chunk of frozen peppers to bring home. The tomatoes and cabbage we ate up a bit more quickly, but the peppers, added judiciously to sauces and stews, lasted until March or April and during most of those four months they were the only green vegetable that was available.

The holidays were approaching again. December 25th would be Family Day, and there was food in the markets, especially staples such as rice, flour, sugar, and oil, as well as cookies. Christmas Day was quiet. Mercie received a lot of toys from family in the U.S. and most of the gifts had arrived on time, as our families had learned how long it took mail to reach us. She had a new doll, a set of doll dishes and pans, some books, and a cat puppet, all of which kept her busy for most of the day.

We prepared a substantial Christmas dinner with chicken *and* ham, rice, peas in a cheese sauce (using canned peas from one of the Soviet families), fruitcake, dark beer (which was much nicer than the usual light beer), wine, and cognac. Steve and Jacky joined us for the feast, in which nearly every component had been bought with dollars or sent from overseas. They brought Mercie a small, motorized motorcycle, a very noisy toy, but a memento of their own real motorcycle. One additional bright spot was receiving a tax refund check for $2,006.07. As I wrote to my mother when I sent the check along to her, we had "won the I.R.S. Sweepstakes." The check was twice what we had expected and went a long way to covering our foreign exchange expenses.

The following week we had a meal with Steve and Jacky to celebrate the New Year, which I greeted in my journal with the laconic comment, "Well, Happy New Year." We enjoyed a lunch of shrimp omelets, a mixed green salad, and chocolate pudding, detailed in my journal as I did with every exceptional meal. We went to bed early, but at midnight we were awakened by screaming and shouting, glass breaking, cans being banged together, and gunshots, as militia and soldiers fired their assault rifles with red tracer bullets into the air. "So, welcome 1984," I wrote. I was not feeling very celebratory at that point.

The evening of January 1st, we joined a crowd of Swedish and Dutch medical cooperantes at the beach near the hospital. It was a gorgeous evening, the sun was setting in a blaze of orange and purple over the Indian Ocean, we cooked hot dogs and ate chocolate cake, and Mercie just lay in the warm water as the tide receded. On another visit to the beach, we watched dozens of tiny crabs dig into the sand, running sideways into little holes, and scrabbling out with their claws filled with sand which they tossed aside. Mercie thought they were eating sand. Another weekend we had a pleasant omelet dinner with the Swedish family, Anders, Marie, and their two children, though Steve was on call for pediatric emergencies and had to leave for part of the evening.

Chapter 23

I was working on the history of the health services in Beira, as suggested by Rui Bastos. I wrote a five-page report, which I turned over to Gama. That account became my first publication resulting from my research, as one year after we left Mozambique a version of my history was published as a general interest story in a center spread of the *Diário de Moçambique*. It was fortunate that Steve Boyle was still in Beira when it appeared and he sent me the article, otherwise I would never have known that it was published. I was especially pleased that, rather than being published in an obscure scholarly journal, it appeared in the local Mozambican newspaper where it could be read by people directly involved in the history I was telling.

With respect to my research, I was re-thinking my ideas about urban life and women's history. A lot of literature about Africa (and elsewhere) emphasized a stark division between urban and rural life, on the assumption that rural conditions were simply left behind when people moved into the city. For men, urban residence may have been a stark separation from rural life, but I was learning that women were continuing their primary rural agricultural work in the city. Women were growing crops all around us. We observed that Beira was really just densely populated *mato* or countryside. Steve was struck by the agricultural appearance of the city when he climbed to the hospital roof one day to look at the surroundings. Most of the women working in factories, including the more educated garment workers, had machambas. Three of the women at the cashew factory had told me they were born in Beira and that their mothers had been peasants who farmed within the city limits.

I wished I could read what others had written about urban women and agriculture. Based on my interviews and observations, I began to think that I had a new contribution to make to African history. It was generally understood that the development of African cities was associated with industrialization and wage labor, but if women were

The Mackerel Years

put at the center when describing Beira's urbanization, it suggested an entirely different process. The urban and rural divide was very fluid and porous and rural influences on urban life more vivid when seen from a female perspective.[1]

Once the new year started, I renewed my efforts to get official approval for my research. I called the OMM office one morning and was informed that provincial director Teresa Romão was in, but when I arrived that afternoon, I learned that she was ill and had not been in the office since she had returned from Marromeu. Gossip was circulating that she had returned with seventy-five kilograms of meat, which some sources implied was evidence of elitism. It might have been a matter of her using her position to get a supply of meat, and quite likely most people would have done the same thing if they had the opportunity. When people did not have access to a desired food such as meat, such stories just increased resentment toward the elites who seemed to be doing well.

I noted a new billboard on the road to the OMM office depicting a man and a woman building a brick wall together, with the slogan, "We will involve women in all spheres of society." At that time there was no corporate advertising, but there were billboards around town with political slogans and exhortations, which I generally was pleased to see. How much better it was to advertise women's equality rather than Coca Cola! I did not miss the common western ads that used erotic images of women to push their products.

At long last, I met with Teresa Romão. She spent about thirty minutes with me and called in Sr. Ramos from Pamela dos Santos's office to clarify exactly whose jurisdiction I belonged to. The upshot was that she shunted me back to Pamela, who was out of the city just then (of course!). Teresa simply did not want to make any decisions and, although I could sympathize with her worries, I also felt that she was *in* a position of responsibility and should just take it! She also disconcerted me by saying that I had only been allowed to attend the September meeting in preparation for the Conferência Extra-ordinária because they had *vergonha*,

Chapter 23

they were ashamed that I was sitting there outside of the meeting. She questioned why, if I had arrived in Beira in July 1982, I waited to come to OMM until September 1983. I explained that initially I was waiting for documents from the university, and that in fact I had started coming to OMM in April 1983, when I had met Maria das Dores. Though it seemed too complicated to tell her the whole history of how I was still sorting out my research project during the first few months, I did defend my politics. She seemed to believe that I was just a random American woman wandering around Beira. I told her that I was a city-level leader of a socialist organization in the United States (referring to the Democratic Socialists of America, though I did not elaborate on how small and ineffectual DSA really was). And I explained that my husband and I had chosen to come to Mozambique because of its socialist politics and that we supported the revolution. In my journal I wrote, "What did she think, we're here for a lark?", a possibility that was less likely with each day of war.

When I got home, I called Steve at work and just began sobbing on the phone, I was genuinely distraught at being put back in Pamela dos Santos's hands, since she had already made it clear that she wanted nothing to do with me. Steve went and found Rui Bastos, the provincial health director who had supported my work previously, and he wrote out a guia for me to go to the Conselho Executivo, the Beira Executive Council, or City Hall.

Nonetheless, the situation escalated when Teresa Romão followed up on her belief that the governor should make the decision about allowing me to do my research. She brought up her discussion with me at a meeting of the provincial directors of programs. Rui Bastos was there from the Health Ministry, and he strongly spoke up for us, defending our politics and our plans. But Governor Marcelino dos Santos determined that he needed to talk personally to me or to Steve. Rui told us that dos Santos was not hostile, "He just does not know you," though he could have chosen to rely on the judgment of others such as Rui or delegated the decision to Teresa. Rui's report added to our anxiety, though I thought, if I did get a guia from dos Santos, then I would have entrée into any archive. Steve, as the person with the cooperante contract, went twice and wasted several hours cooling his heels outside the governor's office instead of seeing patients. He never did meet with the governor, so we gave up. At the time I wrote in my journal that, "I just can't believe all this bureaucracy—and [the City Hall archive] probably won't have the stuff I'd like at any rate," a prescient comment. In the end, all our effort and agony was futile, as I used virtually no documents from the city archives. My dissertation relied almost entirely on the interviews I conducted with working women, and for the most part they had been pleased to talk with me without invoking elaborate bureaucratic hurdles.

We were simultaneously aggravated by problems in other areas of life in Beira. The power was cut again at the beginning of January, in the depths of the hot and humid summer season. After one entire day with no power at all, conditions were deteriorating in our apartment. Francisco had to cook with the charcoal stove and there was soot all over the pans as a result. He deep-fried some half-spoiled carapau in coconut oil, a particularly foul-smelling combination of rotten fish and rancid oil. Old milk bottles were sitting around emitting an odor of decay. Though we had occasional rationed hours of electric power, we did not get regular electricity for two weeks, from January 2nd to January 15th. When it finally returned, we took the opportunity to empty the tub, as the water had gotten dirty over the two weeks. We kept it full as much as possible as a precaution. That day the water supply to the city was cut before we had a chance to refill it. City residents also seemed to be losing control, and I observed a crowd of over two hundred people gather in front of our building to encourage two women who were engaged in a physical fight. Mexicana residents watched from the safety of their

Chapter 23

balconies. The mass of people surged back and forth, eventually emerging with a young woman in their grip, as they took her off toward the office of the grupo dinamizador. I never learned what she was accused of doing.

I noted our mail problems nearly every day in my journal. Sometimes letters from my mother only traveled for two weeks before they reached us, other times we would go for two weeks with no mail at all, and at times letters from the United States took more than a month to arrive. Some days we suddenly had three letters from my mother and other mail as well, a wealth of contact with our family and friends. My sister Barbara sent an issue of *Ms.* magazine, and when I saw the January date when it arrived in January 1984, I thought it had been exceptionally speedy. Then I realized that the magazine was from January *1983* and had taken a full year to get to us!

Steve remarked that when we first arrived, he tended to place most of the blame for Mozambique's problems on South Africa and the impact of apartheid throughout the region. But he had revised that assessment, from blaming South Africa for 90 percent of the troubles to only 40 percent. The bulk of the difficulties he now viewed as being the result of ignorance and excessive bureaucracy. Many obstacles were still a consequence of decades of living under a racist colonial regime that kept Mozambicans from becoming literate and learning how to run a modern society. The weekly newspaper, *Domingo*, carried a story about an official in Polana neighborhood in Maputo who could not read a work card (*cartão de trabalho*) and had sent a worker back to his workplace to get proof that he was still employed. The cartão was perfectly in order and was itself the worker's proof of employment, which the worker knew, and which was confirmed by another grupo dinamizador employee the next day. But many thousands of productive hours were wasted with these obstructive procedures day after day. I was frustrated with my experience, but so were many Mozambicans.

Steve had a particularly disillusioning day in the emergency room. Though each incident was minor, they piled up to make the day extremely dissatisfying. First, a man came in with an injured finger. The nurse who saw him when he arrived used scarce supplies to dress the wound and then sent the man to Steve to be checked. The dressing had to be removed just minutes after it was applied so that Steve could look at the finger. Next, Steve asked another nurse to remove a woman's urinary catheter. After almost an hour of dithering around the nurse admitted that he did not know how to remove it. Similar events happened throughout his day. I hated it when those aggravations mounted up as I felt responsible for Steve's horrible, very bad day. We were in Mozambique so I could do my research and that was not going as well as could be hoped either. Though we were managing to get by, we were more easily irritated with each other and bickering more.

As conditions worsened, we were beset by frequent *pedidos*, requests for everything. I had a lengthy conversation with two men in the bank who were half-jokingly trying to determine how they could work in the U.S. and offered to work in my house for me. I told them about the unemployment rate and the racism that still limited people, but they still were sure that life would be better for them in the U.S. They were certainly correct if they were thinking of general living conditions. After doing interviews in Munhava, I got a ride back into town in an ambulance at mid-morning and the ambulance driver asked about buying Steve's bicycle. It was a common request, as people knew we would eventually be leaving Beira and would most likely leave our bikes behind. He wanted it for his fourteen-year-old son, who had to get up at 4:30 A.M. to catch the bus from the outlying suburb of Manga to the Samora Machel Secondary School in Matacuane neighborhood. A young woman working in the empty *tabacaria*, the kiosk selling sundries in our building, asked for *pappas*, the Nestlé baby cereal that we fed to Mercie. A Mozambican woman I had

Chapter 23

never seen before asked if she could buy wine on our ration card at the loja de cooperantes.

Isac and Sonia, our neighbors, came by our place numerous times with requests, for wine from the cooperative, for beer, and for rice. Sonia said, "Temos fome" (We're hungry). I wanted to reply, "Aren't we all?" Sonia asked for "eno" one time, and we spent twenty minutes looking through our dictionary, unable to understand what she needed. Finally, we deciphered her request; she wanted alka seltzer, which we did not have in any case. Isac and Sonia had a son, Milord, who was about three years old. That year they had a new baby, who they named Stiv, and they asked Steve to be the godfather. That was a traditional system of building support networks, and they did ask Steve to come and see Stiv when he was sick. But we were not in a position then to provide the kinds of gifts expected of godparents. Steve finally told Isac how badly supplied we were ourselves and explained that we simply could not support them to the extent they seemed to expect, and they backed off a bit.

It was demoralizing for us to be in that situation, where we could not help as much as we wished we could. We shared when we could, but sometimes we said no if our own supplies were dangerously low or, as was the case often enough, we simply did not have what they needed. When we told them that we did not have the items they requested, we feared that they did not believe us and that they viewed us as being ungenerous, perhaps even hoarding goods. We did leave some of our belongings with them when we left, including a prized Members Only jacket that Steve gave to Isac. Though we sent gifts for Stiv when we returned to the U.S., we lost touch after a few years. We later found each other via social media and sent funds so that Stiv, as an adult, could replace the roof on his home after the disastrous cyclone that severely damaged Beira in 2019.

It was exhausting to be constantly fielding such requests from friends and strangers. Knowing that we would be leaving in a few months and could remove ourselves from the rough life of wartime Mozambique did not make it easier. We felt helpless. While we were living there, we were not much better off than most of our neighbors. But the conditions of our lives were such that we *were* in a better situation and it would soon improve immeasurably. Everyone around us knew that we would return to the comforts of life in the United States. But while we were living in Beira, we shared that city's scarcity and problems, and unhappily could do little to ameliorate conditions for those around us.

Endnote

1 My findings were published in Kathleen Sheldon, "*Machambas* in the City: Urban Women and Agricultural Work in Mozambique," *Lusotopie* (1999): 121-140; see also a later study, Murtah Shannon, Kei Otsuki, Annelies Zoomers, and Mayke Kaag, "On Whose Land is the City to be Build? Farmers, Donors and the Urban Land Question in Beira City, Mozambique," *Urban Studies* 58, 4 (2021):733-749.

Chapter 24
Talking with Market Women

January to May 1984

I returned to the Conselho Executivo one morning and spoke with Sr. Gomes, who remembered me from my visit the previous year. He was very helpful, accepting the guia I had from Rui Bastos and telling me how important it was to learn about the history of the city. But, he said, "All of the colonial papers were sent to the national archive in Maputo, and we really have nothing left here for you to see." Sr. Gomes told me, "Of course, women and men do all the same work, nurses, electricians, in offices, it is all the same." I thought that "of course" they were not doing the same work, but it was interesting that he believed that such a change had already happened.

    I returned to the city council offices a couple of weeks later with specific questions I had formulated, hoping Sr. Gomes would know where I could find the answers. When I first went to find him, he was out on *treinos* (militia training), which was being stepped up with hundreds of Beira residents jogging in formation through the downtown streets. He was back at work that afternoon, trading treinos stories with his co-workers.

I inquired about municipal archives on land holdings, thinking that I might find out whether women owned property in the city center and what sorts of land and buildings were owned by women. Sr. Gomes discussed my request with numerous people and walked me upstairs to the Construcção sector, which handled zoning regulations and building requests. There I was handed along to three different people, as no one knew how to respond to my request, but thought perhaps the next person might have an idea. As it turned out, their records were simply file cards with the lot number and owner's name, but with no information about the size of the lot or whether it was residential or commercial. Ordinarily, one would fill out a card requesting a specific file which would be delivered to you from their archives. That was not a workable process for me, as I wanted to develop a gendered overview of land holdings, and to accomplish that I would have to ask for every file or organize a random selection. But assuming women had title to only a few lots, I could potentially have spent hours requesting files that were useless for my research. Eventually Sr. Domingos from the city archives came along to escort me into the file room. There I could see that they were not organized in any way that would aid my research.

I asked Sr. Gomes about a report that someone had mentioned to me, that discussed women participating in forced labor on the roads during the colonial era. He said, "I've never seen women doing that sort of work in the city, but maybe one of the older people will know more about that." He called in an older man who had been in Buzi, outside of the city proper.

That man, whose name I never learned, told me, "Yes, women did forced labor on the roads, especially when an administrator or other important person was expected to make a visit. The local chief would collect some women to clean the road, they would work for a few days. The chief would give them food, but they were not paid." "Women did it," Sr. Gomes interjected, "because the men were all away at work, outside of Mozambique or on sisal or cotton plantations."

I asked about women in the markets, hoping to get some statistics, and Sr. Gomes referred me to Comércio Interno. I learned that although the women market vendors paid 10 meticais (25 cents) a day for a license to sell in the formal cement marketplace, the government kept no records of how many vendors there were and certainly not of the gender breakdown among the vendors. All they had was a set of ticket books that held the unmarked stubs of the tickets given to the vendors when they paid their fee. I never got the statistical information I was seeking.

When I returned the next day, I was taken down the street to the main city offices of Comércio Interno, where I spoke with the director. They never really understood my intentions, as foreigners trying to do research were uncommon at that time. But the Comércio Interno director phoned someone I never identified who mysteriously told him he should support me. As a result, his office immediately issued a guia that allowed me to go into any market and interview the vendors. I was not even aware that I was asking for that, as it seemed to imply an entirely new research project which I was not prepared to begin.

Armed with my new guia, I took immediate advantage of the surprise entrée to the markets and started to interview market women. The downtown market, built of cement with a tin roof over the entire structure, held about seventy stalls on the ground floor alone. There were more stalls on the second floor and in an adjacent wooden building, though during the two years that I was regularly visiting the market, most of those stalls were unused. I met with an older man who supervised the cement market. When I explained that I would like to talk to some of the women, he immediately walked out of his office and called the women over. Altogether there were about fifteen, including a tiny old woman who I was hoping to interview because I expected she would have many years of vending experience. But we had trouble understanding each other, partly because she had a lisp. Avó, or Grandmother, as I named her to myself, kept mentioning "when the newspaper came," a reference to an interview that had appeared in the paper in late December. The other vendors seemed pleased with my plan to interview them, and I prepared to return the next afternoon. As we spoke, a crowd of men and boys gathered to observe, only to have the women shoo them away, saying "This meeting is for women only!"

But when I arrived at the market the next day, none of the three older women who had agreed to speak with me was present. I went back again the following morning, but the market was too noisy and we set a new time for Saturday evening, though that time did not work out either. I did talk briefly with Avó before I left and learned that she had worked in the market for fifteen years. She told me, "In the time of the *brancos* (whites) there had been plenty of food, but since Frelimo came it had been *menos, menos, menos* (less, less, less)."

I went to the central market again in mid-April, but that day there were only six or seven women there, including Avó. The only items for sale were a few small piles of ground piri piri and some turnip leaves (*nabiço*). Avó refused to be interviewed, though she told me a condensed comic version of her life while I tried to organize a more formal discussion. She claimed that after twenty years of work she had arranged a small house for herself, but then Frelimo came and took it away. The other women were laughing uproariously, she was so amusing. I enjoyed her performance as well, but it was not what I thought I needed for my research, and I did not note down the specifics of her comments.

I never did have success in conducting more structured interviews with the market women at the cement market downtown. Much later, I realized how I had imposed my structure on the interview process, and I wished I had been more intuitive and flexible while I was in the middle of the research. At the time I thought I needed a specific set of

Chapter 24

information so that I could produce an acceptable study of women and work. Though I was not doing a quantitative study, I tried to gather comparable sets of data about women across a spectrum of work sites.

The vendors that day suggested that I go to the neighborhoods with OMM. My journal response to that was simply "Ha." I did begin to go to some of the neighborhood markets on my own, however. I went to Inhamudima and stopped by the small building that held the health post. One of the young men working as an assistant took me over to the market and then disappeared. An older man selling plastic wallets from a market stall began collecting women and brought a chair over to the shady side of a small cement-block building. Gabriel, a younger man who was the responsável for the market, helped facilitate the procedure as well. Soon children began to arrive until about a hundred of them were milling around, trying to see what was happening. Finally, a dozen women joined me, and I began to explain that I was interested in their own stories about their work and their lives. Gabriel translated into Chisena as I repeated myself endlessly, but my motives remained obscure to them. They kept apologizing because even though I had made arrangements in advance with two days' notice, very few women were in attendance. Eventually they understood that I did not want a meeting with a lot of women, but simply wanted to interview them one at a time.

I requested that we adjourn to the health post, and we walked back there, followed by what seemed like all the children in the entire bairro. About a dozen women were still accompanying me, when I only wanted to interview two or three that afternoon. At that moment one woman arrived late, and after some confused explanations in Chisena she turned to me and pointedly asked in Portuguese, "What is it that you are doing exactly?" All the women were apprehensive and seemed to fear that they would be unable to answer my inquiries, though I gave them samples of the kinds of questions I would be asking.

After these protracted discussions I did manage to complete one brief interview with a vendor named Minalda Maninke. She was originally from Massinga, moving to Beira after her first marriage ended in separation. She had sold oranges, tomatoes, and bananas at the cement market downtown, but as supplies diminished, she shifted to selling manioc leaves at the less-structured market in Inhamudima. Manioc leaves were used to make a sauce called *matapa*, which was served over rice or massa and was one of the most common meals eaten by Mozambicans. When well prepared with coconut or peanuts added it was a very tasty and nutritious dish, but often people had to make do with a plain version that was much less appetizing.

When I went back to Inhamudima the following week, there was a lot of activity, as the vendors were selling piles of dried fish and there were mounds of manioc leaves for sale. I had been feeling unwell and had missed one day that we had arranged for my return, and the day I did show up no one was prepared to take the time to answer my questions. Another day I lingered for a long while in the health post waiting room as a young student wrote in the record book and a mother, father, and their one-year-old child sat on the cot in the corner. Gimo, the nurse I had met previously, then brought me out to meet three women who had agreed to talk with me. They were accompanied by Simon Mutembe, the neighborhood responsável for health, who was prepared to translate for me. We all sat on chairs in the shade along the side of a small building behind the health post, and I balanced the tape recorder on my knees. It was a glorious day after a lot of rain, sunny yet cool with a comfortable breeze. There were very few other people around. Two other men who were chatting on chairs nearby were asked to leave so we could have more privacy. Children came and peeked at us and ran off, and a kitten cleaned itself in the sun.

Chapter 24

The first two interviews went well, though they were brief. The third woman only spoke Chitswa, so that encumbered my attempts at a more easy-going discussion as I had held with the first two. The market itself was tiny and makeshift, with perhaps a dozen wooden stalls, a few with thatched awning-like covers for roofs. Other vendors simply set up mats on the ground. I was never able to get an accurate count of the numbers of male and female vendors, which appeared to be about half and half. Then I lost more time as I spent over a week in bed with another undiagnosed illness. It was not malaria, as my blood test was negative. I took a course of chloroquine just in case, but I continued to be feverish, dizzy, and completely incapacitated with weakness.

I went to other neighborhood markets as well, but with less success. At the Maquinino market, which was the largest of the non-cement markets, all the vendors were men. At the Ponta Gêa market there were immense lines for fish on the day I visited, so I did not try to approach any of the women. I went back to Inhamudima hoping I could work out an interview plan, as I remained optimistic about my research despite all evidence and experience, but the market was empty on the day I rode my bike back down the dusty paths. The servente at the health post who had been helpful on previous visits told me that the reason was *fome* or hunger, and the women vendors were waiting in line for bread.

Another day I rode out to Inhamudima on my bicycle along paths deep in mud from the rain, with big holes gouged out along the edges. At one point I had to detour around a huge puddle, really a small pond that had appeared in the middle of my route. Inhamudima was close to downtown Beira and, given the conditions in that relatively urban neighborhood, I was gaining a better appreciation for the obstacles in rural areas, where no roads were paved and no government service was available to make repairs on the vulnerable dirt byways. As I left that day, picking my way through the muck and walking my bike, another bike rider on his way into the neighborhood commiserated about the boggy conditions, saying, "We're really bad here!"

Despite the limited interviews that I was able to have with market women, it was clear that, as a group, they were much more vulnerable than the factory women and the nurses. They had more precarious marriages and were much closer to living in dire poverty. For most of them, market vending was a desperate option to try to bring a little income into their household. In the end, I did not include market women in my dissertation, as the information I had was too partial to allow for a full comparison. I was able to incorporate some of those findings into my later work on urban women in Mozambique, as their anecdotal stories added to the history of women and work in the cities.[1]

Sr. Gomes had suggested that the Labor Ministry might have information, or perhaps I should go to each individual company. The latter idea was daunting, not least because of my experience at the cashew factory, where they had told me they had destroyed all the records from the years before independence. But I did eventually go to the Labor Ministry, where initially they were very accommodating and told me they could give me preliminary statistics from a survey they were in the process of conducting. When I first went to the ministry, the chief was in treinos, but I was encouraged when those who were there did not ask me for my guia. The bureaucratic mentality was not present everywhere, but the difficulty for me was that I needed to be prepared for it when it did appear. When I returned after a few days, I met with Victor, a section chief who was very anxious about my request. He was worried about security and that the figures were incomplete, though, as I told him, I would appreciate any material they could share with me, as I had nothing. Victor took the guia I had from Rui Bastos and showed it to his director. I was very apprehensive myself, because I feared the provincial director of labor would remember my case being discussed at the provincial directors' meeting and

Chapter 24

might require a guia from the governor. But when Victor came back, he simply requested, "Can you come back at the end of April? We will have more complete data then."

I made repeated visits to the Labor Ministry office throughout May. Once I was told that the office did have statistics, but they were locked in Victor's office, so I would have to return. Finally, during my last week in Beira, Sr. Victor copied out a handwritten set of numbers for me, material that was not available anywhere else at that time, outlining the gender division of labor in basic employment sectors such as industry, agriculture, and government. The information in the unpublished report showed over 24,000 men working in industry, but only 1,380 women holding factory-based jobs. In a city of over 250,000 residents, those numbers reflected the restricted openings for women in the waged sector of the economy.

We went to the beach again one January weekend with Steve and Jacky and a gruff and stocky South African named Alf. He made us uncomfortable as he bragged about having been a mercenary, though he claimed he was reformed and was working at the airport for the transport company IAL. But we had a nice enough time, grilling sausages for a braai, the typical South African barbecue, while Mercie dug in the sand. The ocean was a bit too rough for wading as it was storm season. Later that week we were treated to a fantastic rainbow, a full arc with huge broad bands of glowing colors. The rain clouds were high, and we could see needles of rain falling and dispersing before they hit the ground.

A month later we were surprised to learn that Jacky had left Steve. We had sensed that she was not happy, so we were not so shocked that she left him, as to discover that she had left him for Alf, the self-proclaimed mercenary. Alf was much older than us and we had never felt comfortable in his company. He seemed too glib and I never quite trusted his politics. It was clear she would not return to Steve, but at first I did not believe she would remain long with Alf either, though years later we heard that they were still together. When she stopped by later in the month, I could see a purple bruise circling her upper arm, and my eyes kept straying to it as we visited, but I did not know how to intervene if he was beating her. I never did say anything, and we gradually saw less of her while still spending a lot of time and sharing many meals with Steve.

Living in Mozambique was rough on marriages, as cooperantes were living far from their familiar friends and family and were forced to rely on each other for everything. There was little in the way of diversion, the work was stressful, and everyday living involved constant struggle. We knew of other cooperante couples who had a hard time staying together under those circumstances, though Steve and I fared relatively well considering how different our experiences were. Despite the difficulties, my work often involved meeting interesting women and finding evidence of progress that had been made since independence. Steve had witnessed hundreds of deaths, most of them children, while treating everything from suicide attempts to battlefield casualties to starvation. He was not always easy to live with because his daily anguish from confronting the agony of others left him frustrated and exhausted. But we knew that living there was temporary and soon we would be back in our accustomed life in southern California.

In early January Mercie moved into her new creche, for children from two to four years old. We had talked to her about the change that was coming, explaining that there would be a new creche and new *titias* (teachers, literally "aunties"; it is pronounced *tee-tee-ahs*). She seemed unconcerned and told us, "And new pappas, and new Mercie and new Mommy and new Daddy." It was hard to understand just what her conception was of all the changes, but she was certainly not anxious. When she finally started going to the new creche, she immediately saw other children she had known at the babies' creche, and she settled right in. The creche was closer to our neighborhood and was in

Chapter 24

a one-story building surrounded by a fenced-in yard, so the conditions were much improved over the old place in downtown Beira. Once when I dropped her off, though, there were dozens of children on a porch, many of them crying, and no titia in sight. When a woman in a bata finally appeared, she told me that Mercie's group was relatively large, with thirty-eight children. She did not say how many teachers and aides were assigned to watch them, but it seemed that they were understaffed.

Mercie's creche was closed for over a week because they had no food. We never learned what the specific problem was, but as I remained home with her for many days, my own work was also disrupted. When she finally returned, they had only massa for the children, which we learned Mercie was refusing to eat even though she had enjoyed it for many months. When we could, we fed her a big breakfast of bread with peanut butter and fried eggs (which she called "yolk egg"). I visited another childcare center on a return visit to Beira in 1989, when Mozambique was still poor and food options limited, and I was told that the children had a little song, "Todos os dias, massa só, massa só" (Every day, only massa).

Steve had set up a schedule of visiting all the creches in Beira as part of a Ministry of Health investigation. I accompanied him when he went out to Mobeira, the flour and biscuit factory. That creche was small and seemed to have mainly babies who were all coughing. The director was a young woman who had completed the fourth grade and taken a brief course in early childhood education. She also taught the adult literacy class in the factory. At least they had no problem with food, as they could rely on the production of the factory itself. But there were no toys and not even a real play space.

While we were touring, the mothers came in to feed their babies as the law permitted. All nursing mothers were allowed a half hour in the morning and another thirty minutes in the afternoon to nurse their babies. When they learned that Steve was a doctor, two of them complained that they had no milk. Steve, who had been trained in breastfeeding support in residency, then gently expressed milk from their breasts to demonstrate that they had plenty for their babies. Many women did have a diminished supply of milk as a result of their own malnourishment, but not those mothers. I thought briefly about trying to interview the women workers at Mobeira, but it was in a distant suburb, farther from the city center than Caju in Manga, and getting transport there would have been impossible. When Steve tried to visit the cashew factory creche, he learned that the factory was closed and only seventy workers were still doing maintenance there.

I made several attempts to interview Marcela Sola, the mother of Ana, a cashew worker I had interviewed. Marcela was based in Munhava and I missed one appointment because a torrential rainstorm made the roads impassable. When I arranged another time to meet her, Marcela never did show up and there was no way for me to contact either Ana or her mother to set a new date. That same afternoon I returned to Inhamudima market, where I was supposed to meet a few more vendors. But no one was around. I lamented that I had lost an entire day, ending it overheated and exhausted from biking around Beira, but without a single new interview. Even though the missed interviews resulted from a variety of mixed-up communications and difficulties that were beyond my control, I was discouraged about my repeated failures to accomplish specific research, as my time in Beira was coming to an end.

Endnote

1   Kathleen Sheldon, "Markets and Gardens: Placing Women in the History of Urban Mozambique," *Canadian Journal of African Studies* 37, 2 and 3 (2003): 358-395.

Chapter 25
Tragedy and Kabanga

March to June 1984

In early March, Anders Hellstrom contracted a virus that made him dreadfully sick with fever and weakness. He was a dedicated Swedish physician who was widely admired and friendly with everyone. His wife, Marie, was a nurse who was also well liked, and they had two young children with them in Beira as well. It was not clear just what he had, though some called it the "devil's grippe." He did not want to go to the hospital for treatment. Other cooperante physicians stopped by his house during the week to check on him and, while it seemed he was not improving, no one knew just what to do. On Sunday afternoon we joined a few other friends for lunch at the Limpus house and had a wonderful meal with roast pork, onion soup, and chocolate mousse. Mercie and Inalla were playing together in a sweet way, lying side by side on the floor coloring in coloring books. The adults set up Trivial Pursuit, and we were all competing over arcane bits of information when Steve Boyle stopped by to tell us that Anders, who had been ill for a week, was very dehydrated and he had an intravenous drip set up at home, indicating a serious setback in his condition. An hour later Steve Boyle returned, walking into the living room where we were sitting around. He managed to say, "Anders died," his drawn and pale face revealing his disbelief. Anders had been rushed to the emergency room just down the road from his house, but they had not been able to save him.

It was such shocking news that we did not know how to respond. I felt light-headed and disoriented as I looked around the room at everyone dazed and crying, the colorful plastic triangles and trivia cards abandoned. We worried about Marie and their two children, and everyone was wondering what they could have done differently. Could anyone have intervened earlier and saved him? He was such a good doctor that the other physicians trusted his judgment about how to treat his own illness. Everyone was wishing they had taken a stronger stand and made him go to the hospital sooner. My Steve was already close to the edge emotionally after eighteen months of trying to maintain control in horrible conditions. Before this loss he had written in his journal that "being here makes it impossible to really relax and let go for fear that such 'foolishness' will only make future hassles harder to deal with. If I [keep] a certain undertone of vigilance, hardness, and cynicism it's almost like a talisman which will help assuage the hardships."

On learning of Anders' death, Steve walked out of the Limpus's house and crossed the road to the beach, where he fell onto his knees on the sand in agony and despair. He could barely deal with his own desolation, and he could not face speaking with our friends, no matter how close they were. When I realized he had left, I went out to find him, joining him on the sand as we held each other close and tried to feel safe. He wanted to pack up and leave immediately. But we talked about our options, and he agreed that leaving before his contract was finished would create its own problems. I felt we just needed to hold on for a matter of weeks, and then we could return to the wellbeing of home in California.

Nearly two weeks later there was a funeral for Anders. Marie wanted to have him cremated so that she could take his ashes back to Sweden, but in Beira cremation was not a simple procedure. The only way to accomplish it was to hold a Hindu funeral. Anders' body had been held at the hospital mortuary, so just after lunch on the day of the funeral a

Chapter 25

large somber group of health workers met at the mortuary and accompanied the ambulance with his coffin out to the Crematoria de Hindús, located out past the cashew factory in Manga. The whole area was rundown, with paint flaking off the cement walls and grass overgrown into a hayfield. In an open area, about twenty men of Indian descent dressed in loose white shirts performed the necessary rites, chanting and praying.

Anders' body was in a coffin, but they opened that and uncovered his face before carrying his shrouded body into the crematorium, which was simply an open-sided pavilion. He was laid on a platform, and the South Asian men and some of the cooperantes built the pyre around him by stacking logs. Steve Boyle helped prepare the body by rubbing grease over it, a procedure we watched from a distance but still shuddering, as the intimate act of handling a body in such a way was so remote from our own limited experience of postmortem rituals. The chief mourner, conventionally, was supposed to light the fire, and Marie had also asked Steve B. to do that difficult task for her. She was standing quietly as she watched each step, and I could see that she was trying to remain strong for their two children, though obliged to make the arrangements for this unfamiliar rite in a foreign land. We stayed for a short while, standing in the sunny field some yards from the pavilion, and watching as the flames began to burn around the edges of the pyre. We learned that it would take between three and four hours to burn completely, so we left after a suitable interval. Steve Boyle later went back to ritually douse the fire with water and collect the ashes.

Although I was not familiar with the ceremony and could not understand the words, I was comforted by the commonality of human attempts to alleviate grief. Every society honors the deceased with rituals addressing the cycle of life and death, and Hindus' belief in an afterlife meant that the service included an element of joy for the release of the soul to the next stage of existence. I imagined that the unknown words were meant to bring solace to the bereaved and I accepted them in that spirit. That consolation was manifested by the presence of the Hindu community, helping non-Hindus endure a traumatic event. I left the observance feeling connected to all cultures and, though saddened, I was prepared to continue for the final weeks of our stay. But my Steve found that the foreign aspects of the ceremony and language simply accentuated his alienation in Beira. He had witnessed hundreds of deaths and had been unable to prevent them. Increasingly, he had worried about our own health over the previous two years. The loss of Anders, a young and apparently healthy European colleague and friend succumbing to a mysterious ailment, was the realization of his worst nightmare. Every aspect of the funeral just reinforced the fears he had accumulated about the possibility of terrible things happening to himself, to Mercie, or to me.

Other depressing events, both inconsequential and momentous, also affected our declining morale. It rained steadily for three days, and we woke up one morning to find our kitchen floor covered with over an inch of water that had seeped in from the exterior hallway. Steve Boyle and Jacky were having a conflict over the ownership of the motorcycle, and Jacky and Alf had chosen the evening of Anders' funeral to visit Steve and raise the issue, though they knew very well how he had spent his day.

One afternoon I stepped out onto our balcony and was looking down at the neighborhood when I heard a disturbing thump. I could see a sanitation truck stopped at an odd angle about a block away and feared that a child, perhaps one of our neighbors, had been hit. I soon learned that it was not a child, but an adult, Arnold Piggott, who was from Uganda. He was a laboratory technician, one of the international health cooperantes whom we all knew, working in Beira under contract with the United Nations. He had just been back to Uganda where he had a wife and family and he had told us that he believed conditions in Uganda were

Chapter 25

improving, and he regretted that he had already signed a contract to extend his time in Mozambique. That afternoon he was riding his little motorcycle with another Ugandan named Zulu as a passenger. They were traveling along the side of the road when a sanitation truck began to make a right turn and the truck driver did not even see Arnold and Zulu. Zulu suffered only minor injuries, but Arnold never regained consciousness and died later at the hospital.

And then my Steve, still reeling from Anders' death, got sick with malaria yet again, his third bout. Though it was a milder case than the previous ones, he was understandably frantic and distraught. He benefited from talking with Rui Bastos, who told him, "You're an African now, you've had malaria so much you are one of us." Steve followed his advice for rest and medication and recovered enough to return to work once more.

I had been hoping to attend the national OMM conference, which was initially planned for April 1984. But when I wrote and asked for permission to attend, Signe Arnfred replied that they only planned to invite two non-African foreign women as special guests, one woman from Brazil, and Barbara Isaacman from the U.S., who was Allen's wife. The Isaacmans had a long history of doing research in Mozambique and she had already published a report on women in Mozambique.[1] I bicycled out to the OMM office more than once, but a typical journal entry about those visits reads, "Went to OMM, for their version of my request to attend the April meeting, but Camarada Secretaria hadn't yet arrived and of course no one else had the vaguest idea." A week later I finally met with Teresa Romão, and she confirmed what Signe had written to me, that she could only invite fifteen guests and, as I could see from a list she was holding in her hand, those guests were from other African countries. I felt deeply frustrated, but in the end the conference was postponed until November when I was back in the U.S., and I could not afford to return for that meeting even if I had been invited.

We celebrated Mercie's third birthday with a small party, inviting the Limpuses and Liziêt, Júlio, and Swahili to join us at three in the afternoon. When no one had arrived by 3:30, Mercie set her dolls up and organized her own party. Everyone did come eventually, and we ate Boston cream pie that I had baked, a chocolate cake from Judy Limpus, and a lot of beer, crackers, and Kool-Aid. We had previously invited Júlio, Liziêt, and Swahili for a special Sunday lunch of shrimp curry, but Swahili would not sit down and poor Liziêt spent the whole time chasing after him. His parents were dear friends, but their son was a terror who, on that earlier occasion, had climbed on a chair and ripped a May 1st poster on our wall before Liziêt could grab him. Mercie had watched in awe as he swooped destructively through our apartment. For Mercie's birthday we closed off half the apartment to keep Swahili from destroying everything, but even so he managed to knock over a little brick and board shelf where we kept Mercie's books and toys. She was so happy all afternoon she would just jump and skip from joy, and she initiated numerous renditions of "Parabéns pra você, nesta data querida, muitas felicidades, muitos anos da vida" (Best wishes to you on this special date, many congratulations, many years of life). The song is sung to the same melody as the English "Happy Birthday" song. Balloons and a cheerful tablecloth lent by Liziêt added to the festivities.

For Easter that year, one of our Soviet neighbors brought us a celebratory Easter cake, similar to Italian pannetone, and a hard-boiled egg dyed blue for the holiday. For several months we were surrounded by families from the Soviet Union, as our neighbors on each side as well as those directly above us and below us were all from the Soviet Union. We were amused and even pleased to be living in such open defiance of Ronald Reagan's rhetoric about that country as an "evil empire."

Chapter 25

I wanted to interview a few more nurses, so I rode my bike out to the hospital and found Matilde, whom I had interviewed a few months earlier. I was hoping that she would just make a couple of introductions to other nurses for me, but she thought I should go through the Celula da Partido—the Frelimo Party cell in the hospital. She did not find my guia from Rui Bastos to be sufficient, though he was the provincial director of health. The party secretary was not in his office, and I was unable to ride my bike back out there that afternoon when he was supposed to be available. Steve spoke to him when he was at the hospital and he checked back with Matilde for me as well, so I planned to ride out to the hospital later in the week. Matilde did give me a list of the names of the older nurses, and I realized that I had already spoken with all of them or had made plans to do so. At least I then knew that I was not missing an essential potential informant.

I also had two further interviews while I was at the hospital. I finally interviewed Marcela Sola, Ana Alberto's mother, who was in the tuberculosis ward at the hospital. She spoke Ndau and, though she could understand Portuguese, she did not want to speak it. I relied on a student and a nurse to help with the translation, all of us standing around Marcela's bed on the ward. It was maddening when the three of them debated my questions in Ndau at length and then, as Marcela responded, the interpreters turned and gave me an obviously truncated three-word translation. Nonetheless, I did learn the outlines of her life story.

Marcela was then forty-nine years old. Her father had worked at the sugar factory in Dondo as a sugarcane cutter, and her mother had worked in a family machamba in Beira. Marcela had not attended school as a child and had married young. When I asked how old she had been when she married, she responded that she did not remember, and when I asked how many children she had, she counted on her fingers before telling me, "Eight children." She herself

The Mackerel Years

had a machamba in Beira's Vaz neighborhood where she grew sweet potatoes, maize, tomatoes, beans, cabbage, and rice in rotation. All of it was for her family to eat and she did not sell any in the local markets. Her husband had died many years previously and she had struggled to support her children on her own. Marcela also brewed *kabanga* for sale, an alcoholic beverage made by mixing flour, water, and sugar and leaving it in a wooden pan to ferment for two days. In the colonial era she would sell a mug of kabanga for 12$50 escudos (translated as "sixpence"), indicating the minimal level of her income. She used that income to buy matches, cooking oil, and other necessities. When her daughter, Ana, began to work in a rice factory at age ten, that income was used to buy clothes and shoes for the children. Her life had been filled with hardship, a stark reminder of how most Mozambican women lived. She had never had a day off, as the machamba required continuous attention, even when she was pregnant and caring for small children. When I asked about the situation with her crops following her hospitalization, she simply said "The machamba is stopped, I don't know if my daughter is going there."

I interviewed Maria Samuel that day as well. She was an older nurse who was the director of the new creche at the hospital, so I learned about her experience as a nurse and asked about the creche. She had been educated at a mission boarding school, finishing the fourth grade, and completing nursing training in the early 1960s. She married when she was thirty, somewhat later than most Mozambican women, and had four children. Her husband was a teacher in a driving school. She reiterated what the other nurses had related about the racial segregation and lack of respect for African nurses that was common during colonialism. Her life was also complicated following an automobile accident in which her legs were severely injured, resulting in many months in a Maputo hospital, dependence on canes to walk, and repeated surgeries to repair chronic problems. Though she liked working in the creche, she was troubled by constant pain and had difficulty moving around the rooms.

Chapter 25

    I also had planned to talk with Botelho Moniz, the editor of *Diário de Moçambique*, but he was often called away to meetings and it was hard to connect with him. After a few weeks, we arranged a time to meet and I had a good visit with him. While I was waiting to speak with him, I had an extended conversation with the paper's administrative director, another Sr. Domingos. He asked what struck me the most about Beira, so I talked about all the agriculture that was done within the city and women's role in that work. When he learned what I was investigating, he launched into a thirty-minute discourse on the lack of industrial jobs for women, the way they brought their rural skills into the city, and the need for agricultural technicians to improve production.

    When we were on vacation in Zimbabwe, Botelho Moniz had given a talk to the cooperante community about the history of newspapers in Beira, so I was eager to get the information I had missed. In our conversation, Moniz also discussed the role of newspapers in forming public opinion, a topic that was much debated in Mozambique, where new ideas and approaches that the government wanted to encourage were often publicized through the press. That led to him reflecting on whether the press in Mozambique was independent of government influence. He said they were not censored and that *Diário* was not required to promulgate the government line. Though he felt it was not an official government paper, he did believe the paper should be a mouthpiece for "o povo" and he hoped it was a revolutionary paper that was contributing to the struggle to build socialism. He was not only editor of the paper, but also held a government position as provincial director of information and a party position on the provincial central committee of Frelimo. The paper's official or non-official status was clearly complex. At that time there was only the single newspaper available in Beira and it obviously had extremely close ties with the party and the government.[2] I was also able to read some back issues of *Diário*, mainly from the late 1960s and early 1970s. For the entire month of January 1972 there was nothing on women except front page photographs related to an upcoming Miss Mozambique contest.

It was May Day again, so we all went along to Avenida Armando Tivane (named for a hero of the liberation struggle) to watch the parade in Beira. Len Limpus joined us in the shade and Inalla and Mercie sat on the curb and chatted about the people marching by. The procession was led by a police band, complete with drums and tubas, followed by the local militia, Frelimo leaders, Teresa Romão and OMM, the youth organization, trade unionists, students, athletes, and representatives of various workplaces. We knew many of the health workers going by and I also knew some of the Belita workers who marched as an organized and animated group, chanting and carrying banners. A few of the workplace groups walked by in a dispirited manner, but many others were full of energy.

The groups of workers were followed by a series of floats. RENAB, the ship repair yard, had a giant grey metal worker with a fist holding a hammer in the air. Construction workers from C.I.S. (Construtora Integral de Sofala) demonstrated how to build a small brick structure as they rode by on a flatbed truck. The Health Ministry had an operating room, as well as a physiotherapy group doing their exercises under the direction of a Dutch cooperante named Peter. A hotel float had a bed and a dining table with a waiter. CFM (Caminhos de Ferro de Moçambique) had trains, and the bus company, Ikarus, demonstrated how to construct a bus with a chassis on one float, followed by a half-done bus frame, and finally a finished bus. The judges from the peoples' tribunal wore black robes, bakery workers pantomimed selling bread at high speed, and at the end there were several heavy equipment vehicles and, finally, horses.

In its usual observance of national holidays, Renamo had sabotaged the water lines again. We had a bathtub half-filled with clean tap water, but when Francisco arrived, he

Chapter 25

proceeded to fill buckets from the contaminated well water in front of our building and poured that into the bath before we realized what he was doing. All of that had to be boiled before we could use it for cooking or drinking.

I was being helped by Boaventura Verimbo, whom I had met because he was teaching English at the Escola Comércial high school with Jacky. He had lived in the United States for twelve years, completing a degree in economics. When he returned to Mozambique after independence, the customs officials confiscated his college textbooks. He was judged to be a problem because of his years studying "capitalist" economics in the west and was placed in a detention camp for some time. After we were back in the States, I contacted California State University at Hayward to obtain a replacement copy of his diploma, which had also been taken from him. He had three children, but they were having an especially difficult time. On their ration card covering the four months since January, they had only been allotted one kilogram of sugar, four kilograms of flour, no eggs, and nearly no fish. We gave him what flour, sugar, and powdered eggs we could spare, but we learned after we left that his youngest child had died, and malnutrition was a factor.

Bovy, as he liked to be called, was very willing to help me and assisted once or twice with translations in interviews done in local languages. He also arranged for me to interview his sister, Diana Joaquim, who lived in Chipangara, one of the oldest neighborhoods in Beira, also located close to downtown and next to Inhamudima. She lived right on the edge of a huge expanse of rice fields and there were ducks and chickens in the yard. The first time we went to Diana's house, we learned that one of her daughters-in-law had arrived from the rural areas the night before, reporting that she had given birth prematurely and the infant had not survived. The household was grieving and preparing a ceremony.

I returned to Diana's the following week to watch her make kabanga. We arrived before 9 A.M. on a pleasant cool morning. I met several neighbors and other relatives, including a man who had worked in Johannesburg for thirty-five years in domestic service at the American consulate and in various hotels and homes. He enjoyed speaking English with me for a few minutes. Diana's husband and one of her daughters were there as well. The daughter and her husband had come for a brief visit on Saturday, though the husband had gone to buy cigarettes shortly after their arrival and had not returned. The family did not seem too worried, as they teased the daughter about her husband's absence. I watched the daughter chop some wood to make kindling for the fire to cook the kabanga. The ax was in poor condition, and when the head fell off a younger boy repaired it by wedging a piece of wood into the head to hold it tight against the handle.

Kabanga was made with *farelo*, a flour-like food that was made from *milho* or corn chaff, after the kernels themselves were removed from the cob. The farelo was pounded off the cobs in the pilão and left to dry in the sun. Then it was mixed with water and left for two or three days. The farelo was not edible but was used to flavor the water. The next step was to mix the farelo water with sugar, let it ferment, and then boil it, which was the stage Diana had reached. It was a highly alcoholic mixture, though I did not have an opportunity to try Diana's version.

Other family members included Diana's son, Americo Luis, who worked at the hospital. He lived with his wife in a small house facing his mother's home in the same courtyard. His wife had just given birth the day before. Two other toddler grandchildren were also wandering around the yard, wearing wire "spectacles," which they found highly amusing. Americo invited Bovy and me into his home for bottled beer and fried fish—at 9 A.M.! I followed Bovy's cues and accepted the invitation, though I really wanted to watch the alcohol-brewing process. The top half of the inside walls were painted pale blue and the room was sparsely furnished with a table and a couple of chairs and the usual Xirico radio prominently placed even though it did not work. Americo's in-laws were also visiting because of the new grandchild.

Another of Diana's sons, Gomes, who was about eighteen years old, helped me with the translation when I interviewed Diana, who spoke a variant of Chisena called ChiGorongosi. He had recently traveled to Tete with another relative, and though they sought safety by traveling in a civilian convoy, they had been attacked by Renamo. Gomes had suffered a bullet wound in his leg and had just been released from the hospital a few days before. I regretted that I had had so few opportunities to spend time with more Mozambican families, but I appreciated the glimpse I had that morning of a large but close-knit group, struggling to survive in the face of hunger and war.

Endnotes

[1] Barbara Isaacman and June Stephen, *Mozambique: Women, the Law and Agrarian Reform* (United Nations. Economic Commission on Africa, 1980).

[2] For more on press freedom in Mozambique, see Paul Fauvet and Marcelo Mosse, *Carlos Cardoso: Telling the Truth in Mozambique* (Double Storey, 2003), discussion of the early years of independence, 33-37.

Chapter 26
Cake and Despedidas

May to July 1984

Steve had made the plane reservations in late March for our return to the U.S. By early May we were packing our large trunk, as we needed to have the contents approved by customs before it was shipped. The Health Ministry, which was going to pay for its passage, had originally wanted us to get the trunk to Maputo, but finally agreed to pay for sending it from Beira. We had no idea how we would have gotten it to Maputo where we would have had to deal with the transport agency there in a much larger port. We had gotten to know a few of the Beira shipping and customs agents, but we were still getting conflicting advice about the best way to send the trunk. The company that had handled our bicycles no longer dispatched goods from Beira or perhaps to Los Angeles, we were not sure which. We were leaving a lot behind with friends, but still had items we wanted to bring back, including two years of *Tempo* magazine, which I knew would not be easy to locate in libraries in the U.S.

My sister Barbara sent us a book that she had made with photographs of my close relatives, called "Who's Waiting for Mercie?" It was wonderful to sit and look through it with Mercie, to remind her who her aunts and uncles were and to introduce her to the three cousins who had been born since we left. We also talked about babies born to friends of ours, all the babies we would meet when we returned. Mercie said, "I'll hold them real close and *mamar* (nurse) them!"

We were hoping we could cope with other changes back home, as indicated by two letters we received from friends near the end of our stay, both written using a new machine—a word processor. During our two years in Mozambique, the home computer business had really escalated. When we left we did not know anyone who had one, but by the time we returned it was common and even expected that professionals such as my historian colleagues would be using their computers to prepare written work.

While some parts of the world were advancing technologically, however, Mozambique in the 1980s was stalled. Judy Limpus received a cryptic telegram from an aunt in Australia simply saying, "Call urgently." Judy feared her mother had passed away, but there was no way to call Australia from Beira. Len arranged to go to Maputo to try to call from there, despite stories of decreased flights between Maputo and Beira due to a fuel shortage. At the same time, Steve Boyle went out to a Dutch ship in the Beira port and managed to reach Judy's family by ship's radio. He learned that Judy's mother had been quite ill, but by the time they were able to talk the crisis had passed. The original telegram had taken three days to reach Judy and then she suffered for several more days thinking the worst before learning the true, and less dire, situation with her mother. As I wrote to my mother in a letter that itself took over a month to get back to Connecticut, "sometimes it is hard to believe how isolated a city can be in the late 20th century."

In April we were invited to dinner with Jacky and Alf, which was very awkward. But we met a new cooperante family, Ian and Maureen Frayling and their young boy Seán. Ian was an engineer from New Zealand and Maureen a nurse-midwife from Ireland. As I commented after that first meeting, "They seem quite nice, and are interested in the bikes." Mercenary perhaps, but we knew we would be leaving the bikes and child seat behind, and though we

Chapter 26

would have liked to be able to give them away, we were short of cash and needed to sell them if we could. The Fraylings, who have remained our good friends, were a godsend, as they were able to pay us cash for the bikes and they really needed the child seat as well. We enjoyed several more meals with Maureen and Ian before we left and a lot of our supplies remained with them. They very generously gave us more cash than we had requested for the bicycles so that we had enough foreign exchange to allow us to buy food while we stayed in Maputo.

All through May, we had lunch with people every weekend and it was difficult, as each meal was the last time we would sit down and eat with Hanny, the Dutch nurse who worked with Steve in Munhava, or the Fraylings, who would be staying on for years after we left, or with our Swedish friends, Lars and Cecilia. At every meal we shared with people from Brazil, or Canada, or Ireland, we were also thinking about how we would be returning to our homes in far corners of the globe, with little likelihood that we would meet again. We often were invited to eat with the Limpuses, who had access to scarce provisions through Len's connections in the UN Food and Agriculture Organization and were glad to be able to share that food with others. They had a child-sized table and chairs where Mercie and Inalla would sit, smugly pleased with themselves, eating and chatting like two ladies at tea, as Maureen observed. Mercie did not fully realize that she would be leaving Inalla and would no longer be playing the games they had invented. She was also oblivious to the imminent separation from her friends at creche, though her departure was marked by her favorite teacher, Isaura, who gave her a small basket as a memento.

Figure 17: Mercie and Isaura, her preschool teacher, 1984. Photo by Steve Tarzynski.

We also continued to meet new people, some from equally distant homelands, such as José Soares, a young doctor from East Timor. We made him a meal that included American-style cornbread using local maize flour. He settled in Mozambique rather than go back to his war-torn home country, which was a former Portuguese colony then claimed by Indonesia and suffering from many years of an anti-colonial war. Only after a decisive burst of terrible violence in 1999 was East Timor free at last.

We had a final lunch with Steve Boyle before we left. We relaxed on his veranda with beer, then started with soup and went on to a shrimp and rice course with white wine, a meat (imported from Zimbabwe) and potatoes course with red wine, fruit salad, chocolate, coffee, and finally champagne! He gave us a goodbye gift, a small pau preto pilão, a mortar and pestle carved from black wood. After the meal we went to the beach and met Cecilia and her

Chapter 26

boys. I had indulged in a bit too much of the various wines and lost my balance in the surf while holding Mercie in the shallow waves, getting us both wet and scaring her, but her tears were quickly soothed away by an offer of chocolate cookies. I was also distressed to realize that that would be my final stop at the Indian Ocean beaches that had become so familiar. Though narrow and stony in the area close to Beira, we had often gone to sit along the water's edge, and I stopped to appreciate the view as I walked away that last time.

The saddest goodbyes were at the party organized by the pediatric ward workers. They told Steve on Friday that they were planning a despedida for Saturday, so, after lunch with Steve Boyle and my unscheduled dip in the ocean, we went along to that event. Gama and Manuel Julien came to get us so we would not have to ride our bikes. Julien by then was provincial director of health, as Rui Bastos had moved to Maputo, where he later became one of Mozambique's experts on HIV/AIDS. In 1996 Julien fell ill with a mysterious disease that left him comatose. Despite treatment in South Africa, he never regained consciousness and passed away in 2006. But that night in 1984 we all had a wonderful time together.

There were about forty people at the party, including many nurses, technicians, and serventes, as well as a few doctors. Tables were laden with shrimp, fish, rice, *bolachas* (little cakes), and one large, decorated sheet cake with yellow frosting and silver balls trimming the edge, truly a treat we had not seen for two years. The party was held in a classroom at the hospital, and the blackboard had the words "Boa viagem Doutor Stiv. Longe de si a Pediatria jamais te esquescerá" (Good voyage Dr. Steve. Though you will be far away, the pediatric ward will never forget you). Four men got up and, with their arms around each other, one began pretending to weep. When the others asked why he was crying, he said, "Because Dr. Stiv is leaving (*vai embora*), but though he is leaving, his papers and his prescriptions remain behind."

Figure 18: Pediatric good-bye party for Steve, May 1984.

It was intensely emotional, as were Gama's brief comments. He reminisced about how much Steve had contributed and how he set an example by always studying and teaching. For example, he said, when Steve shared his medical journals and books they were marked up, proving that he had really read all that material. Steve managed to avoid weeping himself as he told them in a broken voice how much he had learned and what a privilege it had been to work there. Dona Fatima, the head pediatric nurse who had worked closely with Steve for the entire two years, reminded everyone of one of Steve's passions by giving him a baby bottle filled with LOA, the high-fat drink of milk, oil, and sugar for malnourished babies. She said it was from all the babies and children whom he had treated and saved, but who could not be there. We could not keep the LOA, but the baby bottle remains on display in Steve's study.

Sunday morning, we were up early, finishing our packing. We were faced with the same problem we had had when we left Santa Monica two years earlier—too much stuff for our suitcases. Bovy stopped by and we gave him a

Chapter 26

lot of our household supplies as well as toys for his children. Mercie had previously helped us distribute a few of her toys to other children. We had given many of our kitchen items to Francisco earlier and, in the end, he took most of what was left. Nonetheless, the suitcases weighed forty kilograms over the admissible weight. Hanny came to the apartment to say goodbye and so did Niall. At the airport we had our own bon voyage group with Steve Boyle, the Fraylings, and the Limpuses. As might have been anticipated, our plane, which was scheduled to depart at 11:50 a.m., did not leave until 3:30 p.m., so we were grateful to everyone for keeping us entertained during those hours. And in a further reminder of the community we had become part of during the two years in Beira, as we were walking across the tarmac to board the plane, a ground crew member who had been the father of one of Steve's patients asked Steve in a humorous manner, "Sr. Doutor, está nos fugir?" (Doctor, are you fleeing from us?). But the flight itself was uneventful and Coke McCord met us at the Maputo airport.

We were lodged in an Institute of Planning house where George Povey was staying, though he was in Zimbabwe part of the time we were there. We shared the house with a Basque family from Spain, Sabino and Francisca and their sweet five-year-old boy, Mikele. They were new cooperantes who were preparing to go to Beira for two years, so we shared what information we could. One night, as they slept, a thief or thieves snuck in and stole all Sabino's clothes, his special architect's pencils, some of Mikele's toys, and $450 in cash, right from the same room they were sleeping in. The burglars had been very stealthy, and Sabino and Francisca never heard a sound. Sabino was left with one old pair of jeans and one torn T-shirt. We had been preparing them for life in Beira with stories about shortages and empty stores, so the sense of being personally invaded that follows a break-in was compounded by the knowledge that they would have huge difficulties replacing the lost possessions.

The Mackerel Years

We had planned on spending two or three weeks in Maputo so that I could finish up the archival research that I wanted to do. The first afternoon I went and talked with the archive director, Maria Inês Nogueira da Costa, and she and her staff were immensely helpful, even though we quickly determined that materials I expected to find there were not available. António Sopa, one of the archivists, told me that the papers I hoped to see were still stored in Beira and he drew a little map to indicate which building near the downtown area housed them. Apparently, no one in Beira knew about that storage place, as I had been told repeatedly that the materials I sought had been sent to Maputo. That those files were still in Beira was bad news for me, as I would not be going back any time soon.[1]

Another day, I had a glass of wine and a good talk with Signe Arnfred about doing research on women in Mozambique. She felt the special conference had been postponed from April until November because the male leadership in Frelimo wanted to regain some control over the whole process. They were not sure what the outcome would be, so they did not hold the meeting when it was originally scheduled. Even Signe, who had been deeply involved in the preliminary meetings, would be gone from Mozambique by November and was planning to pay her own way back for the meeting itself. We both felt a bit frustrated, as we had hoped to find a stronger feminist politics in Mozambique, and we feared that postponing the conference reflected Frelimo's low priority for women's issues. Of course, the war against Renamo was taking precedence for Frelimo. Also, September 1984 would mark the twentieth anniversary of the start of the anti-colonial armed struggle, and additional attention and funding had been earmarked for those commemorations rather than the women's meeting. When I told Signe about the bureaucratic run-around I had faced with OMM in Beira, she revealed that Teresa Romão had asked Marcelino dos Santos to decide about the tea breaks at the provincial meeting the previous November—should they last for fifteen minutes

Chapter 26

or thirty minutes? The idea that even such infinitesimal decisions were referred to someone at the highest level of the government because lower-level officials would not take responsibility suggests the hindrances to development faced by Mozambicans. Signe generously lent me a copy of the report on working women in Maputo that she had done for OMM, and I was able to arrange for a photocopy before we left.

While we were in Maputo, we went to the new Loja Franca, which was overwhelming. It had moved from its former small store front to a new building that was like a department store, with entire sections selling electronics, clothes, and furniture, as well as food that was otherwise impossible to obtain, at least in Beira. The cash registers were digital machines that automatically converted prices and payments from dollars to rands to meticais. The contrast to Beira was astonishing. One of the last things I had thrown away in Beira was an old rusty coffee tin, only to later see the guard from the Mexicana carefully washing it out. Conditions seemed several rungs more comfortable in Maputo, and not only at the dollar store. Everyone was wearing shoes, though it had not been so long ago that people stood in line for days to buy shoes in Beira. I was even bewildered by the amount of traffic on the streets. I had gotten so accustomed to Beira's empty boulevards that I feared darting across the lanes of traffic in Maputo as others did so easily.

Most of our time in Maputo was spent on errands at the bank where we did manage to get some of our money changed into travelers' checks in dollars, which was better for our trip home through Portugal. It appeared that the final 5 percent of Steve's pay would not be available before we left and we feared perhaps never, though in the end we collected those funds on our very last day in Mozambique. There were dozens if not hundreds of cooperantes in Maputo and the finance system simply could not cope with all of them. George Povey had not gotten the foreign exchange portion

The Mackerel Years

of his pay for over a year, so he had changed his CUSO contract so that CUSO paid him $200 a month directly rather than trying to handle it through the Mozambican system.

I spent a day at the big central market, much larger than anything in Beira, with a lot of crafts and food that we had not seen for two years. I wandered happily among the various permanent cement stalls and chose some colorful baskets and woven straw mats as gifts. I also bought several sets of political posters at the Bureau de Informação Pública, the information department that sold government publications. Another errand was to arrange for cassette tapes of Mozambican music. Since none were for sale, Iain Christie, a Scottish cooperante working at Rádio Moçambique, made us a wonderful compilation from the materials at the radio station.[2]

Iain also interviewed Steve about the situation in Beira for the English language service of Rádio Mozambique, and Steve's comments were later included in the monthly official news bulletin, *AIM Information Bulletin* (AIM was the acronym for Agência de Informação de Moçambique, the Mozambique Information Agency).[3] Despite our sense that we knew little about current events *because* we were living in the midst of them, Steve's comments were accepted as authoritative. He reported that there had been no cuts in electric power in the six months since January, though there had been monthly cuts for the eighteen months prior to that. And he described improved morale among members of the military, quoting a soldier he treated for a head wound who requested an early discharge from the hospital because he wanted "to go and kill more bandits."

We had a meal with the Mullers—Mike, Ruth, Marika, and their baby, Seán, whom we had not seen since they moved to Maputo months before. Marika helped us figure out two more of Mercie's creche songs, which had remained mysterious to us because her Portuguese was spoken or sung in a confused toddler version of the language, and we had not grown up with these nursery tunes. One song went, "Um, dois, três, sacos de farinha, quatro, cinco, seis, sacos

Chapter 26

da feijão," (One, two, three, sacks of flour, four, five, six, sacks of beans). The other was "Entramos na nossa sala, cantamos com alegria, saudamos as nossas tias, bom dia bom dia" (We enter our room, we happily sing, we greet our aunties [meaning teachers], good day good day). It was obvious that Mercie had an entirely personal experience at the creche, much of which had not been fully shared with us. Though we had been aware of this from time to time, our ignorance about her day-to-day life became clearer every time we deciphered another song or game that she brought home. After apartheid ended in 1994, the Mullers were able to return to South Africa, where Mike became a government official in water and environmental affairs before moving into research at the University of Witwatersrand.

Len Limpus also happened to be in Maputo on business, and he invited us to join him for lunch at the Polana Hotel, Maputo's most famous and luxurious lodging. We enjoyed the treat of gazpacho and fish and meat courses in a lovely setting on the shaded terrace. As we sat relaxing at our table overlooking the bay, I could imagine Mozambique as a resort destination once again, though such an outcome did not develop for over a decade.

I visited Judith Marshall, whom we had met when we first arrived and had seen from time to time in Beira as she traveled for her work for the Ministry of Education. She was staying with Sam Barnes, an American woman then married to a Mozambican journalist. When I said I had grown up in Connecticut, Sam asked, "What town are you from?" and when I said, "Glastonbury," she asked, "I wonder if you know my cousin, Joel Alvord," who was the president of the Connecticut Bank and Trust. The funny thing was that I *did* know him. His wife, Ann Alvord, had been my sixth-grade teacher, and they were members of my parents' church. A small world indeed.

We met with several other Americans in Maputo as well. Ron Davis was an American athlete who coached track and field in several African nations, and he was training the

The Mackerel Years

Mozambican track team for the Olympics. He was working to improve the skills of Mozambican athletes, a goal that was finally realized in 2000 when Maria de Lurdes Mutola won Mozambique's first Olympic gold medal in the eight-hundred-meter race, her signature event. We met Lisa Brock, a doctoral student from Northwestern, who was doing her dissertation research on Gaza, the nineteenth-century kingdom led by Gungunhana, who had been defeated and exiled by the Portuguese. She introduced us to Albie Sachs, who was living in exile from apartheid South Africa.

Albie was a jurist teaching at the law school in Maputo. He was writing the text for a lavishly illustrated book about the murals of Maputo, and he took us on a tour one day to see all of them.[4] There were about a dozen people in a small convoy, though Steve, Mercie, and I rode with Albie as we had no car of our own. We enjoyed having Albie guide us around the murals and it was especially gratifying to see the big mural at the Praça de Heróis up close instead of just driving by on the way to or from the airport. That was the location of a star-shaped tomb where Eduardo Mondlane was buried and where Samora Machel joined him in 1986. The mural covered a long curving wall adjacent to the tomb and depicted the agony of colonialism and the history of Mozambique's resistance and political struggles in bold graphics and bright colors.

In 1988, Albie was the victim of the apartheid government when he was seriously injured by a bomb that exploded as he opened the door to his car, parked on a street in Maputo. It was the same car in which we had toured the murals. He lost an arm and the sight in one eye but survived to return and participate in the post-apartheid government in South Africa in the 1990s, helping write the new constitution and serving on the South African Supreme Court.[5]

That special drive around the city was slightly spoiled by an American photographer named Sue, who was hoping to use her brief visit to organize a longer stay in the future. We went to the Ministry of Agriculture and were admiring a mural called "A Cry of Happiness" by renowned artist

Chapter 26

Malangatana. The mural, one of his most joyful creations, is marked by a large smiling sun and rainbows arching across the outer wall of the ministry. The images include many scenes of everyday life—children on swings and a slide, women in a village, and, appropriately for its location, farm animals in a field and a tractor traveling along furrowed earth. A soldier guarding the building approached Sue as she photographed the mural and asked to see her authorization. It transpired that her letter did not have the proper carimbos stamped on it, so he told her not to take any more pictures. She tried to take another picture on the sly, but the same soldier heard the click of her camera and made her turn over her film.

Sue also wanted me to tell her about all the wonderful women's cooperatives in Beira. We were seated together in the back seat, and I was forced to turn and face her as I tried to make clear that there was not much evidence to support her expectations. She continued to press me for details about women's activities. She had been to Nicaragua and seemed to have very romantic notions about Third World revolution. Even when I explained that I had lived in Beira for two years, had known many members of the women's organization, and had in fact interviewed dozens of women, she plainly thought that if I had not found confirmation of revolutionary women as she defined them, then I had not made good use of my time there.

I did not want to admit that I had arrived with some of the same idealistic views but had learned to accept the reality as I investigated the current situation. I found myself tersely defending what Mozambican women had managed to achieve, and eventually tried to avoid talking to her as we continued to tour the murals. The accomplishments of Mozambican women might not match the standards of some western feminists, but they had been completed only with great suffering and represented important advances for women in Mozambique. Steve and I were exasperated with what we viewed as her western arrogance, especially because

The Mackerel Years

it impeded our brief opportunity to visit with Albie Sachs, a prominent anti-apartheid activist. Encounters like that made us realize how much we had learned. Mozambique might not have exemplified a socialist paradise, but probably no nation could. The reality was far more complex, with genuine ideals, hopes for the future, and the success of a few important improvements, tempered by incredible obstacles, widespread violence, and terror.

We left Maputo and bid farewell to Mozambique. I wrote the last entry in my journal in Portugal. In Lisbon I was delighted to be able to purchase books and arrange for photocopies of useful documents and reports. I even found two informative geography theses about Beira in university libraries. We bought clothes for ourselves and colorful cotton pants and shirts for Mercie. We were constantly amazed by the abundance, as even beggars on the street were relatively well dressed and wore shoes. One day in the Largo de Carmo, a tree-lined square in upper Lisbon, we relaxed on park benches and watched a young boy wearing shorts feed six *pãozinhos* or little bread rolls to the pigeons. It was possible that the bread was stale, but it looked better than most of the rolls we ate while we lived in Mozambique. Our years of mackerel for supper were finished.

Endnotes

1. The story of how those files were lost and then eventually located is referenced by Eric Allina, in his book that relied in part on those documents, *Slavery by Any Other Name: African Life under Company Rule in Colonial Mozambique* (University of Virginia Press, 2012), viii-ix.
2. For a tribute to Iain Christie's life, see "Nyusi grants posthumous award to one of founders of AIM," *Club of Mozambique* (June 26, 2019), https://clubofmozambique.com/news/nyusi-grants-posthumous-award-to-one-of-founders-of-aim-135011/
3. "Military Actions," *AIM Information Bulletin*, No. 96 (June 1984): 11-13.
4. Albie Sachs, *Images of a Revolution: Mural Art in Mozambique*, photographs, Moira Forjas, Susan Maiselas (Zimbabwe Publishing House, 1983)

Chapter 26

5   Albie Sachs, *Running to Maputo* (HarperCollins, 1990).

Chapter 27
Home and Back Again

1984: Overwhelmed by Brownies

We took our time returning to California, first stopping to visit with my family in Connecticut. They were extremely relieved to have us safely home. I got some sense of how difficult it would be to adjust to life in the U.S. when I wanted to make brownies for a family gathering. I was paralyzed with indecision when I stood in front of the wide variety of brownie mixes at the grocery store. I asked my sister to pick one for me and left the store in confusion. We continued on to Chicago and visited Steve's family as well.

We finally arrived back in Santa Monica, and back to our old apartment that a friend had sublet while we were out of the country. We carried our suitcases and boxes inside and collapsed. Before we had even begun to unpack, the phone rang. It was the Internal Revenue Service, with their representative initially complaining that we were never there to answer the phone. I explained that we had been out of the country for the previous two years and had literally just walked in the door. The agent went on to harangue me for not filing a tax return for the previous year. I replied that we had in fact filed our tax return and had received a $2,006 refund in January 1984. For some reason, he had no record of that, and he simply refused to believe me. I tried to describe where we had been, to justify the fact that

I had no photocopy of the tax return in question to send to him as he requested, but he continued to be obnoxious. Finally, I said, yes, please send us the forms again, we will be happy to re-file, and maybe even get a second refund for a further $2,000! We had to laugh (and did not refile those forms), though we were struck with the irony of returning from two years battling an incomprehensible bureaucracy, only to immediately face a homegrown version of the same obtuse attitudes.

It took us nearly a year before we began to take the overstocked American malls for granted and to function more comfortably in our own society. We had assumed that we would have to adjust when we traveled from the U.S. to Mozambique, but somehow thought there would be no adjustment period when we returned to our own culture and community, but our difficulties in returning indicated the impact of life in Mozambique.

1989: Returning to Mozambique

Our son Ben was born in September 1985, and we were acutely aware of how our lives were shifting into a new phase. I completed my dissertation, "Working Women in Beira, Mozambique," in 1988, and began to publish material in a series of academic articles.[1] I taught briefly at California State University in Long Beach and at UCLA, developing a course on African Women's History.

In 1989, my father passed away from colon cancer. When we returned to California after his funeral in Connecticut, we found a series of phone messages from Sidney Bliss of the U.S. Agency for International Development (USAID), growing a bit impatient with our lack of response. When I reached him, he said, "I don't know who you know, but they want you to go to Maputo as a consultant on gender issues." It turned out that "who I knew" was Melissa Wells, then the U.S. ambassador to Mozambique. A few months earlier the *Los Angeles Times* had published a pro-Renamo article and the paper had published a letter that Steve had

Chapter 27

written in response, that explained the reality of Renamo's atrocities. By then, we were involved with the Mozambique Support Network, a national organization that worked to educate the American public about the war in Mozambique. Steve's letter about his experiences as a physician treating victims of Renamo attacks was seen by Melissa Wells' brother who lived in the L.A. area. When she came to visit her brother soon after that, she contacted us, and we had her as a guest for late afternoon coffee and snacks. I was awed to have an ambassador in my home, but she was a down-to-earth person and was glad to meet others interested in Mozambique. Not long after that I received the call from Sidney, wondering "who I knew." Sidney himself was later relocated from Washington D.C. to Maputo, where he remained as an enduring and committed presence in international aid circles until his death in 2021.

That was how I returned to Mozambique after five years away, staying for the month of August in 1989. Mozambique had joined the World Bank and International Monetary Fund in 1987 and adopted their coercive demands to privatize the economy under a so-called "structural adjustment program." I observed many changes that followed the increase of international aid, the implementation of structural adjustment, and the beginning of the end of the socialist experiment in Mozambique. The markets astounded me with their piles of vegetables and fruit, but the prices had risen to ten times the cost of five years earlier. Paradoxically, few could afford to purchase the food that was finally available. I visited numerous women's projects and interviewed many women in the markets and in sewing cooperatives but found that women's work was still centered in such industries as garment factories and other traditional female sectors.

USAID flew me up to Beira for a week, where I stayed with Maureen and Ian Frayling. They were back in Beira after a stint in Italy and were staying in a compound of prefabricated housing newly built for foreign workers. There was a series of compounds located in fenced-off sandy areas on the road along the coast on the way to the hospital and, though the housing was pleasant, I found the guarded separation of foreign workers from Beira and its African residents to be very alienating and distressing. It signaled a stark change from the days when cooperantes went to Mozambique in solidarity with the Mozambican people. It appeared that many of the new aid workers had no ideological or political commitment to Mozambique but were taking advantage of high salaries paid in foreign exchange for working in a hazardous zone. I went to the Belita factory one day and found Castigo Bie Bie and Ana Maria Helena dos Santos, who were both quite amazed to see me again. I was able to read a few more documents while I was there, and really enjoyed visiting the factory again.

One unexpected experience during that trip was the chance to attend a concert at Machava Stadium in Maputo. The headliner was Eric Clapton, but, like the sold-out audience of Mozambicans, I was more excited to see Brenda Fassie, Sipho Mabuse, the Bhundu Boys, and other stars from South Africa and Zimbabwe.

1994: Mozambique's First Multi-Party Election

I returned to Mozambique again in 1994, when I was an official observer at the first multi-party elections. A peace accord between Frelimo and Renamo had been signed in 1992, and Mozambique had been busy with disarmament, reconciliation, and preparation for the elections. The United Nations had a huge presence, with many international soldiers and police monitoring the peace process. I was one of about three thousand foreign observers brought in under UN auspices just for the elections. The UN observers first endured an orientation in Johannesburg, South Africa, which was notable for the misinformation provided by their historian. He was a Nigerian who openly doubted that Mozambique would successfully develop democracy,

Chapter 27

which I thought was ironic in the extreme, given the sad history of Nigeria's own efforts at democracy.

We were flown into Mozambique on a noisy and uncomfortable C-130 military transport. We disembarked briefly in Maputo to go through customs, and tears of nostalgia filled my eyes when I detected the familiar smoky odor of the town as we walked across the tarmac. I was based in Maxixe in southern Inhambane province, sharing responsibility for three voting posts in Morrumbene with a Hungarian police lieutenant. Finally, I was able to see a more rural part of the country. Towns in the area had been destroyed by Renamo attacks, and buildings without roofs and abandoned agricultural fields were a common sight. The impact of the war, so recently ended, could be seen everywhere.

I observed the tentative first steps to electoral multi-party democracy in Mozambique. I watched as an elderly couple slowly entered the Nhacoho polling station, an elementary school classroom near Morrumbene. The woman's feet were wrapped in rags, and she supported her painful steps with a large pole held in both hands. The electoral officials spent a full minute explaining the voting procedure (as they did with every voter) including how to fold the paper ballots so as avoid smearing the inked fingerprint mark made by illiterate voters, before handing the man and the woman their ballots. As the couple turned toward the voting booths, the man's face filled with pride and purpose.

Frelimo, once a self-described Marxist-Leninist vanguard party and in 1994 still progressive if not clearly socialist, responded to the military situation by making several important concessions to the peace process. In 1990 the national assembly and Joaquim Chissano, then Mozambique's president, introduced a new constitution that ended Frelimo's one-party rule and Mozambique's identity as a socialist nation. That constitution allowed for multi-party elections, though other goals had to be met before elections could be held. When the peace accord was signed between Frelimo and Renamo in 1992, various opposition parties were formed. A lengthy series of negotiations worked out the specifics of Mozambican electoral law.

Renamo began refurbishing its image from an international pariah known for burning schools and clinics and for committing horrific massacres and atrocities to a legitimate political party under Mozambican law. Renamo's leader, Afonso Dhlakama, met with international political leaders and was accepted as a candidate for president of Mozambique, despite a series of obstructionist moves on his part that contributed to delaying the elections originally scheduled for October 1993. Given my own experience of Renamo's brutality, I found it very disturbing to hear a campaign chant that went, "Dhlakama, amigo, o povo está consigo" (Dhlakama, friend, the people are with you) and to see campaign slogans referring to Dhlakama as "nice" (using the English word).

The election was estimated to cost one billion dollars, primarily paid for by the United Nations and the European Union. The UN's extensive presence included five thousand military and civilian police stationed throughout the country supervising all Mozambican military and police activities, with hundreds acting as observers during the actual election days. The EU supplied the election materials, including metal ballot boxes and collapsible voting booths.

Although Frelimo and Renamo were the main contenders in the elections, many other smaller parties also emerged. In the election itself, there were twelve presidential candidates (ten backed by parties and two running as independents) as well as twelve parties and two coalitions of parties fielding candidates for the national assembly. The 1994 election did not include provincial or local balloting, but there was a somewhat cumbersome set of two ballots for each voter, one with the names and photos of the presidential candidates, one with the party names and symbols. Voters could mark an "x" or press an inked finger to the ballot to indicate their choices for president and for assembly.

Chapter 27

The voting process itself demonstrated Mozambican patience and tenacity. Originally scheduled for two days (October 27th and 28th), a third day of voting was added on the 29th, and then a fourth day was needed because the lack of electricity for lights meant that the ballots could not be counted until daylight on October 30th. Each of the 7,500 polling stations had a board of five electoral officials as well as several party monitors. As I made the rounds of my assigned voting posts with my UN partner, we could see that officials remained at their polling stations from October 26th, the day before the election, through the count. Most stations had no electricity, no running water, and limited food supplies. Despite such difficulties, officials and monitors, including mothers with infants and pregnant women, remained at their posts until the election was over. When Dhlakama (true to form) called for a Renamo boycott of the elections on the first day of voting, citing supposed irregularities, the international media reported it as a potential disruption to the entire election. Yet Renamo party monitors at the nine polling stations I observed remained at their posts on the second and subsequent days of the election and Dhlakama rescinded his boycott.

The elections were considered free and fair by international observers. Ballots were cast by 87.8 percent of registered voters. Dhlakama conceded defeat on November 15, having garnered only 33.7 percent of the vote to the 53.3 percent won by incumbent Frelimo president Joaquim Chissano. The assembly votes were much closer, in part because some voters who chose Chissano, positioned last on the presidential ballot, also marked the last position on the assembly ballot—a position held not by Frelimo, but by the Democratic Union (UD, for União Democrática), a coalition of four smaller parties. The apparent confusion was a result of voter illiteracy and of Chissano's campaign, which told voters they should mark the last position to vote for him. That certainly cut into Frelimo's lead in the assembly race; of 250 seats, Frelimo garnered 129 to Renamo's 112; a further 9 seats went to the UD.

Renamo's support arose from dissatisfaction with Frelimo policies as well as fear of continued warfare. Many welcomed the election outcome, which confirmed Frelimo's leadership while allowing Renamo to claim positions within the national government. Though Dhlakama pledged to work with the government, his history of reneging on promises, including his call for a boycott during the election, indicated that continued wariness was warranted. Nonetheless, Mozambique did not suffer from a renewal of warfare such as Angola experienced.

Sadly, the effects of the war persisted, as the presence of up to two million land mines meant causalities continued to mount. Areas adjacent to roads we drove on to get to the polling stations were marked with red signs reading "Perigo Minas" (Danger Land Mines) and people told of deaths resulting from mines hidden in fields.

Figure 19: Kathie near "Danger Land Mines" warning sign, outside Maxixe, October 1994.

Chapter 27

The UN presence was also controversial. Some described the UN role as a "recolonizer." There was evidence everywhere of the high-profile presence of UN forces; the UN police and military, for instance, were much better supplied than Mozambican armed forces and police, and the white UN tanks and trucks were very visible. The attitudes of UN staff were also problematic, and I heard foreign UN staff members make racist and disparaging remarks about Mozambicans. An international scandal erupted when it became known that Italian soldiers in the UN mission in Mozambique were paying girls as young as twelve and thirteen for sex. I observed school-age girls with foreign soldiers and police in the city of Inhambane, and the problem was the subject of popular songs as well. The sudden infusion of foreign exchange was not a wholly positive force in local economies.

Though Frelimo won the elections, their lead was narrow, and they had to confront the reality of widespread critical opinion. Components of a stronger Mozambican left existed in the newly active trade unions, in women's agricultural cooperatives, and among some members of Frelimo, but they were not well coordinated. Cynical responses to the elections came from within and outside of Mozambique, though from different political perspectives. Criticism from the left suggested that the elections were simply an expensive exercise in international appeasement, a response to pressures from the U.S. and others to develop a western-style democratic government. Yet right-wing sentiment wanted Renamo to be included in a "government of reconciliation," a concept Frelimo consistently rejected. Despite these nay-sayers from divergent political perspectives, tens of thousands of Mozambicans put in years of effort so they could hold successful elections. As a national project, the election process was a contribution to peace in that war-scarred land.

1998: International Conference in Maputo

I was able to return in 1998 for an academic conference and to spend a month doing more research for the book I was writing, a history of women in Mozambique.[2] I remained in Maputo for that visit, staying with friends and spending time at the archives and the university. Once again, the changes since my prior visit were dramatic, and even more so when compared with my first experience sixteen years earlier. I was particularly awed by the possibility of buying decorated cakes at the bakery located in the Polana Hotel, though a recently opened shopping center, which included a Chinese take-out restaurant, was also mind-boggling. Bookstores were everywhere, and the new university press was launching an ambitious program of publishing local scholars. Luxury hotels were being built along Julius Nyerere Avenue and the tourist business was beginning to revive. I even joined friends for a weekend in the Elephant Reserve just south of Maputo, where we stayed in a comfortable camp and looked (mostly unsuccessfully) for animals.

The impact of peace and noticeable economic prosperity marked real improvements. Our two years in Beira in the 1980s were part of an international effort to end apartheid in South Africa, as people from around the world supported the Frontline States as a bulwark against that racist regime. Finally, Nelson Mandela was released from prison, and in 1994 he was elected as the first president of newly free South Africa.

But the ordinary working women whom I had known best still lived precarious lives. Many of them lost jobs in the cashew factories, which had closed due to misguided World Bank policies in the 1990s, and they were trying to support their families by selling goods along the curbs outside the formal markets. I interviewed several women who had been part of the anti-colonial struggle for liberation in the 1960s and early 1970s. We shared memories of socialist aspirations that had not endured, and it seemed that both the

Chapter 27

women and their dreams had been forgotten in the rush to bring Mozambique into the modern world of a new century.

Endnotes

1   "Working Women in Beira, Mozambique," Ph.D. dissertation (University of California, Los Angeles, 1988).
2   Kathleen Sheldon, *Pounders of Grain: A History of Women, Work, and Politics in Mozambique* (Heinemann, 2002).

Acknowledgments

Although my memories of those years remain sharp, I made regular entries in a journal at the time and wrote detailed letters to family and friends. Steve also wrote reports and kept a journal, which I have drawn on. Those sources, written while we were still immersed in life in a different culture, have provided detailed information about our two years' residence in Beira. I especially thank my parents, Austin and Sylvia Sheldon, now deceased, and our friends Peg Strobel and Bill Barclay, and Rick and Emily Abel, for saving our letters and returning them to me. James Pfeiffer helped confirm some Chisena words, and the late Jeanne Raisler refreshed my memory on a couple of points concerning her family. Jon Schubert very kindly shared a map of Beira that he had adapted from online sources, allowing me to use it with my own further edits.

I shared early drafts of this memoir with some of those who appear in its pages, and thank Mercie DiGangi and Steve Boyle for their comments. Bill Minter, who was working on a larger project about cooperantes in Mozambique, also read the manuscript and had helpful suggestions. But the book languished until 2007 when I enrolled in a memoir writing class at the UCLA Extension Writing Program. The teacher, Dinah Lenney, was instrumental in helping me rework my approach and revise my writing, and I especially value my fellow memoir writers in that class for their honesty in their critiques and in telling their own stories.

Some small sections were included in published articles, which benefitted by reactions from Nupur Chaudhuri,

The Mackerel Years

Colin Darch, Julie Gallagher, Jonna Katto, Sherry Katz, Betsy Perry, Judith Van Allen, and Barbara Winslow. Later versions of the entire manuscript were read by friends and colleagues; their reactions and suggestions are greatly appreciated. Thank you, Edna Bay, Lily Havstad, Margot Lovett, Laura Mitchell, and Peg Strobel. I am especially grateful for the time, attention, and thoughtful queries and suggestions from my Mozambican friends, Terezinha da Silva and Victor Igreja.

Steve Tarzynski read the manuscript multiple times at different stages of revision, and his shared memories and keen editing eye made this truly our story.

Glossary

bairro do caniço – reed neighborhood

bandidos – literally, "bandits"; a common reference to Renamo forces in the 1980s; alternatively, bandidos armadas (armed bandits)

bata – long canvas coat worn as a uniform in many workplaces

bicha – worm, or a line or queue; there are multiple meanings for both **bicha** and **bicho**

bicho – bug, cockroach

bridewealth – goods or money exchanged at marriage, commonly given to the groom's family by the bride's family

caju – cashew

candonga – black market

capulana – length of cotton cloth worn by women as a skirt and to wrap infants

carapau – horse mackerel

carimbo – rubber stamp used on official documents

cidade de cimento – cement city or neighborhood

conto – one thousand **meticais**; in older Portuguese, one thousand **escudos**; it also means "story"

cooperante – foreign worker, in Mozambique to support the society's development and socialism

creche – childcare center

The Mackerel Years

curandeiro – local healer

divisas – foreign exchange

empregada/empregado – worker, usually used to refer to household help

escudo – Portuguese currency, replaced after independence by the **metical**

farelo – flour made from corn husks

fome – hunger

Frelimo – originally written FRELIMO as an acronym for Frente de Libertação de Moçambique, (Front for the Liberation of Mozambique), it became the Frelimo Party after independence in 1975

grupo dinamizador – dynamizing group; a neighborhood organization that was part of the Frelimo infrastructure

guia – permit or guide, an official permit for travel or to gain entrance to official structures

kabanga – home-made alcoholic drink, usually made from maize or corn husks

kanimambo – thank you in Shangaan

lanho – young coconuts and the water within them

lobolo – bridewealth

loja franca – exchange shop, or dollar store

machamba – cultivated plot of land, usually meaning a small, family-held garden

mandioca – manioc; drought-resistant tuber also known as cassava

mapira – sorghum

massa – porridge made from corn meal, the basic food item of most Mozambicans, usually served with a sauce

matapa – sauce made with manioc leaves, usually served over **massa** or rice

Glossary

metical (pl., **meticais**) – Mozambique's currency after independence

mzungu – European or white person

OMM – Organizacão da Mulher Moçambicana, the Organization of Mozambican Women

papel azul – blue paper used for official documents

pappas – baby cereal

pau preto – literally, "black wood;" used extensively in artistic carvings; other names include *Dalbergia melanoxylon*, African blackwood, grenadilla, or mpingo

pilão – large wooden mortar and pestle used to grind grains into flour

piri piri – uniquely Mozambican chili seasoning and sauce, made using the malagueta pepper (*Capsicum frutescens*)

povo (o povo) – people, often referring to the people as the basis of a socialist society

Renamo – Resistância Nacional de Moçambique (Mozambican National Resistance); also sometimes referred to as MNR

responsável (pl., **responsáveis**) – person in charge of a project or sector

salão de chá – tea shop

selos – stamps, often used for official documents

servente – a medical orderly

treinos – training, referring to the quasi-military training undertaken by all residents

Index

A

Acção Social, 61, 125, 139. *See also* Ministry of Health

African Activist Association, 18-19. *See also* University of California, Los Angeles (UCLA)

African National Congress, 13, 69, 148, 194. *See also* South Africa

Agostino, Francisco. *See* Francisco

agricultural labor, 112, 146, 174-175, 197-198, 202-205, 211, 245, 250, 259, 275, 285-286, 287; green zones, 144, 198

alcohol production, traditional (kabanga), 286, 290, 324

Alpers, Ned (Edward A.), 18, 173, 174, 231

American Friends Service Committee (AFSC), 21, 22

Angola, 12, 26, 35, 42, 193, 194, 316

anti-war activism, 6-7, 8-9

Arnfred, Signe, 40, 216, 228, 283, 300, 301

Arquivo Histórico de Moçambique, 40, 143, 149

B

Bastos, Balbina, 179, 215, 221, 223

Bastos, Rui, 89, 99, 119, 179, 259, 261-262, 267, 274, 283, 285, 297

Beira City Council, 119, 261, 267-269

Beira Municipal Library, 68, 179

Beira neighborhoods: Chingussura 201; Chipangara 289; Inhamízua 201; Matacuane 201, 264; Maquinino 239, 273; Vaz 286. *See also* Inhamudima; Manga; Munhava; Ponta Gêa

Belita garment factory, 222, 227, 239-246, 248-250, 253, 288, 312. *See also* garment workers interviews

bicycles, 32, 33, 57, 72, 128-130, 171, 188, 201, 293, 295

black market, 108, 134, 146, 188

Boyle, Jacky, 75, 84, 104, 124-125, 136, 155, 166, 190, 194, 275, 282, 289, 294; providing meals, 72, 77, 105, 112, 116, 173, 258

Boyle, Steve, 72, 74, 79, 104, 116, 124-125, 136, 155, 173, 190, 191-192, 201, 258, 259, 275-276, 279, 281, 282, 294, 296, 299

bread: for sale, 37, 47, 48, 49, 64, 84, 89, 90, 134, 273; recipe, 62, 105-106

bridewealth, 20, 199, 209-210, 217, 220, 244-245

C

Cabo Delgado province, 22, 27, 28, 190

Canadian University Service Overseas (CUSO), 27, 117, 302

candonga, *See* black market

capulana, 63, 98, 129, 211, 216

carapau. *See* mackerel

cashew factory (Caju), 197-199, 202, 203, 204-206, 213-214, 274, 278

cashew workers interviews, 197, 199-204, 206-213, 259

cashews, 38, 67

Centro de Estudos Africanos, 40, 68-69, 142-143. *See also* Universidade Eduardo Mondlane

Cheringoma, 197-198

childcare centers, 2, 164, 165, 205-206, 243, 277; Primeiro de Junho (infants), 57-62, 87-88, 101-102, 113, 116, 175-178, 207-208; Primeiro de Maio (toddlers), 276-277

Chimoio, 122, 241

Chival, Isac, 75-76, 89, 146, 155, 169, 170, 265

Cohn, Jon, 36, 76, 79, 111-113. *See also* Raisler, Jeanne.

colonialism, 12, 45, 49, 54, 58, 75, 81, 102, 122-123, 149, 182, 200, 205, 206, 225, 229, 253, 286, 304. *See also* Mozambique Company

Comércio Interno, 89, 187, 269

Conselho Executive, *See* Beira City Council

Index

cooperantes, 2, 14, 26, 27, 35, 38, 40, 49, 51, 63, 69, 71-72, 74, 77, 80, 82, 84, 85, 88, 89, 104, 107, 108, 109, 113, 129, 139, 147, 172, 189, 212, 223, 236, 276, 301, 312
cooperantes, American, 14; Steve Gloyd, 40, 191. *See also* Cohn, Jon; Raisler, Jeanne.
cooperantes, Brazilian, 106-107, 108, 174; Iris, 77, 169, 170; Juarez, 49, 109, 155, 188, 213; Júlio, 188, 192, 284; Liziêt 188, 192, 284
cooperantes, British, 72, 133, 139, 154. *See also* Boyle, Steve; Boyle, Jacky
cooperantes, Canadian, 2, 117, 139; Marshall, Judith 40, 303. *See also* Dickson, Gerri; Dickson, Murray; Limpus, Judy and Len; Povey, George.
cooperantes, Cuban, 71, 127
cooperantes, Dutch, 77, 112, 139, 165, 258; Hanny, 71, 295, 299
cooperantes, French; Yacine, 48-49, 213
cooperantes, Irish. *See* Crowley, Niall; Reidy, Melanie
cooperantes, Soviet, 2, 71-72, 127, 170, 186, 187, 195, 284
cooperantes, Spanish, 299
cooperantes, Swedish, 124, 125, 139, 165, 258; Marie Ekman 124, 188, 258, 279; Anders Hellstrom 124, 258, 279-282; Christina Hernborg 125-126; Cecilia Salemark 124-125; Lars Salemark 124, 125, 295
cooperantes, Tanzanian, 127
cooperantes, Ugandan, 282-283
cooperantes, Zambian, 2, 77, 85, 171
creche, *See* childcare centers
Crowley, Niall, 67, 138, 166, 236, 239. *See also* Reidy, Melanie
CUSO, *See* Canadian University Service Overseas

D

Davies, Rob, 193, 194, 196
de Bragança, Aquino, 40, 68, 142, 236-237
Democratic Socialists of America, 141, 261. *See also* New American Movement,

Diário de Moçambique, 65-66, 120, 121, 139, 165, 259, 287-288

Dickson, Gerri, 48, 85, 99, 155

Dickson, Murray, 48-49, 116-117, 155

Dondo, 40, 80, 203, 285

dos Santos, Marcelino, 165-166, 216-217, 21, 224-226, 237, 247, 261, 300

dos Santos, Pamela, 216, 237, 240, 247, 260-261

E

education in Mozambique, 26, 180, 198, 208, 221, 243, 277;

literacy 99, 206, 210, 243, 253, 277;

mission schools, 123, 244-245, 250, 251, 253, 286

electricity, power cuts, 39, 47, 85-88, 104, 105-106, 117, 138, 246, 262, 302, 315

Embaixador Hotel, 46-47, 194

Eswatini, *See* Swaziland

F

feminism, 19, 20, 22, 29, 97-98, 181, 199, 216, 300, 305

Ferrão, Valeriano, 144

First, Ruth, 40, 68-69

food, 2, 37-38, 40, 47-48, 67, 73-76, 77-78, 82, 83, 85, 88-92, 104, 117, 137-138, 146, 172-173, 181, 187-191, 198, 207, 222, 243, 255, 257, 260, 270, 277, 295, 302, 311;
in cooperative shop, 38, 74, 84, 88-89, 108, 172, 189, 265;
in markets, 37, 38, 48, 74, 108, 137, 172, 257, 311, 318;
in Swaziland, 152, 154;
in Zimbabwe, 232, 234.
See also bread; Jacky Boyle, providing food; Loja Franca; prawns

Francisco, 50-52, 62, 65, 73-74, 86, 88-89, 108, 131-132, 155-156, 171, 172, 188-189, 190, 213, 257, 262, 288, 299

Frayling, Ian and Maureen, 294-295, 299, 311

Frelimo (Frente de Libertação de Moçambique), 11, 12, 13, 17, 20, 39, 80, 81, 95, 99, 116, 134, 158, 180, 210, 220, 236, 287, 300;
elections, 1994, 312-317;
Fourth Party Congress, 1983, 41, 66, 97, 99, 113, 141-142, 145, 166, 212, 217.
See also Kanimambo

Frontline States, 13, 193, 318

G

Gama, António, 46, 78, 99, 127, 135, 246, 259, 297, 298
garment workers interviews, 222, 239-40, 244-45, 249-253;
Ana Maria Helena dos Santos, 214, 241, 243, 245, 246, 249, 253, 312
gasoline tank sabotage, 1, 106-108, 133-134
Gaza province, 219, 304
Glastonbury, Connecticut, 4-6, 303, 309
Golf Club, 160-161, 191-192
Gorongosa, 185-186, 217
Grande Hotel, 97-98, 100
grupos dinamizadores, 145, 203, 263
Guebuza, Armando, 61, 139-140, 165-166
guia, 119-120, 143, 247, 261, 262, 267, 269, 274-275, 285, 324
Guinea-Bissau, 12, 142, 255

H

health care in Mozambique, 26, 46, 95, 97, 99, 102, 123, 157-164, 182-183. *See also* Health Ministry; Hospital Central da Beira.
Health Ministry, 22, 26-28, 33, 34-35, 46, 63, 76, 111, 119, 125-126, 127, 163, 172, 199, 261, 277, 293. *See also* Acção Social; health care in Mozambique; Hospital Central da Beira.
Hindu community, 139, 280-282
Hospital Central da Beira, 48, 54, 80, 93-97, 99-100, 119-120. 122-123, 127, 133-134, 135-136, 157, 164-165, 179, 185-187, 244-245, 246, 264, 279-280, 285, 297. *See also* health care in Mozambique; Health Ministry.
Hotel Moçambique, 47-49, 222

I

Inhambane province, 113, 159, 182, 199-200, 209, 249, 313, 317
Inhamudima, Beira neighborhood, 157-162, 271-274, 278, 289
initiation rites, 217-220, 225, 226

J

Julien, Manuel, 190, 297

K

Kanimambo (thank you), Frelimo song, 98, 167, 208, 243
  See also songs, political

L

Labor Ministry, 253, 274-275

Limpus, Judy and Len, 71, 136, 188, 279-280, 284, 288, 294, 295, 299, 303

literacy, *See* education

Loja Franca, 38, 79, 84, 108, 112, 115, 137, 188, 223, 301.
  See also food

M

machamba. *See* agricultural labor

Machel, Samora, 41, 76, 79, 113, 123, 145, 146, 147, 166-167, 205, 206, 218, 221, 225, 237, 256, 304

mackerel, 109, 137, 189, 262, 306

Mafambisse, 191

mail and packages, 82, 115-116, 138, 155, 173-175, 190, 257, 263

malaria, 53, 54, 60, 86, 97, 135-137, 227, 246, 283

Malawi, 106, 116, 193

Manga, Beira neighborhood, 73, 132, 155, 171, 198, 199, 201, 208, 264, 278, 281

Maputo, 68-69, 120, 127-128, 165, 222, 310-312, 313, 318; 1982 arrival, 34-39 passim, 42; 1983 visit, 141-149, 155; 1984 departure, 299-306

markets, *See* food, in markets. *See also* market vendors interviews

market vendors interviews, 269-274

Marromeu, 255, 256, 260

Maxixe, 313, 316

May 1st (International Workers' Day): parade in Maputo, 1983, 145, 147-148;
  parade in Beira, 1984, 288

Mbabane. *See* Swaziland

McCord, Coke (Colin) and Susan, 34-35, 38, 40, 41, 42, 50, 299

Mexicana apartment building, 48-50, 54, 63, 87, 91, 169-171, 201, 213, 262, 301

Ministry of Health. *See* Health Ministry

Mobeira biscuit factory, 227, 277-278

Mozambique Company, 45, 122, 143, 179.
  See also colonialism

Mozambique Support Network, 311

Index

Muller, Mike and Ruth, 67, 69, 72, 79, 81, 87, 91, 135, 190-191, 302-303

Munhava, Beira neighborhood, 72-73, 157, 162, 181, 183, 209, 212, 264, 278, 295

N

Namibia, 66, 193

Nelson, Bob, 28, 32, 170

New American Movement, 19, 29, 141. *See also* Democratic Socialists of America

Nhangau, 139

Northwestern University, 7-8, 10-11, 13, 15, 81, 304

Notícias de Moçambique, 120, 141, 143

nurses and nursing, 93-94, 96, 99, 122, 157-160, 161, 186, 187, 297

nurses interviews, 121-123, 179-183, 209, 285-286

O

Oceana restaurant, 67, 76

OMM (Organização da Mulher Moçambicana), 97-99, 125-126, 148, 181, 197-199, 200, 240, 247-248, 249, 255-256, 260-261, 283, 300-301; Maria das Dores, 126, 197, 199, 215, 240, 261; provincial meeting, 1983, 215-228; Salomé Moine, 215-222 *passim*; Teresa Romão, 260, 261-262, 283, 288, 300

Operação Produção (Operation Production), 212, 223

P

Ponta Gêa, Beira neighborhood, 49, 54, 98, 121, 123, 157, 158, 180, 192, 273

Portugal, 11-13, 17, 22-24, 78, 147, 306

Povey, George, 27, 35-36, 39-40, 141, 299, 301-302

prawns, 39, 67-68, 70, 77, 78, 108, 116, 146, 190, 258, 284, 296, 297

Q

Quelimane, 36, 76, 79, 111-113,

R

Raisler, Jeanne, 36, 43, 76, 79, 111-113, 321. *See also* Jon Cohn.

Reidy, Melanie, 67, 138, 236. *See also* Crowley, Niall.

RENAB (Reparações Navais da Beira), 163-164, 216, 288

Renamo (Resistência Nacional Moçambicana), 39, 79-80, 85-86, 95, 97, 117, 133, 186, 194, 198, 214, 226, 288, 291, 310-311; 1994 election, 312-317 *passim*.
See also electricity, power cuts.

Renner, Peggy, 32, 170

S

Sachs, Albie, 304-307

Sheldon family, 4-8, 25, 33, 42, 79, 115, 117, 155, 173, 229-236 *passim*, 263, 293, 309

shrimp, See prawns

Sitoe, Rogério, 120, 141, 143, 149

socialism, 2-4, 12-13, 17, 20, 21-22, 25, 28, 51, 95, 97-98, 114, 116, 145, 147, 149, 181, 196, 216, 226, 243, 249, 250, 253, 287, 306, 311, 313, 318. See also Democratic Socialists of America; Frelimo; New American Movement.songs, 59, 60, 80, 102, 112, 113, 114, 116, 136, 139, 145, 146, 148, 177, 185, 224, 225, 302, 317

songs, 59, 60, 80, 100, 116, 136, 139, 185, 284, 317;

children's songs, 59, 102, 113, 176-177, 302-303;
political songs, 98, 112, 114, 145-146, 148-149, 218, 221-222, 224-225.
See also Kanimambo.

South Africa, 2, 7, 9-10, 12, 13, 18-19, 25-26, 33, 81, 82, 91, 193-194, 303, 318;
attacks on Mozambique, 1, 68-69, 106-107, 128, 165, 237, 304.
See also African National Congress.

sabotage, 82

Soviet Union, 13, 26, 65, 67, 70, 114, 195. See also cooperantes, Soviet

Swaziland, 106, 136, 142, 151-154, 193

T

Tanzania, 13, 18, 21, 64, 91-92, 117, 127, 221, 237

Tarzynski family, 8-9, 14, 115, 128, 138, 190, 230-231

telephone communications, 117, 127-128, 144

Tempo magazine, 201, 212, 248, 257, 293

Tete, 244, 291

U

United Nations, 36, 51, 71, 142, 151, 282, 295, 312, 314-315, 317

United States Agency for International Development (USAID), 116, 310, 311

United States government policies, 13, 25-26, 28, 195

Universidade Eduardo Mondlane, 40, 68, 193, 318. See also Centro de Estudos Africanos.

University of California, Los Angeles (UCLA), 14, 18, 23, 146, 231, 310

V

Verimbo, Boaventura (Bovy), 289-290, 298-299

Vigilância Popular, 133, 134

W

water supply, 41, 47, 86-88, 192, 243, 262, 288-289

Z

Zambézia province, 35, 122, 185

Zambia, 169, 171. See also cooperantes, Zambian.

Zimbabwe, 1, 26, 45, 106-107, 169, 173, 193, 229-236, 247.